FEAR, MYTH AND HISTORY

The Ranters and the historians

FEAR, MYTH AND HISTORY

The Ranters and the historians

J.C. DAVIS

Professor of History, Massey University

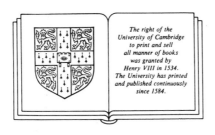

The right of the
University of Cambridge
to print and sell
all manner of books
was granted by
Henry VIII in 1534.
The University has printed
and published continuously
since 1584.

CAMBRIDGE UNIVERSITY PRESS

Cambridge

London   New York   New Rochelle
Melbourne   Sydney

Published by the Press Syndicate of the University of Cambridge
The Pitt Building, Trumpington Street, Cambridge CB2 1RP
32 East 57th Street, New York, NY 10022, USA
10 Stamford Road, Oakleigh, Melbourne 3166, Australia

First published 1986

Printed in Great Britain at the University Press, Cambridge

British Library cataloguing in publication data

Davis, J.C. (James Colin)
Fear, myth and history : the Ranters and the historians
1. Ranters – History
I. Title
273'.7   BT1330

Library of Congress cataloguing in publication data

Davis, J. C.
Fear, myth and history.
Includes index.
1. Ranters – History. I. Title
BX9375.R3D38 1986   284   86-1002
ISBN 0 521 26243 7

BO

... the horrid Villainies of this Sect did not only speedily Extinguish it, but also did as much as ever anything did, to disgrace all *Sectaries*, and to restore the Credit of the Ministry and the sober unanimous Christians: So that the Devil and the Jesuits quickly found that this way served not their turn, and therefore they suddenly took another.

Richard Baxter, *Reliquiae Baxterianae*, ed. Matthew Sylvester (1696)

... they were so few and of short continuance that I never saw one of them.

Ibid.

It is very expedient that there should be heresies amongst us, that thereby those which are indeed of the truth might be made manifest.

John Bunyan, *A Vindication of Gospel Truths* (1657)

Contents

Preface

History appears to the casual observer a realm of solid knowledge, possessed of a high degree of permanence. As its students know, it is nothing of the kind. Topics wax and wane in significance and interest. Controversies which once seemed central virtually disappear from view. What was once obscure, provincial or marginal is brought into the spotlight while the nationally prominent recedes into dark corners of neglect and silence. Bishops, archbishops, professors of theology are forgotten and we listen instead to the tavern or street corner declamations of peasants, artisans and itinerants. There may be justice, as well as excitement, in this. After all, history is, as Milan Kundera reminds us, about forgetting as well as remembering. Revolutions play these games with historical consciousness, both in their own time and ours, with a force and brusqueness which admits of little argument. They not only challenge the *status quo* of the past, its continuity and hegemony, but, reaching through time, they encourage historians to do the same. Even the less spectacular, more conservative, revolutions bear witness to these reversals of historiographical fortune. And this is true of the English Revolution as of others.

In the last fifteen years we have seen a considerable burst of writing about and interest in a once obscure, small and ephemeral group of religious fanatics of the English Commonwealth, the Ranters. Meanwhile, the great fabric of the Church, illegally enduring the revolution and soon to come into its own again, has been virtually ignored. There is exaggeration in my antipodes and the contrast is, of course, too stark, but there is also, I believe, truth, and historians have been eager to defend the inversion which my contrast depicts. Certainly, such extremities of fortune can help us to rediscover neglected aspects of the past but, when the price to be paid is apparently the undue and unwise neglect of other aspects of the past, we may observe a kind of stable equilibrium of attention and neglect. The oscillation taking place before our eyes may tell us more about ourselves than it does about the past. Why do we choose to give attention to certain aspects of the past and how and why are they chosen?

The specific arguments respective to the Ranters, the subject of this book, have fallen under four heads. First is the argument that they represent a plebeian, popular or lower-class phenomenon and that such a phenomenon is important in its own right; that history from below, the history of those ruled over rather than ruling, should be written. Second, the notion that the people make their own history rather than existing as a passive screen for the actions of the dominant or hegemonic groups in society to be projected upon implies that the history of such groups as express alternatives to the dominant culture is of vital significance. Third, an extension of this specific to the Ranters is the claim that they represent an authentic lower-class resistance to the Puritan attempt to impose a repressive Protestant ethic upon English society, an ethic which has had shaping or distorting influence on the English for the last three centuries. Finally there is the argument, only very recently developed, that the cultural and literary significance of these groups is far greater than has hitherto been acknowledged and that their works are worthy of study as important contributions to English literary tradition.

The object of this essay is to examine the historiographical rise of the Ranters and to set it against the documentary record which the past has bequeathed to us. What have historians said of the Ranters? Who were they? How did they identify and distinguish themselves? How did their contemporaries see them? In the process, I shall argue that the Ranters are indeed an interesting phenomenon in the eye of the English Revolution, but not in the sense which has commonly been ascribed to them. They were not so much a real religious movement, sect or group, made up of real men and women identifying themselves with particular beliefs and practices, but existed rather as a projection of the fears and anxieties of a broader society. They were closer to the image of 'folk devils' projected in a 'moral panic' which reached its climax in the wake of the revolution of 1648–9. That image was made up of mythic materials readily to hand and used in ways which were virtually traditional. If I am right in this view, and I must endeavour to demonstrate its validity in the body of this text, the remaining question is how it is that some fine radical commentators, and one great historian, have come to accept as real a highly conservative and admonitory projection or myth from the 1650s. I offer some comment on that problem in the last section of this essay but, although we may be led to the outskirts of some major issues of historical method and purpose, their full examination would require a large book and I must stress that this is no more than an exploratory essay.

I should emphasise too that it is not a presumption of this essay that it may simply be demonstrated, or is sufficient to say, that those who have preceded me in the study of the Ranter phenomenon were misled, wrongheaded or proceeded incorrectly. There is a great deal to be learned from their researches and I am indebted, as always, to Christopher Hill and in this case to A.L. Morton and, in particular, to Frank McGregor. Rather it is a question of perspective. We may agree that it is the primary task of the historian to listen to the voices of human beings enmeshed in, and in some cases distorted by, the documentary artefacts remaining to us. The crucial questions are how that listening process is to inform, and be informed by, the perspectives which we will carry to the ordering of the documentary evidence, and how rigorously all the available evidence will be brought to bear on these perspectives. Some reflections on these issues will be offered at the conclusion of this essay.

It had been my original intention to include in this work an appendix of documents illustrating the thought, and its divergences, of the so-called Ranter group. The function has now been extremely well performed in Nigel Smith's *A Collection of Ranter Writings from the 17th century* (London, 1983). The exception is his omission of the anonymous core text *A Justification of the Mad Crew* which is therefore included here. In addition, since my argument revolves so much around their character, I have included a selection from the sensational yellowpress literature on the Ranters from 1650 to 1652.

My thanks are due again to my good friends Peter Webster and Miles Fairburn, who continue to make me think and have ensured that it is not a solitary habit. Jonathan Scott and Glenn Burgess have contributed much to the argument that they may not now recognise. Michael Hunter, on a visit to New Zealand, generously showed me how to begin thinking again about atheism in seventeenth-century England. John Morrow read the entire text in draft and I have benefited from his criticisms. Many other scholars will, I hope, recognise my indebtedness to them in the text and references. I am also grateful for the support of the following institutions: Robinson College, Cambridge, the Cambridge University Library, the British Library, the Bodleian Library, the library of Victoria University and the Alexander Turnbull Library, both in Wellington, and to the Librarian and staff of my own university. I am especially indebted to my colleagues in the history department at Massey University whose forbearance made persisting with this book possible. In particular Barrie Macdonald's collusion and support, when he was wrestling a major work of his own through the press, is not to be forgotten. Without Sandra, as always, nothing would be possible. Such faults as remain are, of course, mine alone.

Note

Wherever possible, contemporary spelling and punctuation have been followed. Dates have been adjusted to a year beginning on 1 January. Place of publication of seventeenth-century works is London, unless otherwise stated. First reference to works from the Thomason collection is given with the Thomason collection call number and George Thomason's ascribed date. Other seventeenth-century works are cited with Wing or Pollard and Redgrave (P. & R.) numbers.

Abbreviations

The following abbreviations have been used:

B.D.B.R.S.C.	A Biographical Dictionary of British Radicals in the Seventeenth Century, ed. R. Greaves and R.L. Zaller (3 vols., Brighton, 1982–4)
C.J.	Commons Journals
C.S.P.D.	Calendar of State Papers (Domestic)
C.S.P. Ven.	Calendar of State Papers (Venetian)
F.F.R.	Abiezer Coppe, A Fiery Flying Roll (1650; Rota facsimile, Exeter, 1973)
H.M.C.	Historical Manuscripts Commission Reports
L.S.F.	Laurence Clarkson, The Lost Sheep Found (1660; Rota facsimile, Exeter, 1974)
P. & P.	Past and Present
R.W.	Nigel Smith (ed.), A Collection of Ranter Writings from the 17th Century (London, 1983)
W.O.T.R.	A.L. Morton, The World of the Ranters: Religious Radicalism in the English Revolution (London, 1979)
W.T.U.D.	Christopher Hill, The World Turned Upside Down: Radical Ideas During the English Revolution (Harmondsworth, 1975)

1

The historians and the Ranters

i. THE REVIVAL: BIRTH OF A MOVEMENT

In 1970 two historians announced the rediscovery of a more or less forgotten group of religious extremists who had fitfully flourished in the brief period of the English republic.[1] The Ranters were emerging from obscurity. Ironically both historians had previously written of the Ranters, but in each case as subjects subordinate to what was then their main theme.[2] The Ranters were coming into their own, as subjects worthy of study in their own right.

For Norman Cohn, the Ranters, 'almost wholly forgotten', deserved 'a modest niche in history' because they were 'a link in a long series of mystical or quasi-mystical anarchists extending from the thirteenth century to the present day'. In one context they linked the Brethren of the Free Spirit with Charles Manson and the hippy amoralists of California in 1969. In another, they fleshed out and gave substance to the roots of modern totalitarianism in the High Middle Ages.[3] In *The Pursuit of the Millennium* (1957) Cohn had argued that documents on the Ranters from the 1650s could be used, in a retrospective manner, as evidence of the behaviour and belief systems of the Brethren of the Free Spirit (thirteenth and fourteenth centuries) or of the Spiritual Libertines encountered by sixteenth-century reformers like Calvin and Bucer in France and Germany. The Ranters, like the Brethren of the Free Spirit, preached a revolutionary social doctrine, self-deification,

[1] Norman Cohn, 'The Ranters', *Encounter*, 34:4 (1970), 15–25; A.L. Morton, *The World of the Ranters: Religious Radicalism in the English Revolution* (London, 1970). A paperback edition of Morton's book appeared in 1979. Reference will be made to this edition as *W.O.T.R.*
[2] Norman Cohn, *The Pursuit of the Millennium: Revolutionary Messianism in Medieval and Reformation Europe and its Bearing on Modern Totalitarian Movements* (London, 1962), Appendix, pp.321–78. This work was first published in 1957. A.L. Morton, *The Everlasting Gospel: A Study in the Sources of William Blake* (London, 1958), especially Chapter 4.
[3] Cohn, 'The Ranters', 24: for the Manson references see 15, 25; *Pursuit of the Millennium, passim.*

total emancipation, antinomianism and an anarchic eroticism. There were 'many thousands' of them in London and other groups scattered throughout the country.[4] The evidence for this was culled from hostile accounts of heresiographers, Anglicans, Baptists, Quakers and some sensationally lurid yellowpress accounts of Ranter behaviour, as well as from the writings of Jacob Bauthumley, Joseph Salmon, Laurence Clarkson and Abiezer Coppe, all alleged Ranters. Cohn's article in *Encounter* (1970), written when a second edition of *The Pursuit* was in the press, was obviously intended to allow the general argument to reach a wider audience and to underline the affinities which were now seen to exist between the Ranters and the counter-cultural groups of the late 1960s.

A.L. Morton, our second historian, had been, along with a prestigious group of British historians (Christopher Hill, Edward Thompson, Eric Hobsbawm, Donna Torr), a member of the Communist Party Historians' Group which flourished between 1946 and 1956. Members of this group were to have a decisive influence on British historiography. They saw it as part of their rôle to bridge the gap between academic and popular history. Morton was prominent and successful in this area. He had published works on Blake, Owen, the Labour movement, English utopianism and a popular general history of England. *The World of the Ranters* (1970) was a collection of essays exploring facets of radical religious and political movements in the 1640s and 1650s. Central to it were two essays; one on the Ranters, the other on Laurence Clarkson. For Morton, the Ranters were one expression of a radical movement demoralised by the abortive revolution of 1649. While other groups, like the Fifth Monarchists and Quakers, had attracted more attention, Morton suggested that the Ranters were possibly more significant than any of them. They were more menacing, because more urban, than Winstanley and the Diggers.[5] They represented 'the extreme left wing of the sects' but were not themselves to be seen as a sect. There was too much incoherence, too many contradictions, in the central tenets of Ranterism for that, but, as a movement, they were widespread and commanded great attention so that one could speak of 'Ranter theology', 'Ranter doctrine', 'The World of the Ranters'.[6] The defining centre of the Ranters was necessarily hazy, but it was clear that

---

[4] Cohn, *Pursuit of the Millennium*, pp. 321, 323.   [5]   *W.O.T.R.*, pp. 17, 71.
[6] *Ibid.*, p. 73. For Christopher Hill there was to be a 'Ranter intellectual milieu' out of which Muggletonianism, in part at least, sprang: Hill, 'John Reeve and the Origins of Muggletonianism', in Christopher Hill, Barry Reay and William Lamont (eds.) *The World of the Muggletonians* (London, 1983), p. 71.

there was a widespread and significant movement: 'no evidence for any formal organisation or generally received body of doctrine' existed. Nevertheless, there was a movement with a reasonably clear history. It had 'a strong appeal to many Englishmen of the lower orders'; it was 'mainly an urban movement, drawing support from the wage earners and small producers in the towns', but its followers were 'probably both more numerous and more influential than has sometimes been supposed'.[7] It arose out of the 'defeat of the radical plebeian element in the revolution' and represented a shift of aspirations from 'Levelling by sword and spade' to 'Levelling by miracle'.[8] Incoherent though Ranter doctrine might be, its central features were a materialist pantheism, an extreme antinomianism and a 'naive communism'. The movement came 'suddenly into prominence' in 1649 shortly after the crushing of the Levellers. Thereafter the Ranters enjoyed 'a mass following' amongst the poor and marginal classes, especially in London but throughout the country. Though their appeal was to 'the defeated and declassed' there was 'no part of England where their influence was not felt'.[9] The movement peaked in 1650 when, after the passing of the so-called Blasphemy Ordinance on 9 August 1650, it was faced with 'savage repression' and an 'organised police action'. 'Under all these blows Ranterism ceased to exist as a coherent social and religious movement, but its decline was slow and prolonged.'[10] Repression 'did not destroy the Ranter movement, but it certainly checked its growth, drove it underground and forced it to shun rather than court public notice'. It remained 'a main link in the chain that runs from Joachim of Fiore to William Blake'.[11]

There can be no doubt of Morton's success in stimulating fresh interest in the Ranters. He and Cohn had taken them out of the hands of those whose religious disapproval was to the fore and had made the issue of their significance a matter of very long-term trends in English history. But there were disturbing features in Morton's account. Recognising the suspect nature of many of the hostile and extravagantly sensational contemporary accounts of the Ranters,[12] Morton is yet heavily dependent on such material for evidence of the dramatic rise and fall, nature and extent of support, prominence, behaviour and savage repression of the movement.[13] Nowhere is this more apparent

---

[7] *W.O.T.R.*, pp. 92, 110, 111.   [8] *Ibid.*, pp. 71, 85.   [9] *Ibid.*, pp. 17, 112, 111.
[10] *Ibid.*, pp. 17, 103, 110.   [11] *Ibid.*, pp. 107, 112.
[12] *Ibid.*, pp. 76, 81. Cf. his comments on the use of the heresiographer Thomas Edwards in his essay on John Lanseter, *ibid.*, p. 24.
[13] For examples see *ibid.*, pp. 76, 81, 82, 83, 89, 90, 92, 96, 99, 107, 108–9, 110, 111.

than in his depiction of the practical antinomianism of the Ranters, their alleged flouting of all moral conventions. Morton takes his picture of a typical Ranter from a hostile Quaker, Richard Farnworth,[14] and accepts the orgiastic nature of Ranter meetings from what he himself describes as pamphlets of 'the lowest, muck-raking type'.[15] To put it kindly, even while recognising their flawed nature, Morton built his claims for the numbers, members, beliefs, and behaviour of the Ranters upon the incautious use of his sources. Like Cohn, he had, in part at least, been prepared to take hostile and sensational contemporary commentary at face value. The rediscovery of the Ranters was unconsciously beset with methodological and evidential problems and, to a great extent, it has never faced or escaped from them. They are problems which we must consider in greater detail later.

ii. BEFORE THE REVIVAL

A sense of breakthrough or rediscovery of the Ranters was understandable in 1970, given that the great historians of the English Revolution and student textbooks had previously barely mentioned them. For Guizot, Ranke, Inderwick and Gardiner the Ranters were a phenomenon which could be passed over in silence. Similarly Firth, Trevelyan and Godfrey Davies made little or no mention of them. Even in Christopher Hill's textbook, *The Century of Revolution* (1961), the Ranters were in passing associated with the 'lunatic fringe' as illustrations that some limit had to be set to religious toleration – and no more.[16]

Still, 1970 was not the breakthrough or year of discovery that the language of enthusiasm sometimes seemed to imply. The Ranters had been discussed in Barclay's *Inner Life of the Religious Societies of the Commonwealth* and in Masson's monumental *Life of John Milton*. To the former they represented a kind of sectarian madness against which Quakerism, in its sobriety and discipline, provided a barrier.[17] The latter saw them as 'ANTINOMIANS run mad, with touches from FAMILISM and SEEKERISM greatly vulgarized', one of a competing range of 'phrenzies'. Yet Masson knew the Thomason Tracts so thoroughly as to

[14] *Ibid.*, p. 92.
[15] *Ibid.*, p. 81. For examples see pp. 80–1, 90, 91. The cover of the paperback edition is in fact adorned with a woodcut from just such a pamphlet.
[16] Christopher Hill, *The Century of Revolution 1603–1714* (Edinburgh, 1961), p. 167.
[17] Robert Barclay, *The Inner Life of the Religious Societies of the Commonwealth* (2nd edn, London, 1877), Chapter 17.

be aware that they were one of the pamphlet and newsbook phenomena of the early 1650s. There may have been varieties of Ranterism but a shared pantheism, rejection of moral values and scriptural authority, associated significantly with atheism, mortalism or materialism, gave them a common identity.[18]

The tone of religious antipathy permeating Barclay's and Masson's accounts of the Ranters was to remain a marked feature of their treatment until their reassessment by Morton and Cohn. The one serious attempt to break free of the religious perspective was made by an anthropologist, James Mooney, in 1896 but he, sadly, confused Ranterism with John Robins's self-proclaimed reincarnation of the Messiah. As well as perpetuating this muddle, Mooney was ironically dependent for his information on Barclay and so the chances of establishing a value-free perspective were limited.[19]

From the 1930s a number of accounts of the Ranters appeared which continued the tradition of seeing them as a case study in the morbid pathology of a religious disease. They were 'the wildest of the sects', 'a lunatic fringe', reflecting a serious mental as well as moral disorder.[20] Attitudes like this persisted well into the early 1970s.[21] At the same time, however, a more balanced approach was emerging, in passing, in works like Geoffrey Nuttall's *The Holy Spirit in Puritan Faith and Experience* (Oxford, 1947) and, more substantially, in the work of William York Tindall. Tindall's familiarity with the pamphlet literature of the period was so comprehensive as to enable him to place the Ranter phenomenon in a wider context and to see that many of the charges against them were permeated with ulterior sectarian motives. For him the Ranters and the Quakers were the principal non-Calvinist sects of

[18] David Masson, *The Life of John Milton, vol. V 1654–1660* (London, 1877), pp. 17–19.

[19] James Mooney, *The Ghost-Dance Religion and Wounded Knee* (Toronto, 1973), pp. 936–8. This is an unabridged republication of 'The Ghost-Dance Religion and the Sioux Outbreak of 1890', *Fourteenth Annual Report (Part 2) of the Bureau of Ethnology to the Smithsonian Institution 1892–3* (Washington, 1896). An abridged version of this was published by Phoenix Books (Chicago, 1965) which, amongst other things, omits Mooney's account of the Ranters. Compare Mooney with Barclay, *Inner Life*, pp. 419–20. Both are dependent on G.H., *The Declaration of John Robins, the false Prophet otherwise called the Shaker God* (1651), E.629 (13).

[20] C.E. Whiting, *Studies in English Puritanism from the Restoration to the Revolution 1660–1688* (London, 1931), pp. 243, 272–7, especially p. 272; Rufus M. Jones, *Mysticism and Democracy in the English Commonwealth* (New York, 1932; reprinted, 1965), p. 132; Rufus M. Jones, *Studies in Mystical Religion* (London, 1936), p. 467.

[21] G.F. Ellens, 'Case Studies in Seventeenth Century Enthusiasm: Especially the Ranters', unpublished Ph.D. thesis, Columbia University, 1968; G.F. Ellens, 'The Ranters Ranting: Reflections on a Ranter Counter Culture', *Church History*, 40 (1971), 91–107.

the 1650s, but this quasi-quantitative assessment still rested on taking much of the sensational literature seriously.[22] Tindall's account was an important one and a major step in the serious treatment of the phenomenon. Two American doctoral theses, submitted in 1949 and 1956, should have consolidated this, but both have been strangely neglected by scholars in the field.[23] Nevertheless, a more neutral approach was provided, even in passing, in the work of Gertrude Huehns and Serge Hutin. Huehns's study of antinomianism (1951) provided a context for understanding the moral and theological implications of the Ranters' antinomian views, and, while she was too ready to accept as valid the views of heresiographers like Edwards and Pagitt, she raised a number of considerations which have been unfortunately since forgotten.[24] The same, sadly, must be said of Hutin's work on Behmenism in seventeenth-century England (1960). Not only did Hutin confirm Nuttall's distancing of Richard Coppin from the Ranters, but he placed Ranterism against a background of popular pantheism, concern with a third dispensation or everlasting gospel – typified by the Seekers – and the first stirrings of the influence of Jacob Boehme in England.[25]

The Ranters, it is clear, had never been entirely neglected. Their rediscovery in 1970 was not quite as dramatic an unveiling as it appeared to some. Nevertheless 1970 has to be seen, if only in retrospect, as a watershed. From this point on the reputation and significance of the Ranters began to grow. It was no longer possible to write a textbook with only glancing reference to them.

iii. THE RISE OF THE RANTERS: THE WORLD TURNED UPSIDE DOWN

Cohn and Morton had left problems. Cohn's use of a seventeenth-century group as evidence of the practices and beliefs of medieval

---

[22]   W.Y. Tindall, *John Bunyan Mechanick Preacher* (1934; reprinted New York, 1964): see p. 45 for Bunyan's use of attacks on the Ranters as a weapon against the Quakers.

[23]   R.G. Scofield, 'The Ranters in Seventeenth Century England: Their Principles and Practices', unpublished Ph.D. thesis, Harvard University, 1949; A.D. Mott, 'The Phenomenon of Ranterism in the Puritan Revolution: A Historical Study in the Religion of the Spirit', unpublished Ph.D. thesis, University of California, 1956. In his important Oxford B.Litt. thesis of 1968 Frank McGregor mentions neither of them.

[24]   Gertrude Huehns, *Antinomianism in English History: With Special Reference to the period 1640–1660* (London, 1951).

[25]   Serge Hutin, *Les Disciples anglais de Jacob Boehme aux XVIIe and XVIIIe siècles* (Paris, 1960). Morton had, of course, stressed the everlasting gospel in his work of that name two years previously.

heretics was problematic. Was it permissable at all? Both historians had been incautious in their use of sources and, for Morton at least, the central doctrines of the movement remained contradictory and vague, something which made it difficult to distinguish Ranter from non-Ranter amidst the plethora of mid-century religious enthusiasms. Yet the image of a chronologically sharply defined movement with a large, widespread following had been emphatically evoked. Rising in 1649, peaking in 1650, the movement was apparently overwhelmed by fierce and systematic repression but continued to be seen in fitful encounters throughout the century. It was typified by a robust rejection of the forms and ordinances of all churches and sects, and a positive liberation from the sense of guilt and moral repression commonly depicted as the essence of puritanism. It was counter-cultural, and part of its fascination lay in the sense that, in the late 1960s and early 1970s, Western society was witnessing a profound counter-cultural rejection of institutional, social and moral norms and conventions in the name of individual liberation and authenticity. The Protestant ethic and its apparatus, so it briefly appeared, were about to collapse before the trumpets of youth and in the turmoil of their own contradictions. Cohn compared Ranters and hippies and the comparison was extended the following year by Gordon Ellens without apparent incongruity.[26]

It was in this ambience that Christopher Hill's *The World Turned Upside Down* could be read on its first appearance in 1972. It was an ambience of counter-cultural expectation, of the reading of Herbert Marcuse's *Essay on Liberation*, when it was worth while noting that Marcuse, the guru of pop culture and the politics of permissiveness, might have approved of Gerrard Winstanley.[27] For the first time a great historian had written a major work in which the Ranters played a central rôle, their significance reaching far beyond their own century. The breathtaking quality of *The World Turned Upside Down* rested not only on the habitual mastery of Hill's scholarship, the quality of his insights, the verve and moving compassion of his writing but, above all, on the architectonic brilliance of the overall design of the work. What had hitherto appeared as a more or less promiscuously seething mass of heterodoxies took on pattern and social meaning in the groundplan of the book.

In some ways *The World Turned Upside Down* parallels Edward

[26] Cohn, 'The Ranters', 15, 25; Ellens, 'The Ranters Ranting', 105–7.
[27] Christopher Hill, *The World Turned Upside Down: Radical Ideas During the English Revolution* (London, 1972; paperback edition, Harmondsworth, 1975). References will henceforth be made to the latter as *W.T.U.D.* See Chapter 16, section III, 'A counter-Culture?'; for references to Marcuse, *ibid.*, pp. 138, 414.

Thompson's *The Making of the English Working Class*, and is informed by the same underlying convictions. Central to these is the notion that the people make their own history and are not merely a passive screen against which the 'great' act out the events of 'history', or an inert, deferential mass given shape and function by their betters. The overriding concern of Hill's book is with 'the attempts of various groups of the common people to impose their own solutions to the problem of their own time'.[28] These attempts must be taken seriously because they, and in particular those of the Ranters, have something to say to our generation.[29]

The framework for these aspirations of the common people is the continual struggle between them and the dominant classes. The latter wish to establish their hegemony not only by coercive means but in a variety of cultural and even theological forms, through which the subordinate classes will come to think, feel and see themselves as their betters would wish. They will internalise the values of subordination. Against this is set the desire of the people to be free, to make their own history and express their own identity. One may first see these aspirations expressed, according to Hill, in class tensions and, in this particular context, in 'a tradition of plebeian anti-clericalism and irreligion'.[30] In the seventeenth century these expressions of class hostility had been most evident in the phenomenon and fear of masterless men (*W.T.U.D.*, Chapter 3), in the New Model Army (Chapter 4), and in those areas of the country where, for geographical and environmental reasons, the control of the ruling classes had long been weak (Chapter 5). Lower-class self-expression surfaced much more widely in the 1640s and 1650s because of a breakdown of institutional controls in the wake of the revolutionary struggle and because of the incitement given to the lower orders to join in an attack on authority.[31]

Part of the apparatus designed to control these aspirations was Puritanism, which in other respects was a rebellious force itself. Hence the tension within the revolutionary movement and its ultimately conservative outcome. The risks of allowing the people free rein were too great for those who had participated in inciting them to action. In a society with very limited coercive resources, internalised controls, self-control on the part of the masses, were seen to be vital.[32] Puritanism, by internalising the sense of sin, was, in part at least, a sustained attempt to develop such control. The most powerful agency of self-repression, of

---

[28] *W.T.U.D.*, p. 13.   [29] *Ibid.*, p. 16.   [30] *Ibid.*, p. 25.   [31] *Ibid.*, p. 24.
[32] *Ibid.*, pp. 47–8. Hill is here developing arguments from Michael Walzer, *The Revolution of the Saints* (Cambridge, Massachusetts, 1965).

internalising subordination, was sin, powerful enough to undermine the call for a more democratic, less deferential politics by groups in the army and amongst civilian Levellers from 1647 to 1649.[33] After 1649 the Diggers, the Fifth Monarchists, the Seekers and the Ranters could be seen to be seeking ways of liberating the oppressed from the burden of their own sense of sin and sinfulness. The struggle between the Protestant, Calvinist or Presbyterian sense of sin, imposed from above and controlling those below, and an 'antinomian rejection of the bondage of the moral law' was thus not only a theological conflict but a desperate struggle against social, cultural, political and personal repression, the outcome of which has determined at least three hundred years of history and human experience. It was the Ranters who most vigorously, if crudely, led the attack against sin, and gave fullest expression to the longing for self-determination and liberation.[34] There was, Hill claimed, a 'Ranter milieu' expressive of these things, but also a Ranter movement with various wings: those who talked about the end of sin and those who acted out the end of sin, the mystical, quietist wing of the Ranters, and the cursing, swearing wing of the Ranters.[35] While they lacked coherence, leadership, organisation and, consequently, unity, the Ranters did exist as a movement. They functioned and were recognised as a group whose course ran most spectacularly between 1649 and 1651.[36] Theirs was 'a heroic effort to proclaim Dionysus in a world from which he was being driven, to reassert the freedom of the human body and of sexual relations against the mind-forged manacles which were being imposed'.[37]

The framework, or paradigm, within which Hill's Ranters operated was sophisticated and serious; their rôle, though not unique, was central and important. They had secured a place in history. The documentary underpinnings of that place were assembled by a master historian with unrivalled knowledge of seventeenth-century English sources. But two features of the work, relative to the Ranters, were troubling. First, although Hill warned against taking the sensational literature of 1650–1 seriously, he, like Morton, repeatedly used it to illustrate Ranter behaviour, practice and belief.[38] Secondly, and again like Morton, Hill saw little coherence or definition at the centre of the Ranter movement and consequently there is some uncertainty about exactly who should be seen as the central figures of the movement. This is not resolved by the manner in which the figures are presented in *The World Turned*

---

[33] *W.T.U.D.*, Chapter 8, pp. 71–2.
[34] *Ibid.*, pp. 161, 167, 331, 333, 339.   [35] *Ibid.*, pp. 197–8, 202–3, 210.
[36] *Ibid.*, pp. 203, 204, 377.   [37] *Ibid.*, p. 339.   [38] *Ibid.*, p. 317.

Upside Down. After a general section on the movement (pp. 203–10) there follow sections on Abiezer Coppe, Laurence Clarkson, Joseph Salmon, Jacob Bauthumley, Richard Coppin (uncertainly 'a Ranter (or near-Ranter)', p. 208) who denied being a Ranter, George Foster, who 'does not fit neatly into the category of either Leveller or Ranter' (p. 223), and, even less certainly, John Pordage, Thomas Tany and Thomas Webbe.[39] The personnel and the coherence of the core of the movement remained questionable.

Not only did the people endeavour to make their own history, but there were giants of the received tradition of high culture who recognised that effort and were influenced by it. So as Hill's writing continued in the 1970s and early 1980s it became clear that the Ranters were for him part of the milieu which influenced not only John Reeve and Lodowick Muggleton but also John Milton.[40] In 1982 he was arguing that Ranter writings had contributed to a radical reformation in literary modes and style which represented a watershed in the history of English prose, an issue soon to be taken up more elaborately in relation to the Ranters by Nigel Smith.[41] In early 1984, Hill published an essay, 'God and the English Revolution', which restated his vision of the English Revolution.[42] There were three Gods at work in that upheaval; the God who sanctified the established order, the deity of authority and tradition; secondly, the God who stressed justice rather than tradition, a God of scriptural legitimations, heard in the claims of mainstream Puritanism and the more moderate sects; and, thirdly, the God to be found *in* every believer, the God of the spirit and its liberating authenticity. This third was God's revolutionary voice and it was heard through his antinomian saints, pre-eminently Abiezer Coppe, George Foster and Laurence Clarkson. 'In the early fifties the Ranters had abolished sin. But history abolished the Ranters and sin came back in strength after 1660.' God the Great Leveller left England and seems not to have returned.[43] In yet another essay Hill stressed that the fight against religion, conducted as it might, necessarily, have been in

---

[39] *Ibid.*, pp. 203–27. Figures like Tany and even John Robins have continued to be categorised by Hill as Ranters. For Robins see Christopher Hill, *The Experience of Defeat* (London, 1984), p. 45, n.6.

[40] Hill, *Milton and the English Revolution*, (London, 1977; paperback edition, 1979), *passim*; 'John Reeve and the Origins of Muggletonianism', in Hill, Reay, Lamont (eds.), *World of the Muggletonians*, pp. 64–110.

[41] Hill, 'Radical Prose in Seventeenth Century England: From Marprelate to the Levellers', *Essays in Criticism*, 32:2 (1982), 95–118; Nigel Smith (ed.), *A Collection of Ranter Writings from the 17th Century* (London, 1983), Introduction. Reference will now be made to this book as *R W.*   [42] In *History Workshop*, 17 (1984), 19–31.   [43] *Ibid.*, 24–5, 27, 30.

religious terms, was also a fight against repression. It was the Ranters who made the loudest anti-religious noises.[44]

iv. THE CONSOLIDATION OF THE RANTERS

The influence and prestige of Christopher Hill were almost sufficient to ensure that others would begin to take up the theme of the Ranters in scholarly articles, monographs and textbooks. By 1980, the sense of Ranter style had become so definite that Anne Laurence could identify three letters and two poems in the Clarke manuscripts as Ranter material.[45] In 1983 Barry Reay published a study of Laurence Clarkson's own account of his activities as a spiritual wanderer and Ranter, illustrating the religious culture of the subordinate classes in seventeenth-century England.[46] Nigel Smith's edition of what purported to be the principal Ranter texts appeared in the same year. Although they had 'no organisation or programme as such' and the term 'Ranter' was loosely used as one of abuse, the selection of texts was premised on the assumption 'that there was an identifiable body of individuals between 1649 and 1651 which was subject to a thorough persecution by the government'.[47] Such contradicitions are paralleled by the difficulties inherent in the attempt to discuss Ranter style and make general claims for it while stressing the 'highly individualised nature of each Ranter's style'.[48]

Still, the Ranters had arrived, and nowhere is this more apparent than in their treatment in one of the best of the new generation of textbooks,

[44] Hill, 'Irreligion in the "Puritan" Revolution', in J.F. McGregor and B. Reay (eds.), *Radical Religion in the English Revolution* (Oxford, 1984), pp. 191–211. An earlier version of this was given as the Barnett Shine Foundation Lecture for 1974. Hill's account in *The Experience of Defeat* (pp. 42–8) adds little to earlier versions.

[45] Anne Laurence, 'Two Ranter Poems', *The Review of English Studies*, 31 (1980), 56–9. There are enormous difficulties in such ascriptions. Assumptions are made about Ranter coherence, identity and style which just may not be warranted. As Nigel Smith has acknowledged, most of the language of the alleged Ranters is biblical in inspiration, something which does not help to distinguish them from their contemporaries (*R.W.*, p. 23). The effusiveness of their writing could be matched in that of many contemporaries. As Laurence recognises herself, the sentiments expressed in the documents she ascribes to Ranters were commonplace amongst religious radicals in the late 1640s and early 1650s: Laurence, 'Two Ranter Poems', 57.

[46] Barry Reay, 'Laurence Clarkson: An Artisan and the English Revolution', in Hill, Reay, Lamont (eds.), *World of the Muggletonians*, pp. 162–86. A version of this paper had first been given at the Christopher Hill Summer School in Canberra, February 1981.

[47] *R.W.*, pp. 7–8. [48] *Ibid.*, pp. 23, 31, 35.

Barry Coward's *The Stuart Age* (London, 1980). While understandably concerned about the nature of some of the sources upon which the Ranter edifice had been built, Coward clearly felt that their significance required the concession of space. They were a sect 'whose activities were often violent and anti-social' but who shared with the Quakers the distinction of forming an extreme radical wing of the sects which frightened conservative opinion into reaction. They formed 'the hippy-like counter-culture of the 1650s which flew in the face of law and morality and which was considered with horror by respectable society'.[49] With some alacrity the Rump 'revealed its obsessive fear and hatred of the excesses of the Ranters by enforcing observance of the Sabbath', suppressing swearing and cursing, and imposing the death penalty for adultery, fornication and incest.[50] The Ranters illustrate not only the revolutionary potential of mid-seventeenth-century sectarianism but also its capacity to produce a most ferocious backlash. Like Hill, Coward saw the early history of Ranters and Quakers as running close together, but was also concerned to point out that the early history of both groups was bedevilled by the hostile nature of so many of the sources.[51]

As the Ranter image gained currency, not everyone showed the same caution over identity and sources. David Underdown found Ranters in Somerset associated with John Robins.[52] Philip Gura took for granted the corporate identity of the Ranters in an attempt to relate the thought of a New England antinomian to them and the Seekers.[53] Ranter practice was so well established that it could be cited in reference to far distant events and circumstances.[54] The orthodoxy on the Ranters had become that of a 'most extraordinary sect', 'the extreme development of antinomianism and millenarianism in the English Revolution', some of whose writings justified 'sexual licence' and the overthrow of all moral restraint.[55]

---

[49] Barry Coward, *The Stuart Age* (London, 1980), pp. 208, 229, 421, 209.

[50] *Ibid.*, pp. 209, 214, also 217, 222.   [51] *Ibid.*, pp. 418, 209.

[52] David Underdown, *Somerset in the Civil War and Interregnum* (Newton Abbot, 1973), p. 156.

[53] Philip F. Gura, 'The Radical Ideology of Samuel Gorton: New Light on the Relation of English to American Puritanism', *William and Mary Quarterly*, 3rd series, 36 (1979), 78–100.

[54] E.g., Andrew Wallace-Hadrill, 'The Golden Age and Sin in Augustan Ideology', *P. & P.*, 95 (1982), 19.

[55] Keith Lindley, review entitled 'Advancing New Ideas', *The Times Higher Education Supplement*, no. 566, 9 September 1983, 17.

v. A VOICE OF CAUTION

In the midst of all of this, one voice was quietly urging caution. Since the submission of his B.Litt. thesis (supervised by Hill) in 1968,[56] Frank McGregor has been doing some of the best and most scrupulous work on the phenomenon of the Ranters and the radical sects. This work began gradually to appear in print in the later 1970s and early 1980s. It has been typified by sensitivity to the character of seventeenth-century religious sentiment, the context of religious languages and images, caution with regard to the use of sources, and awareness not only of the polemical use of images of deviance, but also of their institutional and corporate values. As McGregor pointed out in 1968, 'The study of English enthusiasm during the Revolution has suffered from the lack of a consistent and comprehensive definition of Ranterism.'[57] From the start, he was reluctant to accept contemporary ascriptions of Ranterism because the term was, on the one hand, such a powerful abusive weapon and, on the other hand, had its uses as a device for procuring discipline and unity within vulnerable sects like the Quakers and Baptists. There was 'a climate of opinion', and briefly in 1650 'a loosely co-ordinated campaign', but there was no Ranter sect.[58] Most of the evidence of their following was unreliable; popular stories of Ranter orgies, their practical antinomianism, impossible to substantiate.[59] Quaker sources provided the most extensive evidence for the survival of Ranterism, but, McGregor argued, they could not be taken at face value because Quaker use of the term 'Ranter' was indiscriminate and deployed principally as a disciplinary device within the Quaker movement itself. 'Ranterism came to represent any anti-social manifestation of the light within', and this in turn could amount to little more than opposition to George Fox and his allies within the Society.[60] Ranterism could be seen as a largely artificial product of the Puritan heresiographers' methodology or of the anxious obsessions of sectarian leaders with unity. It could be given shape by the sectarianising tendencies of seventeenth-century observers when itself far from choate in character.[61]

In McGregor's picture the notion of a Ranter movement, a follow-

---

[56] J.F. McGregor, 'The Ranters 1649–1660', unpublished B. Litt thesis, Oxford University, 1968. [57] *Ibid.*, p. vi; see also p. 137. [58] *Ibid.*, p. 60. [59] *Ibid.*, pp. 85, 90.

[60] McGregor, 'Ranterism and the Development of Early Quakerism', *Journal of Religious History*, 9 (1977), 351, 354, 359, 360–1, 363.

[61] McGregor, 'Seekers and Ranters', in McGregor and Reay (eds.), *Radical Religion*, pp. 121, 122, 137.

ing, disintegrates and becomes a set of shadows thrown up by religious anxiety and sectarian zeal for unity and security. At most Ranterism was an ephemeral phenomenon of a few individuals.[62] Nevertheless, for McGregor there remains a residual core of Ranterism built around a handful of texts produced in 1650 and, despite their differences, expounding 'a reasonably consistent set of doctrines'. Central to them were the belief in a mystical oneness with God, an antinomian denial of the reality of sin to the believer and a moral indifference to behaviour since all acts were inspired by God.[63] Already in 1968[64] McGregor was limiting the essential texts of Ranterism to Abiezer Coppe's *A Fiery Flying Roll*[65] and Jacob Bauthumley's *The Light and Dark Sides of God,*[66] the anonymous *Justification of the Mad Crew,*[67] Joseph Salmon's *Divinity Anatomized* (no copies of which are known to have survived)[68] and his *A Rout, A Rout.*[69] He would now probably substitute Laurence Clarkson's *A Single Eye All Light* for the last.[70] 'These works . . . are the extent of the Ranter's doctrinal literature.' 'With the exception of Bauthumley's tract they are largely a wild mixture of half-digested ideas, conspicuous for their lack of moderation and judgement.' 'At the time they published their Ranter works, Coppe was a Baptist, Salmon and Clarkson Seekers; Bauthumley's previous associations are not known. But these categories mean little.'[71] It would be unfair to quote so extensively from the juvenilia of an early thesis were it not that McGregor's work, then and now, represents the most cautious and sceptical treatment of the evidence which we yet have. In his hand the Ranter movement vanishes and the sect disintegrates, but we are left with a core of

---

62 McGregor, 'Ranterism and the Development of Early Quakerism', 354; 'Seekers and Ranters', p. 129.
63 McGregor, 'Seekers and Ranters', p. 129.
64 McGregor, 'The Ranters 1649–1660', 16–18.
65 E.578 (13, 14), Thomason's date 1 February 1650.
66 E.1353 (2), Thomason's date 20 November 1650. Bauthumley appears, nevertheless to have suffered punishment for this work earlier in March of the same year. See below, p.44.
67 E.609 (18), Thomason's date 21 August 1650. A follower of Abiezer Coppe, possibly Andrew Wyke, has been suggested as author of this. There is no corroborative evidence. Cf. McGregor, 'The Ranters 1649–1660', 17.
68 Salmon's *Heights in Depths and Depths in Heights* (E.1361(4), 13 August 1651) was in part a recantation of opinions expressed in the earlier and now lost work.
69 E.542 (5), Thomason's date 10 February 1649.
70 E.614 (1). Thomason dated this 4 October 1650 but we know that the House of Commons had a copy of the work as early as 21 June of that year (C.J. VI, 427).
71 McGregor, 'The Ranters 1649–1660', 17, 18.

doctrine enshrined in four, possibly five, extant tracts which he is prepared to link under the name of 'Ranter'.

vi. CONCLUSION

There remains a problem in identifying the social character of the Ranter
phenomenon: mass movement, sect, or loosely co-ordinated group of a
handful of individuals? Is that which distinguishes Ranterism in its core
or in its following? For Morton, the ideology might be incoherent and
internally inconsistent, the core diffuse, but the reality of the Ranters
was in the broad movement and what it represented.[72] Likewise, for
Hill, 'It is very difficult to define what "the Ranters" believed, as
opposed to individuals who are called Ranters.' There was no
recognised leader or theoretician and little, if any, organisation. The
views of the principal figures were inconsistent with one another. And
yet there was a group and a movement, with objectives, wings and a history of rise and repression.[73] For them, then, the reality, meaning and
significance of Ranterism was the movement and its rise and fall. The
measurement of the broad phenomenon was more important than the
analysis of the core. McGregor's approach implicitly challenged this.
The broad phenomenon dissolved into shadows in his landscape and a
few figures, with much in common despite some differences, were left
for scrutiny in the foreground. The core was, in practical and evidential
terms, just about all there was.

Until 1970 most historians wrote, if at all, of the Ranters as so
extreme as to be beyond the pale of sympathy – not only antinomian, in
rejecting all ordinances in theology and practice, but scornful of Scripture, pantheistic materialists, sensualists who obliterated the distinction
between good and evil in a crude permissiveness. Since 1970 – or was it
1968? – they have become a movement, earning a paradoxical dignity
from the repudiation of all dignity, a counter-culture or part of one.
McGregor has attenuated the social aspect of this considerably while he
has sharpened the theological aspect of it. His Ranters are a sparse group
with a brief existence, but their theological focus is clear, startling and
enormously significant. In reaction to it, repression came not only
against the sects but within them. In evaluating all of this, we are left
still with a long-running problem, that of the identity of the Ranters.
Should we focus on the core group, the limited number of individuals

---

[72] Cf. *W.O.T.R.*, pp. 17, 92–3.   [73] *W.T.U.D.*, pp. 203–4 and *passim.*

seen by McGregor as united in a set of beliefs with some consistency, or should we concern ourselves with the fringe, the following, the movement, which remains at the basis of the claims of Hill and Morton for the significance of the Ranters in the *longue durée*? Who were the Ranters?

2

Who were the Ranters?

i. THE PROBLEM

Terms like 'Ranter', beginning as terms of abuse, always have a slippery feel to them. They are words which evoke the existence of an identifiable – perhaps undesirable – group, but at the same time they are used indiscriminately, applied to disassociated individuals or unrelated groups. We have seen this distance between word and socially observable fact too frequently in our own day to need more than reminding of the exploitation of words like 'fascist', 'red' and so on. The problem is sharpened by resistance to, instead of acceptance of, the label. People reject it, the more so in that its application to them can appear fortuitous. Words here are witness to some sort of social struggle rather than functioning as precise cognitive signifiers or markers.

The great exemplar of this historiographical and semantic problem in early modern English history is, of course, the term 'Puritan'. Contemporaries used it so indiscriminately as to bring some modern historians, in despair, to call for the abandonment of the term entirely.[1] Our difficulty arises from two concerns: the desire not to be anachronistic, to use terms which are appropriate to the context of the past which we are endeavouring to explore and understand, and, secondly, the desire to describe a social reality, a genuine, coherent and defined phenonemon. It is the tension between the past as a world of contemporary perceptions, which can only be grasped in the words of the past, and the past as a set of social realities which we may explore as we will. When contemporary linguistic usage is too individualistic, arbitrary or inconsistent to enable us to pursue the second goal, we are faced with the difficulty of either narrowing a contemporary meaning, redefining the word in ways

---

[1] For the indiscriminate contemporary use see Christopher Hill, *Society and Puritanism in Pre-Revolutionary England* (London, 1966), Chapter 1; for the suggestion that the term be abandoned see C.H. George, 'Puritanism as History and Historiography', *P. & P.*, 41 (1968), 77–104.

which suit us, however anachronistic, or abandoning its use altogether. It would be a relatively straightforward project to write the history of the word 'Ranter' (and associated words) in terms of the taxonomy of its various meanings and the social and linguistic contexts of the word's usage, a semantic, semiotic and socio-linguistic history.[2] But not all historians are satisfied with this. Behind the verbal smokescreen of the word's usage they detect a real presence, a group who can more usefully be understood if their features are brought into correspondence with the word. This may mean narrowing the meaning of the word in ways which contemporaries did not recognise, hence the historiographical problem.

Certainly there are those who adopt brusque and sometimes arbitrary solutions to this problem. It is, however, a problem worth bearing in mind as we go in search of the Ranters; for the label was one used abusively and indiscriminately and yet historians have made large claims for a movement, group or sect, identified individuals as members or non-members, and have discussed its ideology and variations within it, as if there had existed a cohesive, consistent, clearly defined and self-conscious group. There is a tension between the word 'Ranter', as revelatory of the perceptions of seventeenth-century commentators, and the thing Ranter, as perceived by twentieth-century historians.

This would be no great difficulty if historians themselves had established consistent conventions, operated with an agreed definition of the term and had common practices with regard to persons included in and persons excluded from the group. The most obvious manifestation of this difficulty is the variety of listings of Ranters produced by historians operating without such conventions. For C.E. Whiting in 1931 John Robins, Thomas Tany, Abiezer Coppe, Joshua Garment, Joseph Salmon, Jacob Bauthumley and possibly Richard Coppin were to be counted as Ranters.[3] Three years later Tindall excluded or ignored Bauthumley, Garment and Robins, firmly brought in Richard Coppin and added George Foster, Laurence Clarkson and Edward Ellis.[4] In Morton's *Everlasting Gospel* (1958), the publisher and bookseller Giles

---

[2] Cf. Patrick Collinson's recent caution concerning linguistic conventions and the term 'Puritan': Patrick Collinson, 'A Comment: Concerning the Name Puritan', *Journal of Ecclesiastical History*, 31:4 (1980), 483–8.

[3] Whiting, *Studies in English Puritanism*, pp. 272–7.

[4] Tindall, *John Bunyan, passim*, especially pp. 98–9. One assumes that his reference to Edward Ellis is a confusion for Humphrey Ellis, far from a Ranter, and the author of a description and denunciation of the messiah-like claims of William Franklin and Mary Gadbury: *Pseudochristus* (1650), E.602 (12).

Calvert became a Ranter.[5] In 1970, the same author excluded Foster, and saw Robins, Tany and John Reeve as a type of Ranter but yet not Ranters.[6] In *The World Turned Upside Down* Hill included Coppe, Clarkson, Salmon, Bauthumley and Foster. Coppin was a near-Ranter, although he denied it, and the English Behmenists, John Pordage and Thomas Tany, seem to be loosely associated with Ranter status.[7] While McGregor dismissed Robins and Tany as Ranters in 1968, Hill has continued to identify them as such.[8] As we have seen, McGregor would limit the Ranter ideologues to Bauthumley, Clarkson, Coppe and one unknown writer – and even so their sectarian status might have been other than Ranter when they wrote their 'Ranter' works. Meanwhile the *Biographical Dictionary of British Radicals in the Seventeenth Century* has identified Mary Adams, Bauthumley, Clarkson, Coppe, Foster, Francis Freeman, Mary Gadbury, Anne Gargill and Rice Jones as Ranters and Richard Coppin as a source of Ranter ideas.[9]

Contemporaries were no more consistent. The first attempts to apply the term to specific individuals may not have developed until November 1650. The Blasphemy Ordinance of 9 August 1650, for example, though often alleged to have been produced in reaction to Ranter excesses, makes no reference to the term. The word 'Ranterism' may not have emerged before 1653.[10]

In mid November 1650 Ranters, 'Coppanites' and 'Claxtonians' were seen as identical.[11] In early December the Ranters were still being linked with Coppe, but a fortnight later the association had moved to Pordage, the leading English exponent of Jacob Boehme's ideas.[12] Yet a week later and a Mrs Hull, a preacher named Arthingworth, a Mr

[5] Morton, *Everlasting Gospel*, p. 39. Calvert was again to be accorded Ranter status by McGregor (1968) and, more doubtfully, by Morton (1970).

[6] *W.O.T.R.*, pp. 92, 140.

[7] *W.T.U.D.*, pp. 220–6. Cf. *The Experience of Defeat*, pp. 43–50.

[8] E.g. Hill, 'John Reeve and the Origins of Muggletonianism', in Hill, Reay, Lamont (eds.), *The World of the Muggletonians*, p. 67; see also Hill's review in *The Journal of Modern History*, 56:1 (1984), 133; on Robins, *The Experience of Defeat*, p. 45 n. 6.

[9] *B.D.B.R.S.C.*, under name entries. Gadbury, Freeman and Adams are particularly contentious identifications.

[10] Samuel Fisher, *Baby-Baptism Meer Babism* (1653), Wing S.T.C. F.1055.

[11] [Anon.,] *The Routing of the Ranters* (1650), E.616 (9), Thomason date 19 November 1650.

[12] [Anon.,] *The Ranters Ranting* (1650), pp. 5–6, E.618 (8), Thomason date 2 December 1650; M. Stubs, *The Ranters Declaration* (1650), p. 3, E.620 (2), Thomason date 17 December 1650. Appearing on the same day, according to Thomason, [Anon.,] *The Arraignment and Tryall with A Declaration of the Ranters*, E.620 (3) linked the Ranters with Dr Buckeridge (presumably Pordage) and with Coppe, Claxton and Collins.

Gilbert, W. Smith, an unnamed proclaimer of Charles Stuart as King and 'Ranting Everard's party' were all seen as exemplifying the Ranter phenomenon.[13] One need not go on. In the space of a few weeks all discrimination in the use of the term had shattered. Moreover, it is impossible to find any contemporary accepting the application of it to him or herself. The closest which anyone came to that was Laurence Clarkson in his restrospective account, *The Lost Sheep Found* (1660). But even here we must be circumspect. Clarkson nowhere uses the term 'Ranter'. The most he does is to acknowledge that he was referred to by others as 'Captain of the Rant'.[14]

There is a similar source of confusion in historians' attempts to evoke the social meaning of Ranterism. Was it a sect, a movement, a loose group, or a small set of isolated individuals? For Mooney it was one of the chief sects of the period; for Whiting 'the wildest of all the sects'; for Tindall one of the principal non-calvinist sects of the 1650s and evangelical to boot.[15] Morton in 1958 thought of the Ranters as a sect, bitterly attacked and persecuted, but in *The World of the Ranters* they had become a 'movement rather than a sect', though the cover blurb belied this by calling them 'the most radical of all the left-wing sects'.[16] For Rufus Jones, the Ranters had never been a specific sect but rather 'the lunatic fringe in each sect', or, in another version, 'more or less contagious movements or tendencies of thought'.[17] McGregor too did not see the Ranters as a sect, but more as a climate of opinion, 'a loosely co-ordinated campaign'. They might be described as a movement, but then they were more of a religious mood than a movement.[18] Or, later, there was no sect or movement, but it was still claimed that the Ranters were one of the 'main movements of enthusiasm'.[19]

13 [Anon.,] *The Ranters Recantation* (1650), E.620 (10), Thomason date 20 December 1650.

14 Laurence Claxton [Clarkson], *The Lost Sheep Found* (1660), Wing C.4580. A facsimile of this was produced by The Rota at the University of Exeter in 1974. Extracts were also reproduced in *R W*. Although contemporaries used both 'Clarkson' and 'Claxton', I have preferred the former. The crucial phrase here is in *Lost Sheep Found*, p. 26: 'Now I being as they said, Captain of the Rant . . .'. As we shall see below, this account needs to be weighed very carefully in terms of its polemical function in 1660 before its veracity as autobiography is taken for granted.

15 Mooney, *Ghost-Dance*, p. 937; Whiting, *Studies in English Puritanism*, p. 272; Tindall, *John Bunyan*, pp. 4, 7. Similarly, Cohn, *Pursuit of the Millennium*, p. 15; J.F.C. Harrison, *The Second Coming: Popular Millenarianism 1780–1850* (London, 1979), p. 14.

16 Morton, *Everlasting Gospel*, p. 41; *W.O.T.R.*, pp. 17, 92, cover.

17 Jones, *Mysticism and Democracy*, p. 132; *Studies in Mystical Religion*, p. 452.

18 McGregor, 'The Ranters 1649–1660', 59–60, 104; 'Ranterism and the Development of Early Quakerism', 350.

19 McGregor, 'Seekers and Ranters', p. 129; 'The Baptists: Fount of All Heresy', pp. 58–9; both in McGregor and Reay (eds.), *Radical Religion*.

Personnel and social description remain uncertain. How are we to explore this phenomenon, test the claims made for it and provide evaluations of our own if we do not have agreement as to what to include in it or indeed as to what sort of sociological parameters to anticipate in identifying it? Closely linked with this is the question whether we should seek the identity of Ranterism in a reasonably consistent set of doctrines held, albeit perhaps temporarily, by a very few individuals (McGregor's core), or seek the social identity of the Ranters in the broader movement and perhaps in the common contemporary perception of it (the Morton, Hill approach).

In this chapter and the next, we shall examine the former. Was there an inner group or core whose ideas are consistent enough to give them even an informal or adduced corporate identity? How do we identify that group? I shall argue that no such group existed and that a consistent set of shared ideas has been falsely ascribed to it. Once this is recognised, the group falls apart and we are left with a number of individuals of varying persuasions.

There will remain the problem of the movement. How, and by whom, was it perceived in the 1650s that there was a Ranter phenomenon? And what was the perceived character of that phenomenon? We shall examine these problems in Chapter 4. Why, if there was no coherent centre, did so many people believe that there were Ranters? I seek to answer this question in Chapter 5. Finally, Chapter 6 will offer some reappraisal of the historiographical phenomenon of the Ranters.

ii. APPROACHING THE CORE

Immediately, however, let us turn our attention to the task of identifying a small core of Ranter ideologists, linked by their common doctrines in theology and/or their unity in social programme. Commentators have suggested a variety of essential tenets within Ranterism, not all of them consistent with each other. To simplify matters, however, we may suggest two central features of their thought agreed on by everyone. They were, it is universally alleged, antinomians and pantheists.

The belief that an age of law had been replaced by an age of grace and 'That God sees no sin in those that are his' was evidently about in seventeenth-century England, though its extent is uncertain.[20] The sim-

---

[20] The quotation is from [Anon.,] *A Declaration against the Antinomians and their doctrine of Liberty* (1644), cited in Huehns, *Antinomianism*, p. 8. For conflicting views of how widespread these ideas were see *ibid.*, pp. 28, 66, 68, 71.

plicities of a label like 'antinomian', even when not used abusively,[21] hide a myriad of forms. There was a distinction between what Sedgewick called 'doctrinal' and 'practical' antinomianism.[22] The belief could be held speculatively, that is without necessarily leading to consequences in behaviour and practice. On the other hand, certain forms of behaviour could all too readily be identified with forms of belief which might or might not be held. A second dimension inheres in the extent to which antinomianism was a special problem within Calvinism, applying only to the elect, or, on the other hand, the extent to which we should associate it with the repudiation of Calvinism by those who espoused universal grace. Was antinomian belief an outcome of reflection on Christ and the conclusion that his grace was all sufficient, obliterating sin, or was it a consequence of belief that, in the Creation, God had made all things good, intended all things including what was mistakenly called 'sin'?[23] The latter could, but did not necessarily, overlap with a Socinian position, much to the cost of the few seventeenth-century Socinians.[24]

Even an antinomianism based in the atoning power of Christ's propitiation for sin could lead in a variety of directions. For John Eaton a sense of the liberty of grace strengthened the sense of sin and abhorrence of it.[25] Tobias Crisp, like Gerrard Winstanley, saw the choice of a threefold liberty facing Christians: 'a morale, or a *Civil Liberty*', 'a sensual and corrupt liberty', and 'a spiritual and a divine liberty'. It was the last which should be cultivated; it subsumed the first but rejected the second form of liberty.[26] It may be, as Rutherford suggested of the antinomians, that 'they make all duties a matter of courtesie' towards God,[27] yet duties might remain in a pure turning against evil. In a second case, faith in Christ's assurance of our salvation could lead to an indifference towards forms of action altogether. Thus Francis Freeman claimed that Christ justified us, not our faith in him. The

---

[21] For an example of abusive use see Sedgewick's *Antinomianisme Anatomized*, discussed in Huehns, *Antinomianism*, p. 37.

[22] Huehns, *Antinomianism*, p. 40; Hutin, *Les Disciples anglais*.

[23] For these distinctions see Huehns, *Antinomianism*, pp. 12–13, 42–3.

[24] H.J. McLachlan, *Socinianism in Seventeenth Century England* (Oxford, 1951), especially Chapter 11.

[25] John Eaton, *The Honey-Combe of Free Justification by Christ alone* (1641), Wing E.115, pp. 154, 402.

[26] Tobias Crisp, *Christ Alone Exalted in fourteene sermons* (1643), Sermon VII: Christian Libertie No Licentious Doctrine, pp. 228, 230, 231, 242, E.1106. Cf. Winstanley, *The Law of Freedom*, in C. Hill (ed.), *Winstanley: The Law of Freedom and Other Writings* (Harmondsworth, 1973), pp. 294–5.   [27] Huehns, *Antinomianism*, p. 52.

enigmatic function of faith was to replace the law.[28] Men should not sin though Grace abound, but, should they do so, that too praises God.[29] A third antinomian position was that we should demonstrate the redeeming power of grace and triumph over the sense of sin, by actively committing those acts commonly misunderstood as sin.[30] This is what Sedgewick had called 'practical' antinomianism and it appears to have been extremely rare. Nevertheless, both contemporary commentators and recent historians have identified the Ranters with it. We shall have to be very clear about this for, if practical antinomianism is a criterion for Ranter status then we have a very severe test and other forms of antinomian should not be admitted. On the other hand, if a broader antinomianism is taken we shall have problems with exclusions and end up with a rather heterogeneous collection of people.

There are similar problems with pantheism. It could be linked with Creation antinomianism so that God became either the author of sin, as he was the author of all things, or somehow his being could barely be freed from sin as he was present in all things. Alternatively, God became everything. Sin became nothing, the negation of God. Either way, problems remained. Was pantheism linked with universal salvation or not? Did the notion of God's omnipresence obliterate the distinction between saved and damned? Conflicting answers could be and were given. God's presence, even in events normally regarded as sinful, could free one from a great deal of anxiety. But did it imply that one merely ceased to worry or that, in order perhaps to participate in the fulness of God, one should act out sin?

It is not sufficient therefore to invoke antinomianism and pantheism and assume that we can thereby identify Ranters. Both could mean a variety of things, each with diverse implications. Do the Ranters embrace all of these things – or even many of them? In such a case, they would merge with other groups exploring these various implications and, thereby, would lose their separate identity. They would cease to be a distinct group. The problem is exemplified by the continuing identification of similarities between Ranters and other groups such as Quakers, Baptists, Seekers, Universalists, Behmenists and Atheists.[31]

---

[28] Francis Freeman, *Light Vanquishing Darkness* (1650), pp. 50–1, 52 E.615 (7), Thomason date 29 October 1650. As we shall see, Jacob Bauthumley may also have held this position.

[29] Jacob Bauthumley, *The Light and Dark Sides of God* (1650), p. 35, E.1353 (2), Thomason date 20 November 1650.

[30] These three distinctions are acknowledged and then neglected by Morton (W.O.T.R., p. 77) and McGregor ('The Ranters 1649–1660', pp. 7–8).

[31] For the sectarian blur which commencing with a general concept like antinomianism could, and can, produce, see Francis Freeman, *Light Vanquishing Darkness*, pp. 1–2: 'the highest

Are the Ranters then a distinct group, a distinct species even of pan-theists and antinomians, separated from others by special or defining characteristics and, if so, what are they?

I want to approach the problem initially by means of an exercise in historiographical contextualisation, by clarifying and then testing a series of historiographical hypotheses which seem to have, implicit within them, a set of defining characteristics by which the Ranters are, or should be, known. Let us assume a common way of viewing the Ranters which has been in large measure shared by Cohn, Morton and Hill, as well as by those who have followed them such as Reay, Smith, Coward, McGregor and a host of others. There may be differences of emphasis within this paradigm, as for example that between McGregor and Morton and Hill, but overall there is a common framework. The essence of this is the sense of the Ranters as an antithesis of the Protes-tant ethic, in particular as representative of a struggle against the intern-alised repression of the puritan sense of sin or guilt: 'their ultimate aim was the attainment of freedom from the burden of sin . . .'.[32] By accept-ing property, the Levellers inevitably blunted the revolutionary edge of their cause. By accepting sin, Winstanley ultimately endorsed the need to repress and diverted his vision of a better society into a utopianised totalitarianism.[33] It is the Ranters who, in rejecting sin and repression, epitomised the negation of the Protestant ethic and its accompanying cultural forms which have been major props of the hegemony of the ruling classes ever since. This framework has underlain the claim that they warrant our attention and the significance which has been attached to them over the last fifteen years. They not only tell us something about the seventeenth century but about the nature of English society and its history over the last four centuries. For them to operate within such a framework, they have to be antinomian and pantheistic to the point of rejecting the notion of sin and its repressive concomitants, since, in the seventeenth-century context, the shackles of religion could only be repudiated in the language of religion. The distinctions between sin-ful and holy, between good and evil, heaven and hell have to evaporate

degree of Presbyterians, are almost Antinomians, the highest degree of Antinomians, are almost Independants, the highest degree of Independants, are almost Anabaptists, and the Anabaptists are almost Seekers, and the Seekers are at a stand . . .'.

[32]   McGregor, 'The Ranters, 1649–1660', 47.

[33]   J.C. Davis, 'Gerrard Winstanley and the Restoration of True Magistracy', *P. & P.*, 70 (1976), 76–93; J.C. Davis, *Utopia and the Ideal Society* (Cambridge, 1981), Chapter 7; for a contrary view see Christopher Hill, 'The Religion of Gerrard Winstanley', *P. & P. Supple-ment*, 5 (1978); G.E. Aylmer, 'The Religion of Gerrard Winstanley', in McGregor and Reay (eds.), *Radical Religion*, pp. 91–119.

in their thought. Psychological, theological and social repression would be ended in extreme antinomianism, extreme pantheism and the acting out, at least symbolically, of practical antinomianism as liberation from sin and guilt. To legitimate such a position, Scripture must be seen as a dead letter. Formalism must be rejected along with the scripturally based ordinances on which it rested.

So for Christopher Hill, though there were acknowledged variations between individuals, the tenets of Ranterism could be summarised as follows: God was in everyone and everything; Christ's coming was internal to everyone; evil, sin and judgement had no reality; and, in extreme form, some held that they were most perfect who could sin with least remorse.[34] For Morton, similarly, the Ranters believed that God existed only in material objects, a position which Morton saw as leading either to a 'pantheistic mysticism' and/or a 'crudely plebeian materialism'; that the Bible should be interpreted symbolically or rejected; that the moral law was no longer binding on the children of grace, and consequentially that no act was sinful, 'a conviction that some hastened to put into practice'.[35] Likewise for McGregor, what gave his Ranter core their common element of consistency was a 'mystical antinomianism', a simultaneous sense of oneness with God and a denial of the reality of sin to the believer. Since all acts were inspired by God, the saints' behaviour was a matter of moral indifference. Some emphasised the force of this by acting out sin; Clarkson adulterously, Coppe blasphemously.[36]

Given this context and these distinguishing features, we should be able to begin the process of identifying an agreed body of Ranters. Let us begin, in this chapter, by eliminating those fringe figures who have, for assorted and largely suspect reasons, been associated with or identified as Ranters, thereby merely confusing the issue of the character and significance of the phenomenon. In the next chapter, we shall examine the hard core of established Ranter figures in the light of these criteria.

iii. ELIMINATING THE FRINGE

a. The new messiahs

First and, one would have thought, amongst the most readily discarded should be those new messiahs who claimed to be the reincarnation of

---

[34] Hill, *W.T.U.D.*, pp. 204–8.
[35] Morton, *W.O.T.R.*, p. 70.   [36] McGregor, 'Seekers and Ranters', pp. 129–30.

Christ or God himself. For what they represented was not so much the Age of the Spirit's liberation from the law, as much as a reshuffling of the Age of the Gospel. The ultimate authority over the believer was not to be the spirit within but a new, flesh and blood messiah or God. Joshua Garment's vision of John Robins was thus as Lord of Hosts, judge and lawgiver.[37] Robins was alleged to be revered as God the Father, his wife intended to bear the Saviour.[38] Another messiah, William Franklin, had a protracted history of delusions of himself as Christ or God, reaching back apparently to 1646, and with Mary Gadbury, a close and enthusiastic follower, was tried and sentenced early in 1650. Franklin was alleged to have received a vision saying 'I have made an end of sin & transgression for me and my people.'[39] But what meaning Franklin or any of his followers attached to any of this is never made clear.

Neither seems to meet the criteria of Ranter identity, unless we allow for the contemporary usage as an umbrella term of abuse and religious sensation.[40]

b. The new prophets

The number of those claiming religious authority in the 1640s and 1650s was not inconsiderable, but relatively few took the step of seeing themselves as possessed of a totally new commission, superseding the historical commissions already recorded in Scripture. The ecstatic nature of the language in which these new prophets sometimes sought to express the new commission, their extreme reliance, at least temporarily, on inner promptings, made them look like spiritual enthusiasts

---

[37] Joshua Garment, *The Hebrews Deliverance* (1652), p. 4, E.640 (18). The vision was received in 1650, the tract written in 1651 and published in 1652.

[38] *All the Proceedings at the Sessions of the Peace Holden at Westminster on the 20 day of June 1651* (1651), p. 3, E.637 (18). See also John Taylor, *Ranters of Both Sexes* (1651), E.629 (15); G.H., *The Declaration of John Robins* (1651), E.629 (13); [James Moxon?,] *The Ranters Creed* (1651), Wing R.250. For a sensible discussion of the Robins case in relation to the Ranters see McGregor, 'The Ranters 1649–1660', Appendix A. The following have identified Robins as a Ranter: Whiting (1931), Hutin (1960), Underdown (1973), Hill (1983 on Reeve).

[39] Humphrey Ellis, *Pseudochristus* (1650), p. 15, E.602 (12). Cf. the story of Mary Adams, alleged to have proclaimed herself the Virgin Mary pregnant with the Saviour and to have brought forth a monster. [Anon.,] *The Ranters Monster* (1652), E.658 (6). See also McGregor, 'The Ranters 1649–1660', pp. 174–6. For the allegation of an association with Ranterism see Cohn, *Pursuit of the Millennium* (1962); *B.D.B.R.S.C.* under Adams, Gadbury.

[40] Laurence Clarkson, of all people, was later to argue the diabolism of John Robins: Clarkson, *Look about you* (1659), p. 23, Wing C.4579.

and has even led to their being labelled Ranters. But like Muggleton and Reeve they came ultimately in the name of a new authority, only incidentally in the name of liberation from an old one.

Thomas Tany has been repeatedly identified as a Ranter.[41] From 1649 he was embarked on a millennial mission under direct instruction from God, to call the Jews to return to Jerusalem.[42] In 1651 he was claiming the throne of England in descent through Henry VII and as the true Earl of Essex.[43] It would be incautious to dismiss Tany's antics as those of a madman too readily. He knew that in some respects he was playing the fool.[44] In his *Theauraujohn His Theousori* (1651) Tany developed a mystical pantheism, in which there was no room for the anger or judgement of God. Hell was merely the negation of heaven or separation from oneness with Christ. The thrust of his attack was, however, not on the ordinances of the Gospel or biblical injunctions but on the hypocrisy of Christians not acting upon them.[45] Tany claimed to write and speak as the mouthpiece of God.[46] His authority was to replace that of a discredited Scripture.[47] Tany rejected the labels of Ranter and antinomian.[48] His strange language comes close to a pantheist universalism, but he never entirely rejects the notion of sin – indeed, his greatest vehemence is reserved for hypocrisy, which he saw as a kind of knowing and wilful sinning.

He cannot be accepted as a Ranter under the criteria we are discussing any more than John Pordage, who once gave Tany shelter at his house in Bradfield, can. Pordage was the leading English Behmenist of his generation[49] and had been, since about 1647, incumbent of one of the richest livings in the country. In 1649 he was accused, before the Committee for Plundered Ministers, of holding what amounted to mystical pantheism but on 27 March 1651 was cleared of all charges.[50] Charges against him were, however, renewed and John Tickell, who also pursued Pordage's friend Abiezer Coppe, was also involved in

---

[41] Whiting (1931), Tindall (1934), Hutin (1960), Morton (1970), Hill (1972), Hill (1983).

[42] Thomas Tany, *I Proclaime* (1650), 669 f.15 (28).

[43] Tany, *The Nations Right in Magna Charta* (n.p., n.d.), E.621 (3). Thomason date 1 January 1651. [44] *Ibid.*, p. 8. [45] E.640 (8), pp. 20, 29–31, 15, 70.

[46] [Thomas Tany,] *Theauraujohn Tani. His Second Part of His Theous-Ori Apokolipital* (1653), p. 6. [47] *Ibid.*, pp. 19–29.

[48] [Thomas Tany,] *Theauraujohn His Aurora in Tranlagorum in Salem Gloria* (1655), pp. 10, 25–6, E.853 (26).

[49] Desirée Hirst, 'The Riddle of John Pordage', *The Jacob Boehme Society Quarterly*, 1:6 (1953–4), 5–15; E. Lewis Evans, 'Morgan Lloyd and Jacob Boehme', *The Jacob Boehme Society Quarterly*, 1:4 (1953), 11–16.

[50] Hirst, 'Riddle of John Pordage'; *D.N.B.*, under 'Pordage, John'.

these charges. It seems possible that a motive behind the persecution of Pordage was the desire to oust him from a very wealthy living. Certainly most of the charges were made on the basis of gossip and misunderstanding as to the nature of Boehme's and Pordage's ideas. Nevertheless, he was ejected from his living in December 1654 only to be reinstated at the Restoration.

Of interest to us at this stage is that Pordage was accused of Ranterism.[51] But this needs to be seen in the context of the whole welter of accusations made against him, accusations ranging from witchcraft and sorcery to neglect of a woman parishioner in labour. In their zeal to bring him down Pordage's accusers threw whatever came to mind. Ranterism was just one of a large number of sometimes mutually inconsistent charges. There is an interesting coda to the story. After the verdict, Pordage decided to go to London and appeal personally to Cromwell. Some of his friends condemned this action as being too slavish. Pordage's response was that 'in every Principle according to natural Order and God's Will, there should be Superiority and Inferiority, Rulers and Ruled, Higher and Lower, even as there are' and he went on to defend the maintenance of a ministry through tithes.[52]

Pordage is clearly far removed from the subversive anticipations that we have of Ranterism according to our paradigm. What his tale illustrates is the potential utility of a vindictive charge of Ranterism against an enemy whose religious views are in any way unusual or confusing. Amidst the farrago of gossip and second-hand tittle-tattle that was directed at Pordage, Ranterism was just another item, as credible and lacking in credibility as the rest. We should be on guard against such uses of the term. Certainly they were not uncommon. We can readily find another example, this time unsuccessful, in the case of Thomas Webbe.

c. New victims

Webbe, the parson of Langley Buriall in Wiltshire, was in 1650 accused of adultery with a married gentlewoman of the district, of having encouraged his wife's adultery by preaching Ranter doctrines of sexual promiscuity to her, and of having had a homosexual relationship. He

---

[51] See Pordage's account in *Innocencie Appearing through the dark mists of pretended Guilt* (1655), pp. 14–15, E.1068 (7).   [52] *Ibid.*, pp. 106, 109–10.

was eventually acquitted by an assize jury on the charge of adultery but was ejected from his living by the Committee for Plundered Ministers.[53] Once again accusations and counter-accusations flew thick and fast. And a strange *mélange* they were; from sexual misdemeanour, to contempt of Parliament; from hypocritical repentance to the claim that all preaching is lies; from 'the extraordinary poudring of his head and frizzling of his hair, and other inticements to lust and wantonnesse' to extempore singing and dancing; from the claim to be above all scriptural ordinance, to that of having damaged the parsonage's glebe lands or lacking a legal warrant for his incumbency at all.[54] All we have to go on is an extremely hostile account of charges based mainly on gossip and second- or third-hand reporting. Moreover, Webbe was acquitted on those charges most closely associated with the practical antinomianism identified with Ranterism.

In the context of this type of evidence, little should be made of the reproduction in Edward Stokes's account of a letter to Webbe from Joseph Salmon. The letter, from Coventry and dated 3 April 1650, mentions Abiezer Coppe and probably refers to Jacob Bauthumley, though not by name.[55] Otherwise the letter is the kind of perfervid expression of ecstasy, love and religious paradox that was not uncommon amongst the spiritual enthusiasts of the period. Salmon knew Webbe and could assume that he knew Coppe. This is all that we can safely draw from the letter.

What remains indeterminate here is the degree of malice, or of substance, behind the accusations of Ranterism. Given the heterogeneous nature of the eventual charges and the obvious bias of our principal informant, there does seem to be some warrant for a prima facie case of malice. It is clearly going too far in the opposite direction to accept on this basis and the evidence of heresiographers like Edwards that Webbe was a long-time practising Ranter,[56] or to take for granted the veracity of the charges reported by Stokes against Webbe.[57]

---

[53] The account we have to rely on is again a violently partisan one, produced by an enemy of Webbe: Edward Stokes, *The Wiltshire Rant* (1652), E.669 (5). Webbe's defence, *A Mass of Malice against Thomas Webbe*, appears to be no longer extant.

[54] Stokes, *Wiltshire Rant*, pp. 15, 22, 51.   [55] *Ibid.*, pp. 13–14.

[56] *R.W.*, p. 11. For the suggestion that this might be used as evidence of an organised Ranter movement see McGregor, 'Seekers and Ranters', p. 131; 'The Ranters 1649–1660', pp. 92–5. For the depiction of Webbe's acquittal as a refusal to convict see McGregor, 'The Ranters 1649–1660', p. 94. See also *B.D.B.R.S.C.* under 'Webbe'.

[57] *W.T.U.D.*, pp. 226–7.

iv. TIGHTENING THE CORE

Tany, Pordage and Webbe have all been on occasion associated with
Ranterism and I have suggested that these associations are either invalid
or suspect enough for judgement to be reserved. George Foster, Joseph
Salmon and Richard Coppin have far more frequently and closely been
identified with the Ranters. Let us test them in sequence for their fit
with the historiographical paradigm.

a. George Foster[58]

We know little of Foster apart from the two works which he published
in 1650. Both are millennial forewarnings of a social levelling soon to
come at the hands of a judgemental God. *The Sounding of the Last Trumpet*
announced an imminent overturning of the established order and a
reduction of all people to equality by God: 'cutting down all men and
women that he met with, that were higher than the middle sort, and
raised up those that were lower than the middle sort and made them all
Equall, and cried out, equallitie, equallitie'.[59] Forms of worship and
government would cease and men and women would live in perfect
harmony.[60] The message was much the same in his second work, *The
Pouring Forth of the Seventh and Last Viall Upon all Flesh and Fleshlines*. The
practical Christianity of true charity would lead to the sharing of
possessions in equality. Those who resisted this would soon be judged,
brought low and punished. In the end God would supervise the
emergence of an arcadian perfect moral commonwealth.[61]

There is no antinomian or pantheistic *credo* here; no lack of a personal, objective, historical and judgemental God. The emphasis on
levelling and equality provides one obvious context and it is not a Ranting
one. The limits of his theological preoccupations are millennial and the
personal revelations granted him within the ambience of his reading of

---

[58]   For the identification of Foster as a Ranter see Tindall (1934), Hill (1972), Olivier Lutaud,
       Winstanley: Socialisme et christianisme sous Cromwell (Paris, 1976). Bernard Capp. 'The Fifth
       Monarchists and Popular Millenarianism', in McGregor and Reay (eds.), *Radical Religion*, p.
       187, identifies Foster as 'an idiosyncratic Ranter'. In his entry on Foster for the
       B.D.B.R.S.C., Frank McGregor has suggested that, while Foster was influenced by Ranter
       ideas, especially those of Coppe's *Fiery Flying Roll*, he was too eclectic and millennial in
       orientation to be counted a Ranter.
[59]   *The Sounding of the Last Trumpet* (1650), p. 17, E.598 (18, Thomason date 24 April
       1650.   [60]   *Ibid.*, pp. 21, 46.7.
[61]   *The Pouring Fourth* (1650), pp. 1–6, 13–18, 40, E.616 (4*), Thomason date 15
       November 1650.

Daniel and Revelation. His immediate concerns are social and he should be read in the context of Winstanley and others who looked for an end to covetousness in charity and a society without the injustices they associated with material and social inequality.[62] Unlike Winstanley, Foster's millennialism made him a passive waiter upon the Lord, rather than an activist, and sustained his vision of an earth restored and humanity made perfect in moral performance.

b. Joseph Salmon[63]

Historians have far more frequently bestowed the identity of Ranter upon Joseph Salmon than upon George Foster. The evidence for such an identification is, however, no more convincing. It can, in fact, only be made on the basis of assumptions unsustained by the available evidence.

The case for identifying Salmon as a Ranter rests on two things. First, but somewhat obscurely, comes a tract, no longer extant, called *Divinity Anatomized* which Salmon claimed to have written and from which his *Heights in Depths AND Depth in Heights* (1651) was written to dissociate himself. But, since the beliefs disowned in the second tract are a mixture of tenets held forth in various works, of those 'now charged upon the Author' and, more generally, 'a small parcel of the most crying errors of the times', it is impossible to derive from the recantation exactly what Salmon might have held in the earlier work.[64]

The second ground for identifying him as a Ranter is the evidence of Salmon's imprisonment in 1650 and his associations during that period. Abiezer Coppe's *A Fiery Flying Roll* appeared, according to George Thomason's recorded date, on 4 January 1650. It created something of an immediate sensation. Within a few days Coppe was imprisoned in Warwick,[65] and, shortly thereafter, transferred to Coventry.[66] On 1 February 1650, the House of Commons, which regularly spent Fridays

---

[62] There is no warrant, apart from intuition, for McGregor's supposition that the strongest influence on him was Coppe's *Fiery Flying Roll*, though the common context of both becomes clearer if they are lifted away from Ranter identification.

[63] The following have identified Salmon as a Ranter: Whiting (1931), Jones (1936), Tindall (1934), Hutin (1960), Cohn (1957; 1970), Morton (1970), Hill (1972), Lutaud (1976), McGregor (1968; 1984 – p. 129, n. 19), Ellens (1971), Smith (1983). In 1977 McGregor denied that Salmon openly preached Ranter doctrines: 'Ranterism and Early Quakerism', p. 357.

[64] Jo. Salmon, *Heights in Depths AND Depth in Heights* (1651), pp. 35–6, E.1361 (4), Thomason date 13 August 1651. [65] *C.S.P.D.*, 1649–50, pp. 502, 503.

[66] *A Perfect Diurnall*, no. 6, 14–21 January 1650, 42, E.534 (1).

on religious matters, condemned *A Fiery Flying Roll* and ordered it to be burned by all local authorities.[67] Orders were sent for Coppe to be brought to London, but he requested a postponement on the grounds of ill health.[68] So that, when Joseph Salmon appeared preaching in Coventry, Coppe was still there in gaol.

Salmon was reported to have preached in Coventry on Sunday 10 March, described as 'a comrade of Coppe', 'a most dangerous spirit', guilty of sad oaths and convicted before a magistrate.[69] The previous Wednesday Andrew Wyke, an Essex man, and his companion Mrs Wallis arrived in Coventry to visit Coppe. Captain Beake reported to William Clarke that 'They said the Scripture to them was no more than a ballad, that there was no devil, that it was God that swore in them.' 'Wyke called a soldier of mine a fiend of Hell, a child of the devil. These men are of acute wits and voluble tongues.' By the time this story appeared in the press it had been embroidered so that Wyke and Mrs Willis [*sic*] were now sleeping together, were accompanied by Salmon, claimed their oaths were God swearing in them, kissed the insulted soldier and claimed to breathe the spirit of God into him.[70] Yet again when Bulstrode Whitelocke recorded the story, obviously culled from *A Perfect Diurnall* and half-remembered, it was Salmon who was now the centre of the 'crew'. Coppe had disappeared from sight:

> From Coventry, of the preaching of one Salmon and of his wicked swearing and uncleanness, which he justified and others of his way, that it was God which did swear in them, and that it was their liberty to keep company with women for their lust. That one Wyke, another of his crew, kissed a soldier three times and said, 'I breathe the Spirit of God into thee', and many the like abominable blasphemies spoken by them; for which they were imprisoned till a trial for the crimes.[71]

Such testimony has to be treated with extreme caution.

Nevertheless, Salmon, Wyke and Coppe were now in Coventry gaol. On 15 March Wyke wrote to the mayor and aldermen of Coventry protesting the cruel treatment of his 'kinswoman Mistrisse Wallis' who was not permitted to visit him in prison and could not be expected to

[67]   *C.J.*, VI, 354. See also *C.S.P.D.*, 1650, p. 5.
[68]   *C.S.P.D.*, 1649–50, p. 502; *A Perfect Diurnall*, no. 9, 4–11 February 1650, E.534 (8).
[69]   *A Perfect Diurnall*, no. 14, 11–18 March 1650, 128, E.534 (18). This report, and the one following it, are based on a letter from Captain Robert Beake in Coventry to William Clark. See *H.M.C. Leybourne-Popham* (1899), 57.
[70]   *Ibid.*; cf. *A Perfect Diurnall*, no. 14, 128.
[71]   Bulstrode Whitelocke, *Memorials of the English Affairs* (4 vols., Oxford, 1853), vol. III, p. 163.

make her way home to Essex without him. On 19 March Coppe was taken from Coventry to London.[72]

In the mean time Salmon and Wyke were alleged to have preached every Lord's Day, through the grates of their Coventry gaol, to a crowd of curious bystanders.[73] On 1 April Wyke wrote once more to the mayor and aldermen. The prison keeper had told him that he was prohibited from preaching 'at the grates as formerly' (there is no mention of Salmon), and no one was to speak with him but in the presence of the keeper:

> You profess to the world to walk by the rules of mercy, love and justice, yet you imprison me, against whom there is nothing alleged but for swaring, for which I was fined two shillings, and now you have sent up to the Council of State, by which means I am further detained.

Wyke went on to upbraid the officials for their hypocrisy and to warn them that their time was running out.[74] There is no evidence here of a closely bonded group. Nor is there in Salmon's letter of 3 April from Coventry to Thomas Webbe. This letter makes no mention of Wyke or of Mrs Wallis. It speaks of Coppe with some affection but refers to Jacob Bauthumley's court martial without knowing his name.[75]

By the end of April 1650, Wyke's business was before the Council of State and in late June they ordered his release on the recognisance of Samuel Duncan, a draper of Ipswich, for £200.[76] Salmon was eventually released on condition that he published a recantation, a condition which he fulfilled with *Heights in Depths* in August 1651.[77] Then the records fall silent.

What are we to make of this? The evidence for a coherent, cohesive group is slight in the extreme. Wyke and Salmon were interested in Coppe but barely acknowledged each other's existence. They show no signs of seeing themselves as members of a group, even of the most informal kind. Observers were more inclined to see corporate identity and co-ordinated activity than these individuals were to assume such identity or to engage in such activity. We shall observe this pattern

---

[72] *A Perfect Diurnall*, no. 15, 18–25 March 1650.

[73] Whitelocke, *Memorials*, vol. III, p. 170. Again the accuracy of such reports is doubtful. Once more Whitelocke may have been following *A Perfect Diurnall* (no. 17, 1–18 April 1650, 175).   [74] *H.M.C. Leybourne-Popham*, p. 59.

[75] For this letter see Stokes, *Wiltshire Rant*, pp. 13–14. It is reproduced in *R.W.*, pp. 201–2.   [76] *C.S.P.D.*, 1650, pp. 133, 143, 517, 550.

[77] See Salmon, *Heights in Depths*, An Apologeticall Hint to the Ensuing Discourse, Reader.

again. The willingness of observers to sectarianise, exaggerate and adduce forms of behaviour should be noted. The term 'Ranter' was used by no one in respect of these incidents. So that, to see Coventry in 1650 as experiencing a 'round-up of Ranters' of being 'the main focus of Ranter activity' seems to be to engage in an unwarranted fabrication.[78] The record of events will not bear the weight of such interpretation.

What of the record of Salmon's writings? His first work, *Anti-Christ in Man* (1647), has been described as a Seeker work.[79] It looks forward to a third dispensation when fleshly wisdom, the Antichrist within, will be overcome by the rising spirit of righteousness in each individual. *A Rout, A Rout*, published in February 1649, was a warning to the army that its commission from God would not last indefinitely and therefore that they should press on urgently with the work of reformation. In its stress on the transitional legitimacy of all forms, the variety of instruments which God is prepared briefly to use, it is reminiscent of the millennial framework for interpreting God's shifting providence provided by such writers as John Tillinghast in his *Generation Work* (1653). It is not possible to see here any elements of an antinomian, pantheistic, rejection of sin and hell – any antithesis of the Protestant ethic – which would warrant seeing it as a Ranter work.[80]

Salmon's third extant work, *Heights in Depths*, was the promised recantation. It recounted his arrest and just imprisonment as a blasphemer. His gaolers, and especially Captain Beake, who had petitioned the Council of State on his behalf, had helped him towards a release on condition that he declared himself in print against those things he was charged with. The work opens with a reaffirmation of, or a return to, those quietistic Seeker principles with which Salmon's writing had begun. God was about to confound the formalism of worldly religion, but it was incumbent upon the saints to wait in silence and submissive humility.[81] Indeed, the *leitmotif* of the work is the virtue of a life of spiritual contemplation. For the rest, Salmon portrays himself as a man misunderstood:

Somewhat I have formerly vented in certain papers, which the weak stomacks of many can hardly digest: and truely I could heartily wish, that some expressions had been better pondered; and not so untimely exposed to a publik view: though I also

---

[78] *W.T.U.D.*, p. 218; McGregor, 'The Ranters 1649–1660', 64.

[79] *R.W.*, p. 12; McGregor, 'The Ranters 1649–1660', 64.

[80] Joseph Salmon, *A Rout, A Rout* (1649), E.542 (5), Thomason date 10 February 1649. (Smith reproduces it as one of the chief Ranter works: *R.W.*, pp. 189–200.) John Tillinghast, *Generation Work* (1653), Wing S.T.C. T.1173.   [81] *Heights in Depths*, pp. 6, 26–7.

beleeve, that if they were well chewed (and not so suddenly swallowed without relish-
ing the nature of them) they would be better digested than they are.[82]

There then follows a sequence of statements dissociating himself from
views earlier expressed by him, or of which he has been accused, or,
even more broadly, from common errors of the times. Since the three
categories are not always distinguished, it is impossible to reconstruct
Salmon's earlier views, particularly those which might have been
expressed in the missing work, *Divinity Anatomized*.

So Salmon avers the existence of God as 'that pure and perfect being
in whom we all are, move and live'. The devil, once an angel of light,
has become 'a receptacle of darkness', the 'spirit or Mystery of
Iniquity'. Heaven is to live with and in God. Hell is 'the appoynted portion of the sinner', a place of torment. Scripture, which is used
throughout the tract to validate the positions taken by Salmon, is
inspired by the Holy Ghost, a history or map of truth, a record of God's
dealings with his people in former ages. On sin, Salmon's own careless-
ness has led him to be misunderstood by the 'many headed, ill favoured
monster' of 'vulgar censure'. But he now asserts sin to be a 'contagious
leprosie' from which none are free, a transgression of the law breaching
the unity of men and between men and God. God cannot be the author
of sin, though *Divinity Anatomized* may have come too close to this, since
God is unity; sin, division. Finally, but more opaquely, Salmon asserts
the Trinity. 'I love the Unity, as it orderly discovers itself in the Trinity:
I prize the Trinity, as it beares correspondency with the Unity; let the
skilfull *Oedipus* unfold this.'[83]

It would be wrong to read the whole tract in the light of the evasive-
ness of this last statement. To create a Ranter on the basis of this tract of
Salmon's we would have to extrapolate backwards, into a work no
longer existent, every belief which he here disavows though he claims
some of them have only been reported by the malicious and believed by
the credulous. It is far more likely that Salmon in the early Spring of
1650 flirted with some of these ideas and was attracted by Coppe. He
suddenly found himself swept up by the excitement and outrage attendant on the publication of *A Fiery Flying Roll*, was bewilderingly identified with a party and suffered accordingly. The patient and
sympathetic attitudes of Captain Beake and Colonel Purefoy towards
him might indicate their recognition of this. It is easy to speculate, difficult to be certain. We do not have warrant for believing that Salmon

---

[82] *Ibid.*, pp. 33–4.   [83] *Ibid.*, pp. 38, 41, 42–3, 45, 47, 48, 50–1, 54.

was ever an active member of a group of Ranters disturbing the peace of Coventry and drawing nationwide attention to themselves.

c. Richard Coppin

The relationship between Richard Coppin and the Ranters has produced considerable disarray amongst historians. For Serge Hutin, Coppin was a Seeker compromised by the closeness of his relationships with some Ranters.[84] Christopher Hill, on the other hand, has consistently been prepared to describe him as a Ranter.[85] The description 'Ranter (or near-Ranter)' is the closest Hill was to come to hesitation, but he concludes by stressing the difficulty of finding a more suitable label for Coppin than 'Ranter'.[86] A.L. Morton, however, has become more cautious. Originally he saw Coppin as a Ranter and cited him as evidence of Ranter views[87] but, at the same time, he qualified that view and stressed Coppin's rôle as influence upon the Ranters rather than as one of them: 'while denying that he was a Ranter, [Coppin] was very close to their ideas, influenced Coppe considerably, and gave Ranter theology a sophistication which it often lacks'.[88] This is, of course, larded with question-begging assumptions – a corpus of Ranter ideas, a Ranter theology, a degree of influence over Coppe for which no evidence is ever given – but it falls short of calling Coppin a Ranter. More recently, Morton has depicted Coppin as a universalist, influencing the Ranters, but, by implication, not one of them.[89] Nigel Smith omits him from his collection of Ranter writings. For him, Coppin is often confused with the Ranters because he knew many of them and because his antinomianism was of an egalitarian variety. But 'he took no part in the most demonstrative Ranter activities'.[90]

All in all, this is a sad state of affairs in which to find a writer of some interest, courage and individuality embroiled. The question of his sectarian identity has taken on greater significance than what he actually wrote and preached. Again Frank McGregor offered a sensible way out of this by stressing Coppin's religious individualism and warning against the process of sectarianising figures like him. Nevertheless, he suggests that Coppin does provide a link between antinomian ideas

---

[84]   Hutin, *Les Disciples anglais*, pp. 69, 222–3, n. 145.
[85]   *W.T.U.D.*, p. 191; 'Irreligion in the "Puritan" Revolution', in McGregor and Reay (eds.), *Radical Religion*, p. 205.
[86]   *W.T.U.D.*, pp. 208, 220.   [87] *W.O.T.R.*, pp. 71, 82.   [88] *Ibid.*, p. 73. Cf. p. 97.
[89]   *B.D.B.R.S.C.*, under 'Coppin, Richard'. The categorisation of Coppin as a universalist had been anticipated by Geoffrey Nuttall. See his *The Holy Spirit in Puritan Faith and Experience* (Oxford, 1947), p. 136. Also *D.N.B.* under 'Coppin'.   [90] *R.W.*, p. 11.

current in the late 1640s and 'the ideological amoralism of the Ranters'.[91] I can find no evidence in Coppin's work upon which to base such a linkage.

The most persistent theme of Coppin's teaching is the delegitimation of all authority except that of the indwelling God. Additionally he stressed, from his first printed work onwards, that once we took on the new man through the indwelling spirit we would no longer sin. The context of these thoughts is the seed-bed of the ideas of Gerrard Winstanley or the origins of Quakerism, but not of a rejection of sin and hell, or the amoral acting out of antinomian liberty.

Like so many other conscientious souls of his generation Coppin experienced a variety of religious forms, a pilgrimage which culminated in the ambition to express his own solutions. Two things stand out in his first essays in such expression. The first is not uncommon. It is the condemnation of the hypocrisy of the formal world and formal religion allied with the assurance that God's ultimate instruments will be the poor and ignorant rather than the powerful, learned and worldly wise.[92] God is in everyone but manifest only after a conversion experience. 'We, and the Scriptures, are the grave wherein the glorious God lies buried, and through his Resurrection, in us, we come to a right knowledge of him, our selves, and them.'[93] It is God who initiates this change in the individual soul.[94] The second outstanding thing here is the emergence of Coppin's perfectionist Arminianism. There are, he alleges, two great mistakes commonly made in his day. One is the notion of general salvation, the other, the predestined election of only a few, known and fixed for all time. Salvation, rather, depends upon the balance of good and evil within us, upon our joining Christ within us.[95] There is an emphasis on sin and on the need for a continuing struggle against it in order to win salvation which is hard to relate to a practical or liberationist antinomianism.

In fact Coppin's writings in this vein were not to become controversial until 1651 when John Osborn, minister at Bampton-in-the-Bush, challenged him with the worship of sensual liberty as allegedly

---

[91] McGregor, 'The Ranters 1649–1660', p. 14.

[92] Richard Coppin, *A Hint of the Glorious Mystery of Divine Teachings* (1649), pp. 1–8, E.574 (5), Thomason date 18 September 1649.

[93] *Ibid.*, p. 10 and pp. 13–21. Coppin's scripturalism is worth noting if only because of the frequent identification of Ranterism with anti-scripturalism.

[94] Coppin, *Anti Christ in Man* (1649), p. 48, E.574 (6).

[95] Coppin, *The Exaltation of All things in Christ* (1649), p. 4 and especially Chapter 15, E.574 (7).

practised by Abiezer Coppe.[96] No doubt the fact that Coppe had written a rather innocuous and bafflingly mystical preface to Coppin's *Divine Teachings* did not exactly deter the making of such charges but historians, at least, should be cautious about guilt by association. Certainly, Osborn's initial charges against Coppin were that he had espoused a pantheistic antinomianism, but the debate between the two rapidly shifted on to other grounds and submerged in a dispute over the permitted principles of scriptural exegesis.[97]

Coppin's next work, *Saul Smitten For Not Smiting Amalek* (1653), was directed at the failure of those in power to sweep away formalism and oppression in religion along with the departing Rump. One tyranny of forms was being substituted for another. People should be subject only to Christ. This could only be if they were given religious freedom.[98] Nevertheless, it was necessary to wait upon the magistrate and the Lord for such toleration.[99] Once more it is hard to see the links between this passive insistence on the ultimate legitimacy and freedom of God's indwelling spirit with a Ranterish rejection of all repression, sin and hell. A year later, in *A Man-Child Born*, Coppin argued that man, born in innocency, soon discovered sin. Christ, not ourselves, redeemed us, but Christ Jesus within us made salvation available to all. To acknowledge any other authority but this Christ within was unwarranted.[100]

Those in authority could hardly be expected to relish Coppin's repudiation of any authority but the indwelling Christ, all the more so since he was evidently an effective preacher. It was not, however, easy to convict him of blasphemy despite determined and malicious attempts to do so. On 23 March 1652 he was tried at Worcester Assizes before Baron Wilde on charges of blasphemy brought by rival clergy. The jury were persuaded that he denied heaven and hell but Wilde admonished them for a verdict with which he was dissatisfied and bound Coppin over to appear at the next assize. Eventually, on 10 March 1653, Coppin was tried again before Serjeant Green. After some disagreement the jury found him guilty but he was bound over by Green to the next assize, when Judge Hutton discharged him.[101] It is strange that some

---

[96] John Osborn, *The World to Come* (1651), E.635 (1), Thomason date 7 July 1651.
[97] *Ibid.*, pp. A2, 57–72.
[98] Richard Coppin, *Saul Smitten For Not Smiting Amalek* (1653), Chapters 1–4, 12–15, E.711 (8), Thomason date 20 August 1653.   [99] *Ibid.*, Chapters 5, 8.
[100] Coppin, *A Man-Child Born* (1654), especially pp. 1–2, 5, 14, E.745 (1), Thomason date 25 June 1654.
[101] For accounts see *D.N.B.*, *B.D.B.R.S.C.*, Richard Coppin, *Truths Testimony* (1655), E.829 (8). A further charge against Coppin was dismissed at Gloucester in July 1654.

historians have been readier to accept hearsay evidence and maliciously inspired charges as proof of Coppin's beliefs than were seventeenth-century judges.

In midsummer 1655 Joseph Salmon, who had been preaching every sabbath in Rochester Cathedral, went abroad and Coppin was persuaded to take his place. He was soon seen as a disturbing influence by the local military authorities and the local ministers.[102] The latter, led by Walter Rosewell, Presbyterian incumbent of Chatham, organised a debate with Coppin which took place in the Cathedral between 3 and 13 December 1655. Both Rosewell and Coppin published accounts of the debate. Rosewell complained that Coppin could not be made to stick to the point. What worried him was Coppin's playing to the 'bosome of (a many headed Monster) the rude multitude', especially in terms of an 'unconscionable Liberty of Conscience'. Rosewell alleged that not only had Coppin preached the sinfulness of Christ but that he was a 'Jesuited Familist' and various forms of papist.[103] His account is reliably good evidence for his dislike of Coppin, but no basis upon which to establish the latter's doctrinal position. In his reply Coppin defended his approach to the interpretation of Scripture and returned to his persistent theme that only through the Christ within could true spiritual knowledge come. Christ had taken upon himself man's sinful nature. Only by doing so could he cleanse it and make salvation universal, available for all except the devil. This was validated by a spiritual and allegorising interpretation of Scripture. Heaven and hell were spiritual conditions. In the war between the devil and Christ which took place in everyone, Christ eventually triumphed in all. Only non-belief, rebellion against the spirit of truth, was damning, and this effect was immediate.[104] Wrath, hell and damnation resulted in human despair and those who preached it were no ministers of Christ. Magistrates and ministers upheld each other. Ministers turned with the times. Though magistracy was necessary, it would be better if magistrates confined themselves to the punishment of evil doers, the reward of the good and the restraint of those who sought to interfere with the exercise of the gift of God by any. This should, in particular, extend to women: 'in any assembly of people, a woman creature may have freedom to speak and answer as a man'.[105]

---

[102] *Thurloe State Papers*, vol. IV, p. 486. Major-General Kelsey to the Protector 1655.

[103] Walter Rosewell, *The Serpents Subtilty Discovered* (1656), especially pp. 15–16, E.882 (9).

[104] Richard Coppin, *Michael Opposing the Dragon* (1659), Chapter 1, pp. 8, 12, 13, 19, 32, 50, 83–5, 97, 105, 122, B.L. 4376 de 13(5), Wing C. 6103.

[105] *Ibid.*, Chapter 25 and pp. 141, 143, 148, 222, 243–4.

Alarming though this may have been, it still leaves Coppin closer to a good number of believers in universal salvation, toleration and the primacy of the indwelling spirit than to the Ranter paradigm with its rejection of sin, hell and Scripture. At the conclusion of the Rochester debates, on 22 December, Coppin was forbidden to preach on the following day, the sabbath. He avoided the guard set on the cathedral and preached instead in the fields. On 24 December he was imprisoned in Maidstone gaol but was released some time in the following months without further recorded proceedings. He is an instructive illustration of the alarming dilemma of the shakiness of religious authority in the 1650s. What he was doing and saying was not liked, but it was difficult to stop it legally even under the Blasphemy Ordinance of 1650. In such a situation the pressures accumulated to darken and exaggerate what it was that he did say. Implications were drawn out; heresies and blasphemies extrapolated from statements often vague, bland or mystical enough to be open to a variety of interpretations. We should beware of a too ready acceptance of the confident assurance of such exercises and of collaborating with them retrospectively.

Whatever else he was, Coppin was a man driven consistently by one conviction. That was his belief in the prior legitimacy or claim on our obedience of the indwelling Christ. No authority should usurp that, but, at the same time, this did not mean that there should be no other authority. Coppin insisted on the obligation to submit to the powers that be but he called upon them to complete the work of religious toleration by extending it to all as individuals subject to the Christ within each of them. From 1654, if not before, he believed in the universal efficacy of Christ's saving grace but yet held that men could damn themselves by resistance to or rebellion against the Christ within. Heaven and hell were spiritualised but sin and damnation remained realities confronting the individual. In all of this Coppin is closer to Winstanley, the repudiator of the Ranters, than he is to the paradigmatic Ranter.

v. CONCLUSION

We began with an attempt to introduce some historiographically based clarity to the identification of individuals as Ranters. In consequence, we have to eliminate messianic figures like Robins and Franklin, prophets like Tany and Pordage, the sensational Thomas Webbe and such writers and preachers as George Foster, Joseph Salmon, and Richard Coppin. In part, the argument has been that the evidence, upon which identification of these as Ranters rests, has been suspect or inadequate. Sometimes the evidence that we do have discredits the identification and points in a different direction. Throughout it is important to be aware of a tendency common in the seventeenth century and since to see sects, movements even groups where none existed, or where, at best, the evidence for their existence is wanting or deficient. We must beware of sectarianising or labelling these people in any way which vitiates our careful reading of their ideas and their individuality.

But it is time now to turn to the group – a very small group, it must be admitted – whose status as Ranters has barely been questioned and whose identity as Ranters would appear to be acknowledged by all commentators: Jacob Bauthumley, Abiezer Coppe, Laurence Clarkson and the anonymous author of *A Justification of the Mad Crew*.

3

Examining the Ranter core

i. INTRODUCING THE CORE

It is time, then, to examine those few individuals who are almost invariably claimed to hold Ranter views. I am in fact going to take Frank McGregor's core of Ranters; three individuals and an anonymous pamphlet. Do they hold views consistent with the historiographical paradigm of Ranterism? Do they exist as a group sharing common convictions and acting together on them? If they do, we may consider influences upon their ideology as a whole and this may mean re-examining such figures as Richard Coppin. If they do not, there is no point in such a collective examination of sources. What we would be left to explain would be why so many seventeenth-century observers did believe there was a Ranter movement.

Within the core should be included Jacob Bauthumley, the ex-cobbler who was cashiered from the army, and brutally punished for blasphemy in March 1650; Abiezer Coppe, whose infamous *A Fiery Flying Roll* was condemned by the Rump for blasphemy; the anonymous tract *A Justification of the Mad Crew*, published in August 1650; and, finally, Laurence Clarkson, the self-confessed 'Captain of the Rant', investigated and in September 1650 condemned by the Rump for blasphemy. Not much more than six months, it can be seen, separates all of these events and it is important to remember that identifying the three individuals as Ranters involves isolating *when* they were Ranters. There are two dimensions to this. First, all three of them enjoyed what we might call sectarian careers, that is they moved through a variety of religious forms in the 1640s and 1650s. Coppe had made a reputation as a Baptist before 1650. Bauthumley had been a Seeker. Clarkson's evolution was the classic one from Anglicanism through Presbyterianism, Independency and on into an evolving array of sects. It is essential to know *when* these people were, or might be thought to be, Ranters. To see them as Baptists or Seekers when writing works which we claim to be Ranter is merely confusing.[1] Secondly, we have to look seriously at their denials or recantations of Ranterism. Coppe produced two such works.[2] They have usually been dismissed as insincere or artful. I think that they need to be re-examined, especially in relation to their consistency with the so-called Ranter tracts. In a parallel way, Clarkson's account of his spiritual progress, *The Lost Sheep Found* (1660), has been treated with great credulity as a reliable autobiography, a firm basis for establishing his Ranterism in 1650. Essentially, however, it was a tract of Muggletonian polemical intent, published a decade after the events in question, and it needs to be re-examined in this light. In general we need to re-read these documents with fresh eyes and ears – for the moment – closed to the baying of the heresiographers.

The texts we are concerned with are therefore Jacob Bauthumley's *The Light and Dark Sides of God*,[3] Abiezer Coppe's *A Fiery Flying Roll*,[4] the anonymous *A Justification of the Mad Crew*,[5] and Laurence Clarkson's *A Single Eye All Light, no Darkness*.[6] I intend to examine them each in turn and, in Coppe's and Clarkson's cases, look at each text in terms of the whole corpus of the author's writings. I shall be concerned to establish whether these texts more closely relate to each other than they do to the whole corpus of their author's works. Do they form a distinct Ranter phase or not? What are the common elements of Ranter ideology which these works share? What were the personal links between their authors? What following may they be said to have had as a group? Are we looking at a sect with clear leaders, authoritative texts, disciplinary tests on entry and controls over numbers; or at the looser grouping of a cult distinguished by the followers' faith in their leaders' teachings; or, again, at an even looser phenomenon of consciously common ideas expressed more or less simultaneously without any attempt at organis-

---

[1]   McGregor, 'The Ranters 1649–1660', 18.

[2]   Abiezer Coppe, *A Remonstrance of The Sincere and zealous Protestation of Abiezer Coppe* (1651), E.621 (5), Thomason date 3 January 1651. *Copps Return to the wayes of Truth* (1651), E.637 (4). [Morton gives 11 July 1651 but I see no Thomason dating on this copy.] *W.O.T.R.*, p. 114.

[3]   E.1353 (2), Thomason date 20 November (1650?). But we know that Bauthumley's martial punishment in March 1650 was on the basis of alleged blasphemies contained in this work. *The Perfect Diurnall*, no. 14, 11–18 March 1650, 125, E.534 (18).

[4]   E.578 (13, 14), Thomason date 4 January 1650: facsimile produced by The Rota, Exeter, 1973; edition in *R.W.*, pp. 80–116.

[5]   E.609 (18), Thomason date 21 August 1650. Ascription to Wyke or Salmon has been suggested. I can see no warrant for either ascription.

[6]   E.614 (1), Thomason date 4 October 1650. But the House of Commons had a copy of this work under examination in the previous June. *C.J.*, VI, 427. Cf. *W.O.T.R.*, p. 103, n. 1.

ation and discipline, linked only by shared ideas, mutual awareness and interpersonal relationship; or, finally, are we looking at the independent, largely divergent or distinctive views of unco-ordinated and isolated individuals, seized upon by contemporaries as dangerous, sectarianised as so many groups were and given an identity which the accused, on the evidence available to us, may after all appear to be warranted in denying?

ii. JACOB BAUTHUMLEY

On 14 March 1650, consequent upon a court martial finding of blasphemy, Jacob Bauthumley, Quartermaster to Colonel Cox's regiment, was cashiered from the army, his sword broken over his head, his tongue bored with a red hot iron, his book, *The Light and Dark Sides of God*, burned before his face and copies sent to his native county of Leicestershire and to Hertford for the same treatment.[7] It was a far more brutal and thoroughgoing punishment than anything meted out to Coppe, Clarkson and the others. It may be that the military authorities of the day felt their severity peculiarly justified but, ever since, the disproportion of the punishment has tended to colour our perception of the offence. It has become part of the legend of the 'savage repression' of the Ranters, and consequently, in some quarters Bauthumley's book has been seen as the 'systematic exposition of Ranterism', the most coherent of their works.[8]

In fact our knowledge of his views is confined to the one work which he published. George Fox met him in January 1655 and thought him still a Ranter, but we shall have cause to examine this sort of view more closely in the next chapter. Bauthumley's identity as a Ranter, and consequently our understanding of the character of Ranterism (of which it might be the most systematic expression), rest on *The Light and Dark Sides of God*, a work proscribed in March 1650 but still available in late November of that year when George Thomason acquired his copy.

The work begins, rather prophetically as it was to turn out, with an acknowledgement of the dangers of its misinterpretation. The milieu in which Bauthumley sees it emerging is one in which charges of blasphemy and misinformation about the beliefs of individuals like him already abound. Nevertheless, he was 'inwardly enforced' to write the book 'to ease the burden that lay upon my spirit'. Most readers, Bauthumley thought, would not understand, but, he insisted, 'we

---

[7]   Whitelocke, *Memorials*, vol. III, p. 162: *A Perfect Diurnall*, no. 14, 125.
[8]   McGregor, 'The Ranters 1649–1660', 16, 17.

neither deny there is a G O D; Heaven or Hell, Resurrection or Scripture, as the world is made to believe we do . . . .'. He preferred, rather than a spirit of contention, to acknowledge the 'sweet appearance of God' in all forms of godliness. The propositions he was to advance in his book would be dependent on inward revelation, but he implied that, had he the time, scriptural warrant could be added to support them.[9]

What were those propositions? First, that God's being informs the being of all other things: 'there is nothing has a Being, but thy Being is in it, and it is thy Being in it that gives it a Being . . .'; 'God is in all Creatures, Man and Beast, Fish and Fowle, and every green thing . . .' The worship of a distinct, local God can be therefore no more than a species of idolatry since it denies the nature of God's being. 'Did men see that God was in them, and framing all their thoughts, and working all their works, and that he was with them in all conditions', then they would abandon the outward observances of prayer and formal worship.[10] From this pantheistic view of the divine a number of things follow for Bauthumley. There is a unity in all creatures. Contrary to some scriptural expressions, there can be no passion or variability in God. The Trinity must be 'a grosse and carnall conceit'. The scriptural expression of God is inadequate. Heaven is not a location but merely oneness with God; 'the spiritual presence of Christ'.[11] Bauthumley thus begins with a pantheism which undermines much orthodox doctrine and the basis of formal religious practice.

The question before us is whether this pantheism opened into an antinomianism denying the distinction of sin and virtue, hell and heaven; an antinomianism which, implicitly at least, opened the doors for its practical expression in acting out the rejection of the Protestant ethic. There are in man, according to Bauthumley, manifestations of the power of God which may be called angels. But the devil is also in man, revealed in the proclivity to sin; 'the spirit of envy, malice, cruelty, ever seeking to rob us of that which is most precious to us'.[12] But sin is not so much to be identified with individual acts as with a spiritual condition. It is more 'the defect of Grace and a deficiency in the Creature, than any act as visible to the outward view'; 'a coming short, or a deprivation of the Glory of God'; 'a living out of the will of God . . . .'. 'Sin is properly the dark side of God which is the meere privation of light.'[13]

[9] Bauthumley, *Light and Dark Sides*, The Epistle to the Reader.
[10] *Ibid.*, pp. 3, 4, 6.   [11] *Ibid.*, pp. 7, 9–10, 11, 13, 14, 20.
[12] *Ibid.*, pp. 24–6, 28, 30.   [13] *Ibid.*, pp. 31, 32, 33.

To this point in Bauthumley's work there is no rejection of the category of sin. The crucial question is whether the category has any practical force. Since God does not experience any passion, he is not angered by sin. In particular 'those spiritual and inward acts or motions' that cross the design of God may be unlawful 'and yet, in some respect these also tend to the glory of God, and sin it self doth as well fall in compliance with the glory of God, as well as that which we call grace and goodnesse; for *sinne abounds that grace may abound much more*'.[14] It is important to recognise that Bauthumley is here talking of inner, spiritual states or religious dispositions. Even those which appear contrary to the will of God are to his praise. The statement follows directly from the formality and absurdity of religious observances organised nationally or privately as if God recognised times and places. Underwriting this, nevertheless, is a plea that all might be tolerated.

'Men should not sin because grace abounds; but yet if they do sin, that shall turn to the prayse of God, as well as when they do wel.'[15] This is the difficult phrase in Bauthumley, despite its biblical resonances. His appears to be a pantheistic antinomianism. God is in all things, therefore all things are expressions of his glory. Yet there is a paper-thin barrier against practical antinomianism in his writing. It is difficult, in some senses, to see why a pantheist should believe in sin, or find it a useful category, at all. This is where Bauthumley's mysticism, Behmenist or not, mitigates his antinomianism. Sin being a nullity, God cannot be the author of it. Sin remains as a category, 'an inward lusting after the Creature, beyond that end for which God hath designed it'. While the letter forbids the outward act, the spirit forbids the lust.[16] The point is to concentrate not on the outward symptoms but on the inner states and causes. By this means we can remain in the heaven of God's presence and escape the hell of his absence. But the abjuration of the outward is radical. It extends to the rejection of all religious forms, the denial of a fleshly resurrection. Hell is, in one definition, anxiety about outward forms and formal obligations.[17]

Authenticity should triumph over formalism:

I do not expect to be taught by Bibles or Books, but by God: nay further, I do not do any thing, or abstain from anything, because the outward letter commands or forbids it: but by reason of that commanding power which is God in me . . .

if men were acted & guided by that inward law of righteousnesse within, there need be no laws of men, to compel or restrain men, and I could wish that such a spirit of

[14] *Ibid.*, pp. 31, 33.   [15] *Ibid.*, p. 35.   [16] *Ibid.*, pp. 35, 37, 40.   [17] *Ibid.*, p. 46.

righteousnesse would appear, that men did not act or do things from externall rules, but from an internall law within.[18]

There are strong echoes here of Winstanley's early writings, with their belief that the spirit of righteousness would soon rise in each individual, producing a perfect moral commonwealth of social harmony and justice. Crucially, it remains that God is not the author of sin, which is his negation, the dark side.

There is a certain discomfort in Bauthumley on the issue of distinguishing the promptings of the spirit within from mere imagination and his uneasy answer is to point to the difficulties inherent in following Scripture. 'If any man shall say, that I may be deceived and take that for a discovery of God which is but a fancie of my own Brain: I answer, I may mis-interpret the outward Scripture, and so run as great a hazard that way . . .'[19] It is the Scylla and Charybdis of spiritual enthusiasm and it is important to recognise that Bauthumley is caught on both sides of the divide. On the one hand, formalism is seen as a denial of true spirituality and the omnipresence of God, on the other, the snares of inner religion are recognised and uneasily sidestepped. On the one hand, God is in all things, on the other, sin is somehow independent, a negation of God which, yet again, may in some respects be to his glory.

There is, of course, a confusion at the heart of all of this which too many commentators have obliterated with the imposition of their own logic. The devil is in man as God is. But, if God is in all things, how can he not be in the devil and then what does it mean to distinguish the latter as a separate entity? What is clear in the end is that *The Light and Dark Sides of God* is a work about the internalisation of the spiritual life and of spiritual authority rather than about libertinism, the throwing off of all restraints, internal and external, in the freedom of the spirit.

Like Coppin and Foster, Bauthumley is best seen in the context of Winstanley. All four were concerned with the tensions of an inner dualism to which the imminent rise of the spirit of righteousness within each individual could bring an end. For Winstanley, at least until 1649, such a process could bring the end of covetousness and Kingly Government without violence and coercion. To Foster, it was the guarantee that an age of equality would come and be sustained. For Coppin, it was the way forward to a stable plurality. All of them, and possibly Coppe, should be seen, in this respect, as closer to Winstanley, the repudiator of Ranterism, than to the established paradigm of the Ranters. For it is

---

[18] *Ibid.*, p. 76. [19] *Ibid.*, p. 77.

righteousness, not the abandonment of righteousness, which will be instrumental in the achievement of these things: 'And so I see, that if men were acted & guided by that inward law of righteousnesses within, there need be no laws of men, to compel or restrain men, and I could wish that such a spirit of righteousness would appear, that men did not act or do things from externall rules, but from an internall law within.'[20]

God was seen to be close to Englishmen in 1649 both in presence and in time. He was both immanent and imminent. Bauthumley's writing and his grievous fate are illustrations of the difficulties and dangers of flirting with these themes. But it is important to recognise that, in his writing at least, while playing with the logic of God's immanence, he flinched from the possible conclusion of active antinomianism and actually concluded with a reassertion of righteousness. As his work comes into juxtaposition with the received model of Ranterism, so its omissions and withdrawals are revealing of the gap between the two.

iii. ABIEZER COPPE

At first glance, Abiezer Coppe appears the most obvious and least contentious character for Ranter identification. But a second glance shows an accretion of credulity, of accepted legend, generously interpreted, a second-hand story that invites a re-examination of the record.

A good example of this is the general reliance on that dubious gossip, Anthony Wood, not only for the details of Coppe's early life, but for the first stories of his famed immorality. While at Merton College, Coppe, according to Wood, occasionally kept a woman in his rooms and taking food from the dining hall to her would say that it was for his cat. It is a nice piece of seventeenth-century gossip, but not only is Wood's unreliability well known, and not only is his animus against Coppe obvious, but he matriculated at Merton *eleven years after* Coppe. The notion that Wood's account is to be given the credit of 'first-hand information'[21] rather than be treated with the caution of all college stories passed on by biased retailers of gossip will not pass serious scrutiny. In 1650 Coppe was a sensation and he attracted the attention of sensation seekers. What he said and what others said about him must be sifted and weighed carefully. Central to this process should be an accurate reading of *A Fiery Flying Roll*, a work at once more straight-

---

[20] *Ibid.*, p. 76. On Winstanley Cf. J.C. Davis, *Utopia and the Ideal Society* (Cambridge, 1981), pp. 176–82.   [21] *W.O.T.R.*, p. 99.

forward and more complicated than has normally been allowed. Throughout his writing he played games of inversion, posing as the wise fool, the holy sinner, God's outcast messenger, but to describe him as 'no doubt unbalanced' is to misread these actions and their context.[22]

Coppe was born in Warwick in 1619 and studied at Oxford in the 1630s without taking a degree. Sometime in the 1640s, he became a Baptist preacher of high reputation in the Warwickshire region. By 1649 he had broken with formal religion and a central theme of his writing and preaching over the next two years was to be the repudiation of religious formality of any kind in favour of a practical Christianity, committed to the social works of charity as the highest form of religion. His *Fiery Flying Roll*, which Thomason acquired on 4 January 1650, led to his almost immediate imprisonment in Warwick. On 8 January the Council of State issued a warrant for him to be held in custody for what was described in a curious phrase, as writing 'some blasphemous truths'.[23] On 1 February the work was condemned by the Rump. This was a Friday, the usual day for religious discussion in the House, and it was not unparalleled for the House to proscribe an individual work. All copies were to be seized and destroyed with specimens being burned by the hangman in several places around London.[24] The next day the Council of State ordered Coppe to be sent up to London from Warwick.[25] His transfer was delayed until 19 March because of ill health but in the mean time he had attracted much attention, including that of Salmon and Wyke.[26] Not until four months later did anything further happen, when, on 19 July, Parliament ordered a committee to deal with those responsible for *A Fiery Flying Roll*.[27] Yet two months later they had to urge the same course on another committee.[28] Clearly some of the urgency and priority had gone out of proceedings against Coppe. There was an abortive committee hearing of him, on 2 or 3 October, at which he was reported to have repudiated the committee's authority,[29] but no further action appears to have been taken against him. Early in January 1651 he published *A Remonstrance* dissociating

---

[22]   *Ibid.*, p. 89. See also *D.N.B.* entry under 'Coppe, Abiezer'.

[23]   *C.S.P.D.*, 1649–50, p. 563.

[24]   The resolution was printed as a broadside (Thomason Tracts 669 f.15 (11)). See also *C.J.*, VI, 354.

[25]   *C.S.P.D.*, 1649–50, p. 502. He may have been moved to Coventry gaol as early as 13 January. See *A Perfect Diurnall*, no. 6, 14–21 January 1650, 42; no. 9, 4–11 February 1650, 76.   [26]   *Ibid.*, no. 15, 18–25 March 1650, 141.

[27]   McGregor, 'The Ranters 1649–1660', 82; citing *C.J.*, VI, 444.

[28]   *C.J.*, VI, 474–5, 27 September 1650.   [29]   McGregor, 'The Ranters 1649–1660', 82–3.

himself from the sensational reports of his behaviour and beliefs. He argued that his true beliefs bore no relation to those condemned in the Blasphemy Act. Later in the year (possibly July) he published a further recantation and finally he was released by September.[30]

He was linked with Pordage in the mid 1650s but returned to old themes in a broadsheet, *Divine Fireworks*, published in 1657. After the Restoration he may have practised as a physician under the sardonically assumed name of Dr Higham at Barnes in Surrey. He was buried there in August 1672. But in a final extraordinary twist a verse broadsheet by Abiezer Coppe, *A Character of a true Christian*, appeared in 1680. It was to be sung to the tune of 'The Fair Nimphs'.[31]

Like many of his contemporaries in 1649, Coppe was dwelling with an almost electrifying sense of the imminence of God's second coming, of an approaching millennium or third dispensation. But in his first work, *Some Sweet Sips of Some Spirituall Wine*, Coppe, like Winstanley, saw the second coming in terms of a spiritual renewal and moral reformation of each individual: 'Arise but arise not till the Lord awaken thee, I could wish he would do it by himselfe, immediately: But if by thee mediately His will be done.'[32] Like the Seekers, Coppe argued that religious forms and parties were finished. God would be speaking through individual agents 'and that variously and strangely'. Those who gave primacy to the teaching of the spirit within must therefore embrace pluralism.[33] In Epistles IV and V of the work Coppe produced a letter from a woman disturbed by a dream and uncertain of her interpretation of it. Coppe comments. In the dream the woman saw a world of great natural beauty and harmony. Encountering a friendly tiger, she placed a collar round its neck and took it home. The world of 'glorious liberty' and 'perfect Law' which she had seen shattered. The tiger escaped and the harmony disintegrated. For the woman it seemed to indicate that (like Winstanley's Fall into covetousness) 'appropriating of things to ourselves and for ourselves' brings in bondage.[34] Coppe, after upbraiding the woman for describing herself as 'a weaker vessel', endorsed her view of the dream. The day of the Lord would lead into a world of arcadian bounty and harmony. Even, 'The wormes in us shall give over gnawing . . .' 'Let us not therefore any longer single out any appearance, and appropriate it to ourselves . . . all is yours if you will not set a collar upon the neck of any . . . For while one saith I am of *Paul*

---

[30] *Ibid.*, 84. Coppe, *Copps Return.*   [31] B.L. Lutt. II.35. See also *D.N.B.; B.D.B.R.S.C.*
[32] Coppe, *Some Sweet Sips of Some Spirituall Wine* (1649), p. 3, Wing C.6093.
[33] *Ibid.*, pp. 16, 25.   [34] *Ibid.*, p. 45.

. . . and another, I am of Apollo, &c. are ye not carnall?'[35] Two themes were announced in this work which were to remain constant in Coppe's writing. One was the practical effect of Christian ethics in undermining property and, linked to this, secondly, was the notion of the end of religious formalism.

A Fiery Flying Roll has to be seen as an elaboration of these themes. It is a deliberately controlled but extraordinarily savage attack upon every manifestation of formalism. Form without praxis is the cancer of hypocrisy. The marrow of true Christianity is in its practical charity. The consequences of the wholehearted pursuit of practical Christianity would be the undermining of a property system whose moral basis was covetousness and hard-heartedness. The indebtedness of Coppe to the Levellers, with their emphasis on practical Christianity,[36] and to Winstanley's indictment of covetousness, is clear. But he rejects the Levellers' 'sword' levelling and Winstanley's 'digging' levelling for a levelling based on moral renewal inspired by God's spiritual informing of individuals.[37]

The language of *A Fiery Flying Roll* is deliberately startling. It is meant to communicate the urgency of an imminent divine coming, both inward and outward in its effects, which are not so much immediately comforting as unsettling, disturbing and overturning. In addition, Coppe had to impress upon his readers the awesome, distracting legitimacy of his own prophetic rôle. There is accordingly a good deal of semantic athleticism about the work, but it would be a confusion to suggest that there is anything of the mystical about it.

Rather than a rejection of Scripture, the work is a meditation upon two scriptural texts, Hosea 2:9 (with the Lord's threat to return and recover his corn, wool and flax) and the whole of The General Epistle of James, but especially Chapter 1's injunction to practical Christianity and Chapter 5's warning to the rich.[38] In fact, rather than repudiating Scripture, Coppe rejects the allegorising of these texts. Scripture and spiritual illumination must coexist, dialectically, like a jewel and its cabinet.[39] The thrust of the tract is a balanced attack on formalism with, on the other hand, a condemnation of a sterile religious enthusiasm.

---

[35] *Ibid.*, pp. 56, 60. For the typicality of the association of millennialism and arcadianism see Davis, *Utopia and the Ideal Society*, pp. 35–6.

[36] J.C. Davis, 'The Levellers and Christianity', in B. Manning (ed.), *Politics, Religion and the English Civil War* (London, 1973), pp. 223–50; Barry Reay, 'Radicalism and Religion in the English Revolution: an Introduction', in McGregor and Reay (eds.), *Radical Religion*, pp. 16–17.   [37]   Coppe, *A Fiery Flying Roll*, Part I, p. 2.

[38] Hosea is referred to eight times; James seven times.

[39] *A Fiery Flying Roll*, Part II, pp. 17–18.

The heart of true Christianity is in the self-denying work of charity. 'He that hath this worlds goods, and seeth his brother in want, and shutteth up the bowells of compassion from him, the love of God dwelleth not in him; this mans Religion is in vain . . . he never yet broke bread – that hath not forgot his [meum].'[40] As William Walwyn had argued that the levelling effect of true Christianity would be to 'empty the fullest Baggs; and pluck down the highest plumes',[41] so Coppe warned that 'the mighty Leveller' was coming to infuse men's hearts with a charity which would bring down the established order, both within men and in society at large.[42] Those who resisted would be judged, punished and eventually swept away.[43]

Who are they who stand in the way? The rich, obviously, but also those religious formalists who everywhere diverted religious performance, from its true work in charity, into the niceties of observance and speculation. Coppe conceived of his work as 'a terrible threat to the Formalists'.[44] The formalities of religion were amongst those things which had been set on high and which must be cast down in the day of the Lord.[45] The meticulous, intolerant observances of the 'precisian' were no more than hypocrisy, 'for under them all there lies snapping, snarling, biting, besides covetousnesse, horrid hypocrisie, envy, malice, evill surmising'.[46] Not only are Anglicans, Presbyterians and Independents wanting in this regard, but so too are the gathered churches of the sects, the 'anti-free-communicants', who set themselves apart and mask their hypocrisy behind a contentious preoccupation with forms.[47] Even so, and it is important to recognise this, Coppe's attack does not stop here. Strutting through his work is a character, 'the young man void of understanding', alias the 'well-favoured Harlot', who also rejects the formal churches and their ordinances, favouring the sufficiency of the spirit within. These antinomian speculators or 'Spirituall Notionists',[48] in so far as they do nothing, are also the enemy, clothing religion in hypocrisy. A prime objective of the second *Roll* is to discover 'the secret villainies of the holy Whore, the well-favoured Harlot (who scorns Carnall Ordinances, and is mounted up into the notion of Spiritualls)'.[49] It too, scorning Scripture, 'speaking nothing but Mystery, crying down carnall ordinances, &c. is a fine thing among many, it's no base thing

---

[40] *Ibid.*, Part II, p. 22. Coppe's square brackets.
[41] William Walwyn, *A Still and Soft Voice* (1647), pp. 8–9.
[42] *A Fiery Flying Roll*, Part I, Chapter 1.
[43] *Ibid.*, Part I, Chapters 2–6.   [44] *Ibid.*, Contents; Part II, p. 9.
[45] *Ibid.*, Part II, pp. 10–11 (mispaginated in the original).   [46] *Ibid.*, Part II, pp. 11–12.
[47] *Ibid.*, Part II, Chapters 6–8.   [48] *Ibid.*, Part II, p. 15.   [49] *Ibid.*, Part II, title page.

(now adaies) though it be a cloak for covetousnesse, yea though it be to maintain pride and pomp; these are no base things. These are things that ARE, and must be confounded . . .'[50]

The extraordinary thing here is that Coppe is denouncing the very image with which he has been mistakenly identified. The antinomian dabbler in the liberty conferred by inner illumination is anathema to him, another devious formalism which chokes the practice of living by Christ. For a moment he is depicted even as the carrier of sin's bacillus, the deceiver of the Last Days:

I see a brisk, spruce, neat, self-seeking, fine finiking fellow (who scornes to be either Papist, Protestant, Presbyterian, Independent, or Anabaptist) I mean the Man of Sin, who worketh with all deceivablenesse of unrighteousness, 2 *Thes.* 2. Crying down carnall ordinances, and crying up the Spirit: cunningly seeking and setting up himself thereby.[51]

Formal ordinances are indeed to come down; not for avid inner religion, but for the righteous performance of a practical Christian charity.

Coppe's well-known story of his encounter with a beggar[52] illustrates that there can be no holding back, no limit, in the practical exercise of Christianity. The hypocrisy of conventional religion is its fertility and subtlety in finding restraints. Compared to the wickedness of this, cursing and swearing, 'base impudent kisses' and lust are innocuous offences.[53] As Christopher Hill acknowledges, 'Coppe agreed that adultery, fornication and uncleanness were sins', but he regarded the wickedness of those who hypocritically preached Christianity while evading their real obligations as Christians as so much worse.[54] Coppe's tragedy is that he has nevertheless been transformed by historians into the 'leader of the drinking, smoking, swearing Ranters'.[55]

Coppe's vision was therefore of a soon to be purged and reformed society. The spirit of Christ would cast down the mighty and the wealthy, sweep away the hypocrisy of formal religion and open the hearts of men and women to a life of true charity, of true righteousness. It is a noble vision and one deeply rooted in the Christian tradition. Moreover, it owes nothing, in this version, to pantheism, antinomianism or liberation from the restraints of a religion which demands self-effacement. Indeed, through the work runs a heavy insistence on the

---

[50]   *Ibid.*, Part II, p. 11 (mispaginated as 9).
[51]   *Ibid.*, Part II, p. 17.   [52]   *Ibid.*, Part II, Chapter 3.
[53]   *Ibid.*, Part I, pp. 8–9; Part II, p. 13.   [54]   *W.T.U.D.*, p. 212.   [55]   *Ibid.*, p. 210.

arduous and even frightening social obligations of Christianity. It is an insistence which is abroad in the later 1640s and culminates in different ways in Walwyn, Winstanley and Coppe. The echoes of Winstanley are particularly strong in Coppe:

> The true communion amongst men, is to have all things common, and to call nothing one hath, ones own. And the true externall breaking of bread, is to eat bread together in singleness of heart, and to break thy bread to the hungry, *and tell them its their own bread* &c. els your Religion is in vain.[56]

In one of his typical, and yet scriptural, inversions Coppe insists that this rigorous self-denial and service 'is perfect freedome and pure Libertinisme'. With its performance, 'Sin and Transgression is finished and ended.'[57]

Such a vision was critically alarming precisely because it could be argued to have some warrant in the teachings of Christ. It therefore had to be dissociated from them and it is not at all surprising that accusations of blasphemy and immorality swiftly followed. What is surprising is the historians' credulity in the face of these charges and their unwillingness to examine Coppe's denials seriously. As we have seen, Coppe was swiftly imprisoned after the appearance of *A Fiery Flying Roll* but was dealt with lethargically, even by seventeenth-century standards, thereafter. Beyond Parliamentary condemnation, he was never, as far as we know, officially found guilty of anything, including any offence under the Blasphemy Ordinance of 9 August 1650 – which is, of course, supposed to have been occasioned by the sort of Ranter excess Coppe is alleged to have incited and taken part in.

His *Remonstrance* and *Return* of 1651 can be read as the sincere protestations of a man whose social and ethical message has been blanketed under a welter of accusations of blasphemy and immorality without the issue ever being brought to the test in court. But the historians have thought otherwise. Because he is identified as a Ranter, his 'recantations' must be suspect. Ambiguity is held to typify their protestations.[58] Read in this light, his guilt is presumed and any assertions of innocence are to be regarded with suspicion. Moreover, the burden of proof has fallen on Coppe. Nigel Smith, for example, finds him wanting in that he denies accusations of immoral behaviour but 'with no sup-

---

[56] *A Fiery Flying Roll*, Part II, p. 21. My italics.   [57] *Ibid.*, The Preface, A1; p. 1.
[58] *R W.*, p. 27. Cf. *W.O.T.R.*, pp. 107–8; *W.T.U.D.*, pp. 212–13; McGregor, 'The Ranters 1649–1660', 83–4; Hill, *The Experience of Defeat*, p. 44.

porting evidence'.[59] *Copps Return* is held 'to read like the parody of an apology, as if Coppe is mocking the authorities'.[60]

The point which must be made is that doubts about Coppe's sincerity in 1651 only have some substance if we assume that *A Fiery Flying Roll* is a blasphemous work and that Coppe himself advocated and perhaps exercised practical antinomianism. But that tract will not bear such a reading and the evidence for Coppe's personal immorality or leadership of the drinking, smoking, swearing Ranters is dubious in the extreme or non-existent. If we read his tracts of 1651 without prejudice, without assuming his blasphemous amoralism, a very different picture emerges.

In fact both works are misread if they are looked upon as penitent recantations. Coppe, as we have seen, preached a disturbing social gospel in *A Fiery Flying Roll*. In response, that gospel was ignored while his opponents heaped charges of blasphemy and immorality upon him. Attention was diverted. Coppe's replies of 1651 are attempts to deny what he believes was falsely charged against him while reasserting his status as a prophet and reiterating his social message. They seek to bring his original message back into focus. Like the authors of the Blasphemy Ordinance he desired to propagate the Gospel and to suppress profanity and wickedness. He had, he claimed in *A Remonstrance*, been a great attacker of idolatry and this is borne out by his identification of idolatry with formalism in *A Fiery Flying Roll*.[61] To show his hatred and detestation of the opinions listed in the Blasphemy Ordinance, he goes through them in order. He does not believe that any creature is God, though 'God Christ is in the creature'. He denies that God dwells in the creature and nowhere else, but he affirms the omnipresence of God. He affirms moral righteousness but abhors hypocrisy. He disavows practical antinomianism and asserts the existence of heaven, hell, salvation and damnation. No liberty should be owned but that of the Sons of God. Sinful liberty is detestable.[62] There is nothing here which is in the slightest inconsistent with the opinions expressed in *A Fiery Flying Roll*. In a postscript to *A Remonstrance*, Coppe refers to the sensational literature which has appeared on the Ranters and which associates him with such a movement and with immoral behaviour. Most disturbing is that

---

[59] *R.W.*, p. 27.   [60] *Ibid.*

[61] Coppe, *A Remonstrance*, pp. 2–3, E.621 (5), Thomason date 3 January 1651.

[62] *Ibid.*, pp. 3–5. Cf. 'An Act against several Atheistical, Blasphemous and Execrable Opinions, derogatory to the honor of God, and destructive to humane Society' [9 August 1650], in C. H. Firth and R. S. Rait (eds.), *Acts and Ordinances of the Interregnum 1642–1660* (London, 1911), vol. II, pp. 409–12.

two of the tracts claim to be published by public authority.[63] They are 'scandalous, and bespattered with Lyes and Forgeries'.[64]

Copps Return to the wayes of Truth appearing later in 1651 was clearly a more urgent attempt to obtain release, but fundamentally it was a rehearsal of the same points and a repudiation of the same errors as *A Remonstrance*:

> There are many spurious brats, lately born: and because their parents have looked upon me as a rich Merchant they have took on them the boldnesse to lay them at my door, &c. Some of them (indeed) look somewhat like my children. But however, to put all out of doubt, Whether they are mine, or no: I will not be so full of foolish pity, as to spare them. I will turn them out of doors, and starve them to death. And as for those which I know are not mine own: I will be so holily cruel, as to dispatch them.[65]

To endorse the whole, Coppe reproduces an exchange of letters between himself and John Dury in which the latter tries to test out Coppe's sincerity. In his reply Coppe asserts that sin is transgression of the law and exists independently of men's imagination. He denies ever holding that sin was the 'nearest way to perfection'. It is an absurd opinion.[66] Both in his reply to Dury and in an appended letter to Marchamont Nedham, he disavows any blasphemous opinions which may be insinuated in *A Fiery Flying Roll*.[67] What he does not concede is any blasphemous intent in that work, and a careful reading of it would seem to vindicate the consistency of his position. Dury was evidently impressed.

In 1657 Coppe published an obscure broadsheet returning to the theme of the imminent day of the Lord, when there would be judgement, retribution, and condemnation of those who had condemned others and an overturning of the established order. 'The end hath the *beginning* found.'[68] In his final, posthumously published work, *A Character of a true Christian*, there is an air of patient resignation but also

---

[63] The two tracts were probably: [Anon.,] *A Blow at the Root* (1650), E. 594 (14), Thomason date 4 March 1650; Anon., *The Routing of the Ranters* (1650), E.616 (9), Thomason date 19 November 1650. It is in the latter that Coppe is alleged to have behaved eccentrically before a parliamentary committee, to have gone to Coventry, with two 'She-Disciples' with whom he slept simultaneously, and to have engaged habitually in cursing. Coppe and Clarkson are here alleged to be the leaders of the Ranters. For this sort of material see below, Chapter 4.   [64] Coppe, *A Remonstrance*, p. 6.

[65] *Copps Return* (1651), To the Supream Power, The Parliament, E.637 (4).

[66] *Ibid.*, pp. 19, 23.   [67] *Ibid.*, pp. 21, 28.

[68] [Abiezer Coppe,] 'Divine Fire-Works or Some Sparkles from the Spirit of Burning in this dead Letter' (1657), B.L. 669 f.20 (45), Thomason date 21 January 1657.

an emphasis on Christian love and charity which is consistent with the earlier work.[69]

Like other alleged Ranters, Coppe, at least in terms of published works, spent more time in disavowing blasphemy than he did advancing his own views. In the atmosphere of 1650–1 blasphemy was a sticky and dangerous smear. Examining his earlier writings, however, we find no evidence that Coppe can be made to conform to the received Ranter stereotype. He was never a pantheist. Rather he was a millennialist who placed a heavy reliance on God's historical rôle and the imminence of a second coming. He did not, so far as his writings bear witness, advocate a practical antinomianism. There was sin and it would be punished. The most heinous of sins was formal pretence of Christianity without the practical moral force of charity; in other words, hypocrisy. Its most obvious manifestations were the hardness of heart associated with wealth amidst material deprivation and the pride and intolerance of those who claimed to have perfected the forms of religion while neglecting its substance. But those 'Spirituall Notionists' who saw ordinances at an end to the neglect of all moral obligation were equally condemned. Pre-eminent were the sin of pride, its partner, hypocrisy and its consequence, inequality. The fear engendered by Coppe's *A Fiery Flying Roll* must have been the old nightmare of social levelling, but it was more effectively dealt with and diverted by the charges of blasphemy and immorality. If only the blasphemous and immoral could be shown to hold such views, they could be safely ignored. Coppe's message should be read in the context of the search for a socially redemptive, practical Christianity, pursued before him by Levellers and Diggers. It was more effective for his opponents to read him, at the time, in the context of the pantheistic, practical antinomianism of a fabrication, 'the Ranters'. Coppe's fate and his tragedy has been to be misread in that illusory context ever since.

iv. A JUSTIFICATION OF THE MAD CREW

The anonymous work of August 1650, *A Justification of the Mad Crew*,[70] made no reference to any other alleged Ranter works, nor is it referred to in any of those works. The strength of the case that it is one of a core of Ranter texts[71] must therefore rest on internal evidence alone. It rep-

---

[69] 'A Character of a true Christian' (1680), B.L. Lutt. II. 35.

[70] E.609 (18), Thomason date 21 August 1650.

[71] McGregor, 'The Ranters 1649–1660', 20; McGregor, 'Seekers and Ranters', p. 129, n. 19.

resents an example of a work whose Ranter identity must rest solely on its conformity with other works in the canon.

Like other works of radical delegitimation, *A Justification* plays with inversions of the perceived world at what is proclaimed to be a millennial moment. Weakness is become strength, madness wisdom as God reveals himself to things formerly cast away. While the world, in practice, worships many gods, the mad crew worship only one God.[72] This God is in all things and served by all things and persons, even sinners. To the innocent there is no good–evil distinction; such perceptions were only acquired by eating the fruit of the tree of knowledge.[73] To God all men are one because 'they are himself, they are not apart from him'. But yet those who seem righteous will go to hell, the apparently wicked to heaven.[74] In heaven there would be no marriage, all things would be held in common and the righteous would live in perfect purity, perfect freedom.[75]

The antinomianism here is that of the pure to whom all things are pure: 'I have acted in such purity in such a devine way, that I have not known it by its name of impurity or unholiness, it hath all been risen in me to an immortal and incorruptible being.'[76] The call is to purity of heart, not to the liberation of practical antinomianism. Moreover, though God is in all things and in all men there has been a fall from innocence and there will be a judgement, though this might invert the expected order. The pantheism of the work is curiously ambivalent and falls short of Bauthumley. Nor does it share the social radicalism of Coppe. From its perspective, rich and poor, cavalier, roundhead and Leveller are all one to God. What these works have in common is a repudiation of formalism, but that was too common an exercise in the late forties and early fifties to permit a case for group identity to rest on it alone. For the rest the dissimilarities impress and are more obvious than the similarities. There is no warrant for setting *A Justification* alongside the works of Bauthumley and Coppe as presenting 'a reasonably consistent set of doctrines' distinguishing them as a cohesive Ranter core.

v. LAURENCE CLARKSON

The case of Laurence Clarkson is a much more critical and central one and will have to be dealt with at greater length. Two pieces of evidence

---

[72] *A Justification*, title page, pp. A2, 3–5.
[73] *Ibid.*, pp. 7–8. [74] *Ibid.*, pp. 9–11. [75] *Ibid.*, pp. 13–21. [76] *Ibid.*, p. 25.

are crucial to identifying Clarkson as a pantheistic antinomian theorist of the Ranter type and as an active, leading member of a Ranter group. They are his *A Single Eye All Light, no Darkness* (1650) which led to his swift arrest and examination by a parliamentary committee, and his much later account of these years in *A Lost Sheep Found* (1660), written when he was a Muggletonian and contending for leadership of that group. The former is our best evidence of his beliefs in 1650; the latter our best source for his possible rôle in Ranting activities.

A Single Eye All Light

We do not know exactly when *A Single Eye All Light, no Darkness* appeared. George Thomason acquired his copy on 4 October 1650 but, on Friday 21 June 1650, John Weaver reported to the House of Commons from committee 'the several abominable Practices of a Sect called Ranters' and, at the same time 'some heads of a Book called, "A Single Eye"'. No overt connection was made between the two.[77] The following month, however, it was reported in *The Impartial Scout* that on 12 July

> divers of those called *Ranters* were apprehended near White Chappel London; but upon examination, acknowledging the wickedness and greviousness of their Tenets and Actions, and promising never to commit the like errours again, their present faults were remitted, and their persons set at liberty; Their *Ring-Leader* was one *Clark* . . ., formerly an Anabaptist, and after turn'd Seeker, and now Rantipoler.[78]

On 19 July Weaver's committee was urged by the House to enquire with greater speed into *A Single Eye*, but it was 27 September before Clarkson's confession to authorship was reported. It was then resolved that Clarkson be sent to a house of correction for a month, then to be banished, and that all copies of his tract be seized and burned.[79] Neither resolution was effectively implemented. Clarkson was not banished and copies of his work continued in circulation. There are problems in validating the precise sequence of events here and in verifying the Clarkson–Ranter link, but we shall return to them later.

Who was Clarkson, and what were his views prior to the publication of *A Single Eye*? Ignoring, for the moment, his later, retrospective

---

[77] *C.J.*, VI, 427.

[78] *The Impartial Scout*, no. 56, 12-19 July 1650, 238 E.777 (29). Like many of the day's newsbook reports it should be treated with caution, especially as there is no independent evidence confirming the incident.

[79] *C.J.*, VI, 444, 474–5. See also *A Perfect Diurnall*, no. 42, 23–30 September 1650, 535–6.

account, let us concentrate on the record of his printed works. His first tract, no longer extant, may have been *The Pilgrimage of Saints*, published in January 1646.[80] Whatever its contents, it was soon followed by *Truth Released from prison to its Former Libertie, Or, A true discovery, who are the troublers of Israel; the disturbers of Englands peace.*[81] This argued the warrant of the humble, possessed of inner illumination, to preach. Social deference should be no barrier to the witness of the spirit. Social disorder was caused not by these inspired folk but by persecuting and intolerant authorities. The surviving evidence of Clarkson's preaching and publishing career begins then with an emphasis on the legitimacy of the teaching of the inner spirit and a defence of spiritual enthusiasm.

His next tract, however, yoked an anti-deferential stance with an insistence on social and political responsibility. *A Generall Charge, or Impeachment of High Treason in the Name of Justice Equity, against the Communality of England as was presented by Experienced Reason, Anno 1647*, has often been described as a Leveller or pro-Leveller work, but there is good reason to doubt such a description.[82] As the title itself hints, there is much parody of the Levellers' language and epecially of their emphasis on equity. The tract also offers a critique of constitutional radicalism, something the Levellers were becoming wedded to by this stage of 1647. Constitutional change, Clarkson argues, will alter nothing as long as people go on behaving deferentially. It is the very point which recent commentators have criticised the Levellers for neglecting. For a system of a truly representative nature, the behavioural bonds of deference had to be broken. It is in this context that Clarkson repudiates constitutional details, emphasising instead the need for a radical transformation of behaviour and attitude. The communality were called to civic *virtu* and responsibility, hence their impeachment. The ills of England in 1647 were their fault and nobody else's because they were both the greatest power and the greatest authority in the land. They should choose 'self-denying' men to do their business and if these failed they should replace them.[83] Deference must end:

---

[80] Barry Reay, 'Laurence Clarkson: An Artisan and the English Revolution', in Hill, Reay, Lamont (eds.), *World of the Muggletonians*, p. 168.

[81] E.1181 (6), Thomason date 5 March 1646.

[82] L[aurence] C[larkson], *A Generall Charge*, (1647), E.410 (9), Thomason date 7 October 1647. For examples of its depiction as a Leveller tract see Reay, 'Laurence Clarkson', p. 169; *B.D.B.R.S.C.* under 'Clarkson'; Hill, *The Experience of Defeat*, pp. 42–3.

[83] *A Generall Charge*, pp. 1, 10.

who are the oppressors but the Nobility and Gentry; and who are oppressed, if not the Yeoman, the Farmer, the Tradesman and the Labourer? then consider, have you not chosen oppressors to redeeme you from oppression? . . . your slavery is their liberty, your poverty is their prosperity; yea, in brief, your honouring of them, dishonoureth the communality . . . unlord those that are lorded by you.[84]

But the reformation of behaviour invoked here is everything. There is no suggestion of a radical transformation of social structure or governmental institutions. Indeed one of the charges against the commonality is that it has allowed the King to be divided from his wife, family *and his prerogative.*[85]

Nothing in this tract prepares us for *A Single Eye*, Clarkson's most notorious tract and the one upon which claims to identify him as a Ranter theoretician must rest. What was it about this work which aroused such hostility and yet led to such an indecisive punishment?[86]

First, the work must be seen against the background of a growing interest in mysticism. From 1645 onwards the works of Jacob Boehme were appearing regularly in English translation and attracting English followers. The language of mysticism was beginning to pervade English spiritual enthusiasm.[87] In particular, Clarkson's choice of title and theme may have been influenced by the 1646 edition of a translation of Nicholas of Cusa's *Vision of God* under the title of *The Single Eye*.[88] This work pursued the common mystical task of showing that antitheses may in fact be the same thing; the finite infinite; the static in motion; darkness light and so on. God is in all things; his redemption universal. None of these sentiments was particularly uncommon by the late 1640s.

Two things are striking about Clarkson's *A Single Eye*. One is the vigour, one might almost say recklessness, with which Clarkson plays with inversions. The second is the scriptural frame of the work. It is virtually a meditation on Isaiah Chapter 42 and in particular the millennial inversions foretold in verses 15 and 16.

I will make waste mountain and hills, and dry up all their herbs; and I will make the rivers islands, and I will dry up the pools. And I will bring the blind by a way *that* they knew not; I will lead them in paths *that* they have not known: I will make darkness light before them, and crooked things straight. These things will I do unto them, and not forsake them.

[84] *Ibid.*, pp. 11–12. [85] *Ibid.*, pp. 12–13.
[86] Cf. his own statement in *The Lost Sheep Found* (1660), pp. 31–2, Wing C.4580.
[87] Hutin, *Les Disciples anglais*, pp. 38–9. Alastair Hamilton, *The Family of Love* (Cambridge, 1981), pp. 137–8.
[88] [Nicholas of Cusa,] Ὀφθαλμος Ἁπλους *or The Single Eye* (1646), E.1212 (1).

It is this volatile combination of mysticism, millennialism, inversion and scripturalism which made the work so startling and the treatment of Clarkson so ambivalent. But to describe him as anti-scripturalist is to miss this basis of his work.

God is the Single Eye reconciling the pre-lapsarian and post-lapsarian Adam; bringing heaven to a fallen world, reconciling good and evil. The immediate sense of an informing God within the saint has led Clarkson to the view that God is about to reveal himself more directly though most people will remain unwilling to see. Clarkson's commission is to make clear the nature of God and to warn against the continued idolatry of worshipping a local god, subject to passions, a projection of human identity: 'they imagine him as themselves, not infinite but finite'.[89] How can darkness, as promised in Isaiah, be not simply banished but be itself made light? God is light. In making light, therefore, God made nothing but himself. All that is light is nothing but God.[90] Similarly, all powers come from God. What then of 'Power in the wicked' or 'the Power of darknesse'?[91] This is the point where Clarkson's vigorous inversions run through his invocation of a pantheistic God into a dangerous flirtation with practical antinomianism.

Since all power comes from God, even wicked power must come from him. Light is the source of darkness. Even the crucifixion was according to the will of God. The darkest acts of sin arise from the light source of power God:[92] 'there is no act whatsoever, that is impure in God, sinful with or before God . . . Darknesse, is but only in reference to the Creatures apprehension, to its appearance; so nothing but imagined Darknesse . . .'[93] This imagination or apprehension is Adam eating 'of the Tree of knowledge of good and evil'. There is a problem here as to where such imagination, contrary to the nature of God, can have come from, but Clarkson glides past it. The notion of sin arises out of the imagination of (fallen?) man, not out of a right understanding of the nature of God. To those who can partake fully of the purity and singleness of that nature, there can be no such thing as a sinful act. It is not clear whether on balance Clarkson takes this to mean that the pure will never perform certain types of act or that they may perform all types of act without impurity, and the dialogue form which he slips in and out of does not help here. But what is clear is that Clarkson comes very near to a psychological, and possibly a theological, justification for practical antinomianism:

[89] L.C., *A Single Eye* (1650), pp. A2, 1. This work is reprinted in *R.W.*, pp. 161–75.
[90] *Ibid.*, pp. 2–3.   [91] *Ibid.*, p. 5.   [92] *Ibid.*, pp. 6, 5, 7.   [93] *Ibid.*, pp. 7–8.

therefore, remember that if thou judge not thy self, let thy life be what it will, yea act what thou canst, yet if thou judge not thyself, thou shalt not be judged . . .'[94]

To see all things as one is the only resurrection and the only freedom from self-judgement, reproach and torment:

therefore till acted that so called Sin, thou art not delivered from the power of sin, but ready upon all the Alarms to tremble and fear the reproach of thy body.

The object is to become 'Representative of the whole Creation', at one with God in reconciling all things unto oneself.[95]

A Single Eye undoubtedly raises the issue of a radical pantheism leading not so much into an antinomian liberty as an antinomian obligation or psychological necessity. It may be his pluralism – his sense that for each person the experience of God is distinct – that inhibits him from actually enjoining others to liberation from sin by acting it out, but there is no such injunction here. Spirituality is to realise one's unity with God. Guilt is a kind of separation from God induced by our own psychological states, not by our acts, which must in themselves proceed from God. To be at one with God we must be liberated from those attitudes. This is the core of Clarkson's unorthodoxy. The nature of his writing, opaque, convoluted and distorted by the fitful adoption of the dialogue form, does not permit us a much more definite or precise interpretation. Nevertheless, what must be acknowledged is that there is here a mystical pantheism which allied with an antinomianism pushed to practical conclusions comes so close to the Ranter typology as to be virtually indistinguishable. And, as we shall see, it may very well have been Clarkson, this tract and the reaction to it which unleashed the whole Ranter sensation.

Nevertheless, conceding the Ranterish nature of *A Single Eye* does not admit the existence of a cohesive Ranter core, a coherent group. Rather what comes out of our examination of the tract are its dissimilarities to those works with which it is usually associated. There is no claim in the tract that it is part of a group of works sharing common aims and approaches. It is radically distinct from Bauthumley's *Light and Dark Sides*. For the latter, God's pantheistic presence does not extend to those acts called sinful, for they negate his being. Sin does have an objective, rather than a psychological manifestation, for Bauthumley which it does not have and cannot have for Clarkson. The latter's pantheism is more radical and embraces a practical antinomianism foreign to Bauthumley.

---

[94] *Ibid.*, p. 12.   [95] *Ibid.*, pp. 13–14. See also pp. 15–16.

Equally, the preoccupations of Coppe are entirely different from those of Clarkson, as revealed in *A Single Eye*. There is in that work no hint of levelling, no focussing on social justice. Indeed, practical Christianity would lose its distinct moral meaning in the framework of Clarkson's thought. Avarice, hardheartedness and malice would presumably become as morally neutral as adultery, theft and drunkenness. Coppe reinforces a sense of certain types of acting and non-acting as sinful. Above all, hypocrisy is a barrier to righteous performance. To Clarkson, all acts and non-actings have become morally indistinguishable. The only offence of hypocrisy is to ourselves. It is that imagination which insists that we have separated ourselves from God when we are, in fact, an inseparable part of his universal unity.

The gulf between these three writers in these three particular works is then very great. Their objectives, approaches and tenets are so diverse as to outweigh any similarities between them and belie the notion of a consistent core or a group identity.

b. The Lost Sheep Found

In 1660 Clarkson published a work, *The Lost Sheep Found*, of which the first half is cast in an autobiographical frame. A number of historians have treated it as an accurate record, a reliable account of events.[96] Two disturbing considerations should be brought to bear on this. The first is that the context of this work is Clarkson's publication of several works of Muggletonian apologia in 1659 and 1660. The second is that to see any kind of autobiography, in this period or others, as essentially an accurate, factual narrative is to engage in a form of naivety. Far more is invariably going on than the simple recording of the facts of a life. Moreover, early modern biography and autobiography are loaded with rhetorical, theatrical and polemical purposes and devices over which 'the facts' by no means necessarily predominate. Indeed, 'the facts' may be so subservient to the main purpose of the work as to permit fictional characters to emerge. The William Roper in Roper's *Life of More* would be one example, as the James Boswell in Boswell's *Life of Johnson* would be another. Is the Bunyan of *Grace Abounding* really the truth about John Bunyan? Would we rely on that text alone for our biographical evidence of him?

The problem is compounded by the prevalence, conventions and

---

[96] The fullest instance is Reay, 'Laurence Clarkson', but see also W.O.T.R., Chapter 5; Paul Delany, *British Autobiography in the Seventeenth Century* (London, 1969), pp. 84–8. Cf. McGregor on the reliability of Quaker autobiographies, 'Seekers and Ranters', p. 128.

polemical purposes of the genre of spiritual autobiography in the seven-teenth century. Coppe, Salmon, Coppin, Foster and Bauthumley, of only those figures we have already mentioned, produced elements of autobiography. But these autobiographical fragments were never pre-sented as neutral records of fact. They follow well-known and recognised conventions. The spiritual pilgrimage essential to them is designed to demonstrate the validity of a presently held truth.

The Lost Sheep Found is a much more carefully crafted and constructed work than has been generally allowed. Its immediate context is a sequence of Muggletonian writings of which it is the culmination and which formed the basis of a bid for the leadership of that sect by Laurence Clarkson.[97] The first of these writings, *Look about you* (1659), was preoccupied with discovering the devil and partly devoted to a repudiation of Ranterish principles. The devil was a reprobate Angel who had seduced Eve and copulated with her

in which and by which she found so much delight (that after that) she enticed her hus-band, who had copulation with Eve, as man with woman in these days; so her innocent soul and body being defiled by that reprobate Dragon-angel, after which her hus-band Adam going in unto her, was also defiled, as a sound woman should receive into her body a diseased man, not only her womb is defiled, but she pollutes her husband also; as the Pox or Gangreen doth eat through the whole man, so Eve's soul and body being defiled, did putrify the seed of Adam . . .'[98]

Sin was no longer a state of mind but an inherent propensity, made potent by the lust of woman, and transmitted biologically. So the seed of the devil was dispersed in millions of men and women: 'there is no other devil but what is in men and women'. Attributing sin to an external devil was really a way of evading responsibility.[99]

There follows a lengthy survey of false views of the devil, including those of pantheists and Ranterish blasphemers.[100] Two worlds or two seeds existed, the pure and the wicked: 'there is two distinct whole worlds, to distinguish between the divine glory of Election, and the everlasting shame of rejection, a cursed Cain, a blessed Abel'. These distinctions will continue to the end of the world. Even today there are 'black ranting devils' who engage in all uncleanness or say 'there is nothing that I can think, speak, or do, but God is the author of it', or

[97] See, for example, Christopher Hill, 'John Reeve and the Origins of Muggletonianism', in Hill, Reay, Lamont (eds.), *World of the Muggletonians*, pp 97–8.

[98] Clarkson, *Look about you* (1659), p. 2. The same work appeared with a different title page as *The Right Devil Discovered* (1659). Cf. Wing. C.4579 and C.4583.

[99] *Look about you*, pp. 17–19.   [100] *Ibid.*, pp. 29–30.

who hold that men can only be freed from sin by sinning.[101] But the day of Christ is at hand. Time for repentance is short.[102]

The tract does a number of things. It dissociates Clarkson from a host of previously held views. It insists on the objective and ever-present reality of sin and calls to repentance from it. At the same time, it condemns a whole spectrum of religious belief and performance. The tract's weakness is that its initial stress on the importance of the teachings of the new prophet, John Reeve, is not systematically related to the themes discussed in the body of the work.

The Quakers Downfal (1659)[103] defends the third commission of Reeve and Muggleton much more directly. At the same time, it has to be seen as part of a challenge to Muggleton for leadership of the movement. Not only is the third commission defended against Quakers and Arminians, but a special rôle is claimed for Clarkson himself:

> I write this by the same spirit of inspiration as the Prophets and Apostles did theirs; nay furthermore I affirm, that being called forth by vertue of this last Commission, infallibly to bear record to this last Witness of the Holy Ghost or Eternal Spirit, the knowledge of which doth interpret the mystery of the two former commissions . . .[104]

Of course, this delegitimates all other authorities and in this tract Clarkson begins to work through the implications of that. Since his commission is direct, the most obvious challenge to it is from similarly based authorities. Those, like Quakers and Ranters, who believe in direct inner illumination must be shown to be wrong in terms of the First, Second and Third Commissions – the Old and New Testaments and the writings of Reeve and Muggleton. Clarkson proceeds here by arguing particulars: the corporeal nature of God and Jesus, the two seeds of good and evil and so on, and the continuities of treatment of such issues through the three commissions. He continued the same approach in another tract, _A Paradisical Dialogue Betwixt Faith and Reason_ (1660), though the emphasis was shifted to an attack on the Church of England, as nonsensical and blasphemous, and to an adumbration of the distinguishing tenets of the Third Commission.[105] _The Lost Sheep Found_, also published in 1660, falls into this context as a polemic within and on behalf of what was later to become known as Muggletonianism.[106] The

---

[101] _Ibid._, pp. 3, 57, 58, 92–3, 99. Violence of language is also a sign of the sons of Cain, p. 102.   [102] _Ibid._, pp. 125, 136.   [103] Wing C.4582.

[104] Clarkson, _The Quakers Downfal_, pp. 3–4.

[105] Wing C.4581. See especially Chapter 16 and pp. 113–20.

[106] The Friends House Library copy is in fact bound in together with the other three works of 1659–60. See also _The Lost Sheep Found_, p. 3 where his other writings in support of the Third Commission are alluded to.

autobiograhical elements are subordinate to these themes, but to demonstrate that we shall have to examine the work and its structure in some detail.

The title page itself incorporates the notion of a story to be told as a type for every church: 'As all along every Church or Dispensation may read in his Travels, their Portion after this Life'. Clarkson's story is effective as such a type because he is a special commissioner, 'the onely true converted Messenger of Christ Jesus, Creator of Heaven and Earth'.[107] Clarkson's life is therefore presented in this work as a type the purpose of which is to give recognisable historical meaning to an argument which rejects two antitheses. The fundamental proposition is that the authority of the old churches is spent, their time is over. But Clarkson no longer wants to accept the sectarian consequence that inner illumination or 'Reason' replaces the authority of institutional faith. The sects have also to be inadequate and all of this must lead towards the inevitability and necessity of an authoritative Third Commission. As an additional objective is to demonstrate Clarkson's central rôle in that commission, an autobiographical form or a biographical type has obvious advantages. Clarkson had found a formula in the autobiographical type which enabled him to stress the significance of the Third Commission without giving the laurels to Lodowick Muggleton as John Reeve's partner.

It is, however, important to note, first of all, that almost a third of the work (pp. 34–51) is given over to the exposition of the importance, authority and teaching of the Third Commission. The rest (pp. 1–33) is a preparatory history of the times focussed on an autobiographical type and designed to show two things: first, the inadequacy of the Second Commission and its Scriptures, given their indeterminacy and inner contradictions on many important matters; second, the folly and instability of the search for a spiritual authority through reason or self-reliance which is ultimately negative and egotistical.[108] It follows that

---

[107] *The Lost Sheep Found: Or, The Prodigal returned to his Fathers house, after many a sad and weary Journey through many Religious Countreys, Where now, notwithstanding all his former Transgressions, and breach of his Fathers Commands, he is received in an eternal Favor, and all the righteous and wicked Sons that he hath left behinde, reserved for eternal misery; As all along every Church or Dispensation may read in his Travels, their Portion after this Life. Written by Laur. Claxton. the onely true converted Messenger of Christ Jesus, Creator of Heaven and Earth.* LONDON: Printed for the Author. 1660.

[108] On reason see Lotte Mulligan, ' "Reason", "right reason" and "revelation" in mid-seventeenth-century England', in Brian Vickers (ed.), *Occult and Scientific Mentalities in the Renaissance* (Cambridge, 1984), pp. 375–401. 'Right reason', that is human ratiocination reinforced by scriptural authority, would also be insufficient for Clarkson because the scriptural basis – of defunct First and Second Commissions – was so dubious.

what is required is a secure faith built on an unambiguous Third Commission. In fact, Clarkson had a polemical interest in emphasising the
blackness of the principles of the Ranters, amongst others, to show
where the folly of reason might lead. So that even Clarkson, like many
others, uses Ranting principles as a bogeyman, and consequently may
have caricatured and exaggerated them. Despite this, it is worth noting
that he is very vague about his – or anybody else's – adoption of a practical antinomianism as part of his Ranting principles and that there is no
suggestion in the work of a Ranter movement, sect or group. Rather the
stress is on individuals. 'My one flesh', obviously a group, is never identified as Ranter.

The object of the work is to follow a spiritual progress

through each Dispensation and that for no other end, than that Reason, or the Devils
mouth might be stopped . . . to consider what variety of by-paths, and multiplicity of
seeming realities, yet absolute notions, the souls of the Elect may wander or travel
through, seeking rest . . .(3)

The biographical type is chosen in order that 'thou mayest in me read
thy own hypocrisie and dissimulation in point of worship all along'(4).
The allegorical value of a life of spiritual pilgrimage is therefore pre-
dominant in this account and we must expect the details of the account
to be shaped to that purpose. What should also put us on guard is the
logic of the progression which the account follows. It forms a kind of
dialogue in error between defunct formal authorities and the perversity
of reason.

So, in the 1630s, the young Clarkson is presented as a pure adherent
of the Church of England, a disciple of the best preaching *within* the
Church. But faced with choices over the forms of communion he began
to question the basis of forms altogether: 'increasing in knowledge, I
judged to pray another mans forme, was vaine babling, and not acceptable to God . . .' (4–5). Such knowledge, the fruit of reason and confusion within the Church of the Second Commission, is immediately
shown, within the context of seventeenth-century standards of order, to
have socially undesirable consequences: 'the next thing I scrupled, was
asking my parents blessing' (5). Nevertheless, like himself, the nation
has grown too wise to accept the confused crudities and simplicities of a
restored episcopate(7). Presbyterianism, his second stage, had the
advantage over episcopacy that it was free from superstitious rites and
ceremonies and its doctrine was more lively. But Clarkson found for-
malist preoccupations were just as strong. He was tortured by doubts as
to his election and appalled by the Presbyterians' hypocrisy in urging

men to fratricidal conflict in the Civil Wars despite the teachings of the Second Commission(7-8). We should note here Clarkson's use of scriptural authority to endorse each position which he takes up and then discards. The clear implication is that the Scriptures of the First and Second Commissions – the Old and New Testaments – are ambivalent, cloudy and can produce a wavery torment or instability both personally and nationally. A new and clearer commission or testament is required.

Clarkson moved on then to Independency. It seemed to possess clearer doctrine and a more moderate spirit, but, soon, differences over baptism, confusion over admission to the sacrament and doubt as to who is saved and on what basis became oppressive (8–9). Once more, Scripture seemed to point in a new direction. This time it was towards Dr Crisp and the antinomianism further clarified by Mr Randel and Mr Simpson (9–10). It is significant that Clarkson depicts the antinomians as a sect (10), something recent historians have been reluctant to concede. Sectarianising was a way of tidying up the retrospect. There seems no warrant for our believing in the existence of such a sect, and Clarkson himself was ambivalent about it ('part form, and part none'). Its real importance is as a stage in the polemic, and surprisingly the antinomian stage comes before the Baptist one and well clear of the Ranters.

It was, Clarkson tells us, at this time that he began to preach, first with the army at Yarmouth and then around East Anglia. But this preaching is again presented as part of the hypocrisy and confusion inherent in all positions justified by the Second Commission:

> I thought I was in Heaven upon earth judging the Priests had a brave time in this world, to have a house built for them, and means provided for them, to tell people stories of other mens works.(11)

At this stage he came under the influence of John Tyler and the Baptists, for whom again he saw scriptural warrant. Following, with them, Christ's ordinances and living in a kind of apostolic order (12–13) led only to unsubstantiated charges of naked and multiple baptism and an attack upon the legality of his marriage (13–17). Imprisoned as a consequence, he was confronted by the issue of the legitimacy of the succession of baptismal authority. Did the authorisation of baptism cease with the apostles? Despite, however, the pertinence of the question, Clarkson still did not grasp that it brought into question everything still being done under the authority of the Second Commission, including preaching and praying (19). There were other positions for reason to exhaust in the old Scriptures yet.

'Sixthly I took my journey into the society of those people called Seekers, who worshipped God onely by prayer and preaching' (19), but who had no outward form of organisation or sign of membership. As we read carefully on, we see that this is yet a further stage in the disintegration of all spiritual authority and certainty:

for notwithstanding I had great knowledge in the things of God, yet I found my heart was not right to what I pretended, but full of lust and vain-glory of this world, finding no truth in sincerity that I had gone through, but meerly the vain pride and conceit of Reasons imagination, finding my heart with the rest, seeking nothing but the praise of men in the heighth of my prayer and preaching, yet in my doctrine through all these opinions, pleading the contrary, yea abasing myself, and exalting a Christ that then I knew not.(20-1)

Religious profession became a trade, 'preaching for monies'; his very whereabouts determined by the play of fortune; his relations with others a matter of exploitation and hypocrisy (21–2): 'there was not any poor soul so tossed in judgement and for a poor livelihood, as then I was'. 'I concluded all was a cheat yea preaching it self'(23). Getting money was a matter of 'subtilty of reason' and his main employment(24).

Spiritual authority outside the self, independent of reason and imagination, had practically ceased to exist. The inner resources of the individual were inadequate to the provision of spiritual stability and security. We are wondering how far this process can go when Clarkson encounters the group 'My one flesh' (24–5). Three points are important, from our point of view, about this encounter. First, the term 'Ranter' or 'Rant' is not used in relation to this group, and Clarkson kept the two experiences distinct. Secondly, the image of 'My one flesh' is by no means clear. In particular, we are not told what they believed before Clarkson joined them. Finally, nowhere in this section of the work is there any indication of the pre-existence of a Ranter group which Clarkson could be said to have joined.

At his first encounter with the group (25), Clarkson was told, somewhat enigmatically, that if he had arrived earlier he might have seen 'Mr. *Copp*' 'who then had lately appeared in a most dreadful manner'. He was invited to a further meeting but before recounting the experience Clarkson was careful to state his religious position at that time:

Now observe at this time my judgement was this; that there was no man could be free'd from sin, till he had acted that so called sin . . .

But he had not published these views or put them to the test. And so 'I took my progress into the *Wilderness*.'

At the meeting Clarkson was invited to speak and voiced his opinion that freedom from sin could only be achieved by acting it out 'in purity'. Scriptural support for this is offered, in *The Lost Sheep Found*, as one more piece of evidence of the failure of the Scriptures of the Second Commission to provide a barrier against the wilderness: 'till you can lie with all women as one woman, and not judge it sin, you can do nothing but sin'. The group, 'My one flesh', were impressed and one of them, Sarah Kullin, invited Clarkson to go with her and make trial of the doctrine, but Clarkson does not say that he went. Nevertheless, his following grew.

Significantly, it was at this point that Clarkson distinguished himself from Coppe. 'Now Copp was by himself with a company ranting and swearing, which I was seldom addicted to.' The suggestion is that the nature of their activities and a physical distancing separated Coppe and Clarkson. Whatever the exact nature of Clarkson's activities, his point in *The Lost Sheep Found* is that they could be endorsed by Scripture: 'onely proving by Scripture the truth of what I acted; and indeed *Solomons* Writings was the original of my filthy lust . . . not then understanding his Writings was no Scripture' (26). In Clarkson's view then, the Scripture principle also separated himself and Coppe, but the more important point being reiterated is the deceptiveness of that principle, given the inadequacy and uncertainty of the Scriptures of the Second Commission.

At this stage in the story, he published *A Single Eye* and only then became the Captain of the Rant when most of the principal women of 'My one flesh' joined him. His body was shared with these women but his money still went to his wife. This was the height of his recounted ranting: 'at last it became a trade so common, that all the froth and scum broke forth into the height of this wickedness, yea began to be a publick reproach . . .' Whatever this means precisely, Clarkson decided to break with this way of life and went into the country and to his wife. But the hypocrisy of a life based on a wavering inner spirituality or an inadequate textual authority was inescapable. Even as he preached, 'the very notion of my heart was to all manner of theft, cheat, wrong, or injury that privately could be acted, though in tongue I professed the contrary'. As God had made all things good, so man had invented mine and thine and the evils that went with them. Perhaps Winstanley's denial of the validity of private property rights was, therefore, justified.

But, no; this was yet another man-derived authority, the devil's kingdom of which reason was the lord,[109] and as reason was egotistical so Winstanley's crime had to be self-love(27).

In this fashion Clarkson's dialogue continued, but the resources of the Second Commission and an inner spirituality were reaching exhaustion. 'I saw all that men spake or acted, was a lye . . .' No moral boundary was left. Men were no better than beasts. Clarkson took to an amoral life, wandering the country with Mrs Star, filled with scepticism. But, in the ultimate paradox, Scripture even endorsed the collapse of all faith, 'concluding with *Solomon* all was vanity' (29):

> I judged all was a lie, and that there was no devil at all, nor indeed no God but onely nature, for when I have perused the Scriptures I have found so much contradiction as then I conceived, that I had no faith at all, no faith in it at all, no more than a history, though I would talk of it, and speak from it for my own advantage . . . (32)

This is, in a sense, the crux of the work. The scriptural authority of the Second Commission is spent. When people rely on their own spiritual resources they end in restless hypocrisy, confusion and wickedness, as the story of the type Clarkson has illustrated. The conclusion forced on us by this dialectic is the need for a new commission, a new and clearer authority, external to the restless egotism and pragmatism of human will. The Quakers' claim to a righteousness reconciling spirit and law must fall because it is based on both sets of weakness – the old Scripture and the inner spirit (33). Finally, Clarkson began to hear of the two witnesses of the Third Commission and to read the writings of John Reeve. Faith could triumph over reason because the necessary renewal of authority on which it might be based was occurring. 'I write not now as I have done formerly when I was in *Egypt* or the *Wilderness*, but I write infalibly, without the help of any . . .' (38). 'So ye *Baptists, Ranters,* but especially the *Quakers* like vagabonds run with the letter and doctrine of Moses . . .' (39). It is his only use of the term 'Ranter' in the whole tract, and it is significant that it is used to lump Ranters with those dependent on the Scripture of a defunct and discredited commission.

In looking at *The Lost Sheep Found* as a source of information about Ranterism and Ranting activities in 1650 a number of considerations should weigh heavily on the side of caution. Least amongst them is the lapse of ten years. Most important is a recognition of the polemic essential to the work, and the typological device of the autobiographical character. The central purpose is to demonstrate the overwhelming necessity of faith in the Third Commission. To that end, the inadequacy

---

[109] Cf. *ibid.*

of the authorities of the Second Commission and of reliance on reason have to be demonstrated. This is achieved through a picaresque spiritual odyssey of a central character, the author himself (or, should we say, the author posed as a type?), in order thoroughly to illustrate these themes and their relevance to contemporary reality and circumstance.

So the 'autobiography' demonstrates how 'all along in the second Commission there was a great number of false, to the small number of true'(52). At the same time, it shows that the attempt to resolve the problems of the Second Commission by the application of reason were doomed because of the nature of reason:

O what a changeable, desiring, unsatisfied seed is Reason . . . so that where Reason is lord its operations are never satisfied, no not a year, a moneth, or a day, but inventing new fashions, new delights, new mischiefs, sometimes it will be ruled over, and sometimes it will rule itself, *as these late transactions will confirm what is written,* so that well may the imagination thereof be compared to a bottomless pit, for indeed it knows not what it would be, nor what it would have, never long contented but either too full or too empty, too rich or too poor, too wise or too foolish, too high or too low . . . (58; my italics)

How better to illustrate this than with the 'history' of the type Laurence Clarkson?

My principal argument therefore is that we must see the use of this autobiographical type as part of the polemical thrust and structure of *The Lost Sheep Found* and that this should qualify our willingness to accept it, independently of other sources, as a reliable account of actual events in 1650 upon which we can base a history of those months. Clarkson's primary purpose was not autobiographical in any purist sense. Hence the leaps and chronological vagueness of the work. It seems doubtful that anyone would accept his account as an adequate depiction of Anglicans, Presbyterians, Independents, Baptists, Seekers or Quakers. There is nothing in the text, or other evidence, to lead us to conclude a peculiar reliability on the topic of the Ranters.

Since *The Lost Sheep Found* has been so commonly treated as a reliable documentary source for a history of events, a number of other points should, perhaps, be made. First, in Clarkson's account the experience of 'My one flesh', or as Captain of the Rant, are separated. Between the two come periods as Baptist and Seeker. Second, if Ranterism is identified with a practical antinomian breakthrough into sexual promiscuity (amongst other things), then there are problems with this account. For it is while he was a Seeker that Clarkson's career of overt fornication began (22). Third, what do we really learn from this account about the group 'My one flesh'? There is no clear image of what they believed when Clarkson encountered them. Rather, he depicts himself as their instructor. Are they a movement, a sect, a group, or an *ad hoc* gathering? Are they practical antinomians? One of them, Sarah Kullin, suggested, though Clarkson points out that this was his inference, that they put his doctrines to a sexual test. But Clarkson does not tell us whether they did or not. It is unclear how 'My one flesh' and Clarkson's spell as Captain of the Rant are linked. Most accounts have merged the two, but Clarkson implied that they were distinct and that only some of the former followed him as the latter. Fourth, his account suggests that he was only briefly linked with either. He rapidly dissociated himself from their wickedness and was soon preaching a different message (26–7). Fifth, the immorality which Clarkson ascribes to himself has its limits. When he returns to his old group in London it is to be adulterous in a stable liaison, but not promiscuous (27). Later still, when he denied his adultery his denial was accepted (30–1). The impression created, for what the impression is worth, is that he was not notorious for boundless immorality.

Finally, and of central importance from our point of view, there is a distinct sense of the absence of a cohesive core, a coherent group in Clarkson's account. He repeatedly stresses individuality rather than group identity: 'was not these men your disciples? They were not mine, but their own' (30). Bauthumley is not mentioned. Nor are the so-called central texts of Ranterism. Coppe appears, but only as an individual missed, a relationship denied.[110] 'Do you know one *Copp*? Yea I know him, and that is all, for I have not seen him above two or three times' (31). Ranting principles and Captaincy of the Rant are mentioned, but there is no reference to 'Ranters' in the 'autobiographical' section of the work. This comes later and once only when, as we have seen, Ranters are grouped with Quakers, Seekers and Baptists, all flawed by their dependence on the Scripture of the Second Commission and the application of reason to it.

How shall we sum up? There is some warrant for scepticism and considerable warrant for caution in approaching *The Lost Sheep Found* as a documentary source for the events and affiliations of 1650. It provides no evidence whatever for the existence of a coherent, cohesive group of like-minded Ranters such as has been depicted by some historians. There is clear evidence that, in *A Single Eye*, Clarkson flirted with the doctrines of practical antinomianism. In *The Lost Sheep Found* there is at

---

[110] Cf. Cohn's description of the close association between Clarkson and Coppe: 'The Ranters', p. 20.

best dubious evidence that in practice he may have briefly taken these ideas further. The group nature of such beliefs and practices remains doubtful and hazy. There is no evidence to connect either beliefs or practices with those of Abiezer Coppe, Jacob Bauthumley, the author of *A Justification*, with George Foster, Richard Coppin, Joseph Salmon or any of the other figures we have examined.

vi. CONCLUSION

If we take McGregor's Ranter core (Bauthumley, Coppe, the anonymous author of *A Justification*, and Laurence Clarkson), we find no evidence of any close direct links between them as individuals forming a group and their works prove disparate, lacking the consistency of a group possessed of a shared ideology. The Ranter core shatters and disintegrates.

The primacy of the indwelling spirit, the pantheistic sense that God is in possession of or infuses all things, the *frisson* of millenarian perception, the juggling of inversions, these common features of the mid-seventeenth-century landscape of spiritual enthusiasm cannot be confined to a Ranter group and, accordingly, they are not adequate discriminators for identifying such a group. In terms of pantheistic antinomianism, only Clarkson can be said to have come close to such a position. Even he changed his mind, recanted after a fashion, and his later account of these years will not permit us the reliable reconstruction of a Ranter group, especially one made up of these individuals. Bauthumley differed from Clarkson about God as the origin of evil and was, in any case, ambivalent. Coppe's preoccupations, social rather than theological, were markedly different from the others. In his own view, which appears on the evidence justified, he was and has been misread. In this his experience, though not his views, followed those of Coppin and Salmon. None of them dismisses the validity of Scripture in 1650; though clearly, by the time of his Muggletonian phase in 1660, Clarkson was committed to discrediting the Second Commission.

Such evidence as there is, therefore, suggests that the Ranters did not exist either as a small group of like-minded individuals, as a sect, or as a large-scale, middle-scale or small movement. Yet in 1650 and continuing spasmodically thereafter contemporaries claimed the existence of Ranters and believed them to be a dangerous threat to social, moral and religious stability. There was a Ranter sensation. What was this sensation and how are we to explain it?

4

The Ranter sensation

i. INTRODUCTION

If there was no core, no sect, no mass movement of Ranters, what was it that Englishmen in 1650, and the years following, were so alarmed about; so much so that they produced an outpouring of dramatic accounts, earnestly defended themselves from association with Ranterism, accused others, revised the law and – so it has been alleged – embarked on a savage repression? If there were no Ranters, why did so many Englishmen apparently believe that there were?

In this chapter I shall attempt a description of contemporary beliefs in and perceptions of the Ranters; in the next, an explanation of those beliefs. There are three tiers to the phenomenon to be described; tiers which to some degree interlock. First are the 'yellowpress' accounts of a Ranter movement, towards which historians, on the whole, have adopted a sceptical attitude, but which they have ambiguously used as a source of information. Second come some allegedly more serious and reliable accounts. Third are the reactions of sects, like Baptists and Quakers, and their leaders to what were perceived as encounters with the Ranters.

ii. THE SENSATION

According to David Masson, who believed in the reality of a Ranter sect, 'low printers and booksellers made a trade on the public curiosity about the Ranters, getting up pretended accounts of their meetings as a pretext for prurient publications'.[1] Few would disagree with this, although historians' attitudes to what use may be made of such materials have been wavering and ambivalent. Here a chronological description of this sensation is presented to demonstrate its uselessness as evidence

---

[1]   Masson, *The Life of John Milton*, vol. V, p. 18.

of a real movement and its value as an indicator of contemporary fears and anxieties.

There were, of course, numerous religious sensations in the 1640s and 1650s and throughout the seventeenth century. For example, in May 1650, Humphrey Ellis reported William Franklin's claim to be the restored messiah.[2] What is initially significant about the sensational reporting of a Ranter movement is that it did not begin until October 1650. Coppe's *A Fiery Flying Roll*, its condemnation, his arrest, the arrests of Salmon and Wyke, the punishment of Bauthumley – all had happened at least six months earlier and none had been sufficient to set off a sensation.[3] The first pamphlet of a long sequence which claimed to depict the horrible tenets and excesses of a Ranter movement appeared on 11 October 1650, exactly a week after George Thomason acquired his copy of Clarkson's banned work *A Single Eye*. Was it Clarkson's work, illegally available again in early October, which, with its approximation to practical antinomianism, sparked the whole thing off? Earlier, official references to Ranters occurred in June 1650 and might be linked with the circulation and examination of *A Single Eye* by the Commons in that month. On 21 June Weaver's committee reported 'the several abominable Practices of a Sect called Ranters' and then went on immediately to report the 'Heads of a Book called "A Single Eye" '.[4] A week later *The Impartial Scout* reported the punishment for blasphemy of two troopers of Colonel Rich's regiment, 'companions of those called Raunters'.[5] Given the sectarianising tendencies of the day and the religious anxieties which abounded, could it be that Clarkson's idiosyncratic tract was sufficient to spark off first an official reaction and then a sensation about a new, dangerous and diverting sect, its doings and its beliefs?

Be that as it may, *The Ranters Religion* (11 October 1650), published by authority, was the first overt, sensational account of and attack upon the Ranters as a new and pernicious sect or movement. In one fell swoop, it established many of the conventions which the sensational literature was to follow. It was short, racy, disapproving and at the same

[2]   Humphrey Ellis, *Pseudochristus* (1650), E.602 (12), Thomason date 27 May 1650. Ellis had been predicting the arrival of false Christs since 1647. See Ellis, *Two Sermons* (1647), Wing E.580.
[3]   *A Perfect Diurnall* (no. 34, 29 July – 5 August 1650, 394) had reported the punishment of a dragoon in Scotland for blasphemy, the cause of his blasphemy being 'a ranting humour' brought on by too much drink. There is no suggestion at this time, however, of a Ranter movement.
[4]   *C.J.*, VI, 427.   [5]   *The Impartial Scout*, no. 53, 21 June – 28 June 1650, 219.

time prurient. The title page was adorned with a woodcut of naked men and women and the deliberation of a pornographic appeal was underlined by a comparison with Aretino: the reader was to look at the filthiness in order to abominate it.[6] So the Ranters are depicted as believing that God is pleased by acts of sin and is indeed the author of them. A resurrection is possible, but it will be determined astrologically. All women should be in common and oaths, drinking and sexual promiscuity are to be encouraged. Three keys are held by God: the key to the womb which admits us to the world; the key of liberty which authorises us to fulfil our lusts; and a third key, which is a small bone in the back, will be instrumental in the resurrection. There is a knock-about, titillating and scandalising air about these publications which does not preclude their serious treatment but does mean they should not be taken too solemnly as sources of reliable information.

The image of the Ranters as practical antinomians was endorsed late in October by Raunce Burthall in *An Old Bridle For a Wilde Asse-Colt*.[7] Ranters were to be identified with prophesied anti-christians or false prophets. If there were no such thing as sin, Burthall asked, why do we see the fruits of sin in thorns and briars, pain in childbirth and the necessity to kill God's creatures for food? Ranters could offer others no liberty since they were themselves slaves to carnality and bestiality. Only subjection to the law could free men from such slavery:

we confesse all action, as it is action, (even in devils) is of God, and so tis good; but how can this free either devils, or men, that are subjected, under a Law; for their actions, must not be meere actions, but regular, according to Law.[8]

There is a tension in the seriousness of Burthall's polemic against these prophesied Antichrists and it arises out of what are perceived as possibly shared premises.

The Routing of the Ranters (19 November 1650) represented a return to the sensational theme and, like *The Ranters Religion*, claimed to be published by authority. The cover illustration showed a group of five men arranged around a table furnished with writing materials, while one of them, somewhat inconsequentially, whipped himself.[9] The Ranters, 'alius Coppanites, or Clartonians', were a group newly sprung up. They

delight not only in gluttony and drunkennesse, chambering and wantonnesse, and the like, but deride holy Scriptures, deny Christ, blaspheming, and as it were spit in the face of God himself.

---

[6] *The Ranters Religion* (1650) title page, An Advertisement to the Reader, E.619 (8), Thomason dating 11 October 1650.   [7] E.615 (9), Thomason date 31 October 1650.
[8] *Ibid.*, p. 15.   [9] E.616 (9).

Their chief leaders were 'Copp' and 'Claxton'. Their meetings were orgiastic with a hint of diabolatry.[10] There is a heavy emphasis throughout the pamphlet on sexual promiscuity combined with the spectre of the unbridled appetite of women and its social consequences.

From this point on, it was clear that there was a market for this sort of material and the production of it accelerated. On 2 December *The Ranters Ranting*[11] made its appearance, claiming dissatisfaction with *The Routing of the Ranters* but using much of the same materials. It is a lurid account of two meetings in London, a diatribe against Coppe, and, rather ludicrously thrown in for good measure, an account of a Welshman's fratricidal and matricidal acts and of his consequent fate. The journalistic exploitation of the sensation was getting into full swing. As it did so, we may note an increasing association of the collapse of the polarities of good and evil with the influence of atheism.

Gilbert Roulston, who produced the next sensational account of Ranterism, claimed to have been an ex-Ranter, but we are more certain of his identity as an ex-royalist hack who fulminated against 'Round-Heads' in the 1640s.[12] His *The Ranters Bible*[13] was collected by Thomason on 9 December 1650 and carried the sectarianising tendency to excess by finding not one but seven sects under the Ranter heading. It is hard not to see this as sheer fantasy. For example, the Seleutian Donatist subsect of the Ranters were, according to Roulston, sunworshippers and star-followers; the Marcian Ranters held that there were two gods, one good, one evil, and engaged in a pitched battle with other Ranters.[14] What, in the author's mind, held all of this together was the spread of atheism and the consequent collapse of orthodoxy and moral order.[15]

The author of *The Arraignment and Tryall with a Declaration of the Ranters*[16] (17 December 1650) attempted to portray both the variety and widespread nature of this religious and moral collapse, while showing that its antecedents went back as far as the Donatists of the fourth century. Coppe, 'Claxton', Pordage (misnamed 'Buckeridge') and the new messiahs were indiscriminately linked under the 'Ranter' umbrella. On the same day, 17 December 1650, appeared M. Stubs's *The Ranters Declaration*.[17] This was a rehash of *The Ranters Religion* with the addition of some new promiscuity stories, the notion 'of the new Generation of

---

[10] *Ibid.*, pp. 3–4.   [11] E.618 (8).
[12] See his *The Round-Head Uncovered* (1642), E.108 (9); *The Round-Heads Catechisme* (1643), E.1205 (1); *The Round-Heads Remembrancer* (Oxford, 1643), E.105 (13).
[13] E.619 (6).   [14] *Ibid.*, pp. 4–5.   [15] See especially *ibid.*, p. 1.
[16] E.620 (3). This also claimed to be 'published according to order', title page.
[17] E.620 (2). 'Licensed according to order', title page.

Ranters', some material on Pordage and the startling possibility that some Ranters worshipped the deceased Archbishop Laud.

Three days later (20 December 1650), what has to be seen, in seventeenth-century terms, as a major press phenomenon continued with the publication of *The Ranters Recantation*.[18] In yellowpress fashion, the author claimed that it was the inadequacy of previous accounts which had impelled him to relate his more responsible version. With that we are led straight into accounts of sexual licence and the sermons of two reputedly Ranter leaders, Arthingworth and Gilbert, of whom we hear nothing elsewhere. Arthingworth preached that there were no gods but himself, that it was lawful to drink, swear, revel and lie with any woman and 'That there is no Sabbath, no Heaven, no Hell, no Resurrection, and that both Soul and Body dies together'. He called for a Turk's head or piss pot and 'upon a great flash of fire, vanished, and never was seen more, to the great admiration of the Spectators'.[19] Such burlesque exits typify the humour of this literature and must condition our view of its reliability as evidence of anything resembling actual events. Sensation is all. So, according to this author, Ranters had been arrested at Coventry for proclaiming Charles Stuart king. Whatever was shocking, salacious or outrageous was good copy, though naturally accompanied by solemn demands for harsher punishments and firmer social discipline.[20]

Farce was not far away and came on stage with the production by Samuel Shepherd, another hack writer, of *The Joviall Crew, or, The Devill turn'd RANTER* on 6 January 1651.[21] 'All the world now is in the Ranting Humor' the work proclaimed, and proceeded to illustrate this in dramatic form with a short play about the danger of wives' contempt of their husbands' authority and the consequent cuckolding of the husbands. The amoralism of the Ranters had come to equate with the inversion of the double standard.

Later in the same month, two further tracts consolidated the exploitation of the Ranter image as a basis for fantasy. Samuel Tilbury's *Bloudy Newes from the North*[22] (20 January 1651) recounted the plot of Ranters at York to murder all those who would not join them. Again, Ranters were held to declare for Charles Stuart as well as engaging in the usual immoral practices. The same mixture of Ranterism embracing royalism and practical antinomianism was presented the following day in *Strange Newes from Newgate and the Old-Baily*[23] (21 January 1651). In

---

[18] E.620 (10).   [19] *Ibid.*, pp. 2, 5.   [20] *Ibid.*, pp. 5, 6.   [21] E.621 (7).
[22] E.622 (1). 'Published according to order', title page.
[23] E.622 (3). 'Published according to order', title page.

fact, the material was becoming exhausted. The woodcuts adorning *Strange Newes* were taken from *The Ranters Ranting* and stories fabricated or rehashed to go with them.

The attempt to link Ranterism with support of the Stuarts may have had something quite deliberate about it. There is evidence of official concern that royalist propaganda could exploit stories of antinomian excess in belief and practice to discredit the Commonwealth. As early as October 1650 *Mercurius Politicus*, the semi-official newspaper of the Commonwealth, had reported the sentences on Clarkson and Major Rainsborough with the comment that the

> severity of which *Votes* may serve to stop the slandrous mouths of those that publish abroad such vile reports of this Common-wealth, as if they intended to countenance impious and *licentious* practises, under pretence of *Religion* and *Liberty*.[24]

Certainly, the representatives of the Stuarts in Venice and elsewhere had presented the emergence of the English republic as a threat to all religion, morality and social order.[25] In January 1651, *Mercurius Politicus* had a report from Leyden that the King's agents there were spreading

> Stories of exorbitant practices of some men in power among you, and to make his party merry with *Canterbury* tales of *Ranters*. I had thought the Ranters had all been Kings men, and spued out of your land: for I have seen good store of them here.[26]

Ranterism was a powerful and dangerous slur and its force had to be directed away from the Commonwealth towards its enemies. The reports of papers like *Mercurius Politicus* were both a warning and exactly such a diversion. Lurid as they were, tracts like *The Ranters Recantation,, Bloudy Newse*, and *Strange Newes* may, by their identification of Ranterism with the cause of the Stuarts, have been more than casually serving the same purpose. Is it possible that, within the sensational material on the Ranters, we can glimpse a struggle to control, exploit and interlock a series of powerful images: antinomian or atheistic collapse of moral and religious order with royalist excess or Puritan disintegration?

However that may be, after January 1651 the sensational focus shifted to the pseudo-Christs and, though the term 'Ranter' sometimes went with the shift, it was losing its coherence. In *The Declaration of John*

---

[24] *Mercurius Politicus*, 17, 26 September – 3 October 1650, 286–7.
[25] *C.S.P. Ven.*, XXVII, 1647–52, pp. 136–40.
[26] *Mercurius Politicus*, 33, 16–23 January 1651, 546. See also the account of an accord between Ranters and royalists in *The Faithful Scout*, 128, 2–9 September 1653.

Robins[27] (2 June 1651) woodcuts from Stubs's *Ranters Declaration* were used and an anecdote about a Ranter was told but the main drift of the pamphlet was to link John Robins, who claimed to be the third Adam, with the Shakers. John Taylor's *Ranters of Both Sexes*[28] (3 June 1651) was, in fact, an account of the trial of John Robins and his associates, as was *The Ranters Creed*. Ranterism was becoming identifiable with the broadest blasphemy as its focus moved away from pantheism and practical antinomianism. *The Ranters Monster*[29] (30 March 1652) dealt, amongst other things, with the prodigious deformities of the child produced by Mary Adams, who claimed to be the Virgin Mary with child by the Holy Ghost.

By 1652 in *The Character of a Time Serving Saint*,[30] Lionel Lockier could complain that the term 'Ranter' was no more than a label used by formalists to discredit those who sought a true Christian community. In a sermon preached in the same year, but not published until 1657, Robert Abbot engaged in a positive riot of confusion.[31] Ranters were associated with moral perfectionists, Adamists, extravagance in dress, delight in vain company, settled obstinacy and neglect of spiritual observance. In other words, the Ranters had become everything that Abbot did not like and, since his aversions were legion, there was plenty of room for them to operate. By 1653, in *A Total Rout, or a Brief discovery*, the Ranter had become no less than that cynosure of moral weakness, a gentleman at loose on the town.[32] Late in the same year, *The Black and Terrible Warning Piece: Or, A Scourge to England's Rebellion*[33] deciphered the hand of the devil in recent events and especially in the spread of error. Ranterism was, to this author, an illustrative epiphenomenon, but curiously its most significant outbreak was at 'Hammel' in Germany in 1484 when 130 children disappeared.

More seriously, Ranterism moved in the 1650s into a perceived loose association with Quakers, Seekers and Shakers and it may, ironically, have been, as we shall see, the sects themselves who kept such associations alive. In rather tired fashion, a broadsheet list of blasphemies of 1654 had in the thirtieth and last category 'Ranters, Quakers, Seekers and Blasphemers [who] do daily broach sad and fearfull Blasphemies'.[34]

---

[27] E.629 (13).
[28] E.629 (15). See also *The Ranters Creed* (1651), Wing R.250. Morton gives May as the date but I can see no evidence for this. *W.O.T.R.*, p. 114.   [29] E.658 (6).
[30] B.L. 669 f.16 (53). Reproduced in H.E. Rollins (ed.), *Cavalier and Puritan Ballads and Broadsides Illustrating the Period of the Great Rebellion 1640–1660* (New York, 1923), pp. 320–4.   [31] Robert Abbot, *The Young Mans Warning-Piece* (1657), Wing A.70.
[32] B.L. 669 f.17 (56).   [33] E.721 (7).
[34] 'A List of some of the Grand Blasphemers and Blasphemies' (1654), B.L. 669 f.17 (83), Thomason date 23 March 1654.

J.M.'s *The Ranters Last Sermon* (August 1654) blurred together Ranters, Quakers and Seekers under an anti-scriptural, practical antinomianism with a strong dash of diabolatry.[35] In Thomas Underhill's condemnatory history of the Quakers, *Hell broke loose*,[36] of 1659/60, Quakers and Ranters were deliberately confused wherever possible.

The Ranter sensation, if we mean by that a sensation about antinomian flouting of moral conventions, systematic impiety and pantheistic complacency, lasted a bare three months, from October 1650 through to late January 1651. In that time, a vigorous outpouring of lurid accounts must have been sustained by a ready, if not avid, audience. Amidst the reckless fabrication and repetitive exploitation of material we should note two themes running through the sensational fabric – the influence of atheism and the relationship between Ranterism and royalism. Both are themes to which we shall later return. After January 1651, the Ranters continued to be a sensation, but the definition of their image blurred and finally disintegrated. 'Ranter' was fast becoming just another smear word. For a while it was saved by the new menace of the Quakers rising in public consciousness from 1653 onwards. For some time Quakers, Ranters and Seekers were to be lumped together in hostile commentary. Quakers themselves kept the notion of a Ranter movement alive both by their struggle to free themselves from association with it, and paradoxically, by their attempts to use it in disciplining their own adherents. Such ambiguity had its precedents and we must now look at these in the more serious, less sensational contemporary accounts.

iii. MORE SERIOUS ACCOUNTS

In order to survey these more serious reactions, it is necessary to begin before the sensation burst upon the scene. It is important to recognise the widespread anxiety about the last days which pervaded the atmosphere of 1649 and 1650. It was an anxiety exacerbated by tensions within the sects themselves and more generally by uncertainty as to the meaning of true religion in its Calvinist and neo-Calvinist forms. These fears will be examined more closely in the next chapter, but it is necessary to look at some of them here as anticipating and then fixing the perception of a Ranter phenomenon in the minds of earnest men of religion.

---

[35] E.808 (1), Thomason date 7 August 1654. Morton, mistakenly in my opinion, gives 2 August 1654: *W.O.T.R.*, p. 114.

[36] E.770 (6), Thomason date 13 November 1659. For further association of Quakers and Ranters see *Mercurius Politicus*, nos. 245, 246; *The Faithful Scout*, no. 140.

The widespread expectation of the last days, and the millennial upheavals associated with them, is too well known a feature of seventeenth-century English life to need comment here.[37] It was at once an anxiety about the devastations of Antichrist without, the fear of papists or episcopalians,[38] and at the same time a fear of disintegration from within, of a scattering of the gathered churches, brought on by a lack of watchfulness and a running to excess. Edward Ellis in his *A Sudden and Cloudy Messenger* (1649) warned that the Scriptures prophesying the disturbances of the last days might apply to the sects themselves, the army, the City of London, the godly ministry – all those props of the Good Old Cause as it was coming to manifest itself in 1649.[39]

What form could this disintegration from within take? One answer came from a group of Particular Baptists, themselves locked in anxious quarrel with the General Baptists, and its importance to us in this context is that it prefigured the popular image of the Ranters before that name had even emerged. A group of Particular or Calvinist Baptists, led by John Spilsbery, published in late February 1650 a tract entitled *Heart-Bleedings For Professors Abominations*.[40] It was directed at their co-religionists and associated sects. In 'the last Ages of the World' reliance on the indwelling spirit alone could lead to the denial of Christ, of Scripture, of sin: 'there is no sin but what contradicts a mans own light, (which is a mans onely law) and sin is onely sin to him that thinks it so, and there is no hell but that torment that men sustain through crossing their own light'.[41] God's will could then be for saints to curse, swear, be drunk and full of all uncleanness. The anxiety which impelled this publication by this group was that it might be their teaching which indirectly could lead to excess of this kind.[42] The later, popular, image of the Ranter was already being articulated. To use the language of

---

[37] See, for example, Bernard Capp, *The Fifth Monarchy Men: A Study in Seventeenth-Century English Millenarianism* (London, 1972); P. Toon (ed.), *Puritans, The Millennium and the Future of Israel: Puritan Eschatology 1600–1660* (Cambridge, 1970); Paul Christianson, *Reformers and Babylon: English Apocalyptic Visions from the Reformation to the Eve of the Civil War* (Toronto, 1978); Katherine R. Firth, *The Apocalyptic Tradition in Reformation Britain 1530–1645* (Oxford, 1979).

[38] Christopher Hill, *Anti Christ in Seventeenth-Century England* (London, 1971); Robin Clifton, 'Fear of Popery', in Conrad Russell (ed.), *The Origins of the English Civil War* (London, 1973), pp. 144–67.   [39] E.592 (13).

[40] E.594 (13). Thomason date 28 February 1650. For Spilsbery and the Particular Baptists see Frank McGregor, 'The Baptists: Fount of All Heresy', in McGregor and Reay (eds.), *Radical Religion*, pp. 23–63; L.F. Brown, *The Political Activities of Baptists and Fifth Monarchy Men in England During the Interregnum* (London, 1911), pp. 3–4, 5, 58, 123, 160, 202; *B.D.B.R.S.C.*, under 'Spilsbury'.

[41] *Heart-Bleedings For Professors Abominations*, pp. 3–4, 7.   [42] *Ibid.*, pp. 12–15.

sociology, it comes close to a prediction of deviance which was later to be projected, exemplified and amplified.

By March 1650, Coppe's case and his *A Fiery Flying Roll* had achieved sufficient notoriety for fears of this kind to focus around them. Even so, his doctrines were seen as no more than the latest and isolated instance of a general phenomenon. *A Blow at the Root or Some Observations Towards A Discovery of the Subtilties and Devices of Satan* (4 March 1650) exemplifies this. The devil's design is aimed principally at the people of God, using deceptions which closely resemble divine light and truth and taking advantage of the disorders of times of reformation. In particular, Satan had led men from separatism into Anabaptism, thence into Seeking, on into Levelling and from there into the doctrine of the *Fiery Flying Roll*.[43] The association of Coppe with Levelling rather than with practical antinomianism is noteworthy, but what is central to this tract is the fear of potentialities *within* sectarianism and their links with emphasis on the indwelling spirit. Unguarded, they could lead to every kind of moral and theological disorder. The answer lay in prayer, adherence to Scripture, reliance on Christ, avoidance of disputes, consultation with godly Christians and observance of the fate of those who had gone astray.[44]

We can see the same problem manifested, from a somewhat different direction, in the publication in December 1650 of Edward Hyde junior's *A Wonder and yet no Wonder: A Great Red Dragon in Heaven*.[45] Hyde was an unusual defender of 'the old true Protestant Religion of the Church of England' and especially of its liturgy[46] but, at the same time, was sufficient of a religious enthusiast to argue in 1651 that Christ was within us and that a hireling clergy, namely one dependent on tithes, was to be treated with contempt.[47] *A Wonder and yet no Wonder* was a detailed exegesis of Revelation 12:3, 4. Jesus might be within us, but false prophets would put Scripture aside and claim the legitimacy of an immediate relationship with God. Then the saints could be led astray in a variety of ways and Hyde endeavoured to catalogue them. Amidst

---

[43] *A Blow at the Root* (1650), Chapters 1–4, pp. 151–2, E.594 (14), Thomason date 4 March 1650. Was Coppe singled out because of his earlier reputation as a Baptist? The juxtaposition of Levelling and *A Fiery Flying Roll* in the sequence is significant.

[44] *Ibid.*, pp. 138–44. [45] E.1361 (2).

[46] Hyde, *Allegiance and Conscience Not fled out of England* (Cambridge, 1662), To the Reader. See also, by Hyde and John Ley, *A Debate Concerning the English Liturgy* (1656); Hyde, *Christ and his Church: or, Christianity Explained* (Oxford, 1657), E.633 (1); *The True Catholicks Tenure* (Cambridge, 1662).

[47] Hyde, *The Mystery of Christ in Us* (1651), pp. 14–18, 42, 84, 183, E.1372 (4), Thomason date 28 May 1651.

his list we find the proposition that 'all manner of wickedness is lawful, and so we may commit it . . .'; according to Hyde, a serious misreading of Scripture.[48] It remains striking that, at the very height of the Ranter sensation in December 1650, Hyde made no reference to a Ranter movement, or to specific Ranters. His concern is a general one, associated with all forms of enthusiasm and penetrating even Hyde's own Anglicanism.

What we have, then, is a very broad anxiety about the potentiality of sectarianism, or even an undifferentiated religious enthusiasm, to slip out of control into all sorts of moral and doctrinal disorder. Amongst these varieties of disorder are types which approximate, in almost predictive fashion, to the Ranter model, though, as we have seen, there is through to December 1650 no reference to a Ranter movement, and when Coppe is referred to it is in association with Levelling, not Ranting.

In fact it is only when the yellowpress Ranter sensation had almost run its full course that this more serious and introvert literature absorbed the Ranter phenomenon and made it a central feature of its anxieties. In late January 1651, when, as noted earlier, the sensational image of the Ranters was virtually exhausted and was losing its focus, John Holland published *The Smoke of the Bottomlesse Pit*.[49] Here the serious literature of sectarian anxiety took the notion of a Ranter sect or movement from the yellowpress sensationalists at the last moment of the latter's interest. Although Holland's postscript confesses that he had gathered the opinions under discussion in a confused manner, his full title makes an oblique reference to *A Justification of the Mad Crew* and his work is probably best seen as a loose critique of the nine 'Principles' of that work. The Ranters are pantheist; see Christ as only a form or shadow and dismiss the atonement; stress their indwelling divinity, dismiss the distinction of good and evil; find Scripture 'a fleshly History', irrelevant if not pernicious to Englishmen; reject the applicability of ordinances and deny the notion of a last judgement consigning souls to an outward heaven or hell. Certainly, as Holland admitted, the views assembled were more heterogeneous than the framework of the critique, *A Justification of the Mad Crew*, would bear. Nevertheless, his juxta-

---

[48] *A Wonder and yet no Wonder*, pp. 34–5.
[49] E.622 (5), Thomason date 22 January 1651. The author is described on the title page as 'John Holland Porter' and there has been some uncertainty as to whether 'Porter' is a surname. It may be an occupational description, either in reality or allegorically. Whatever the case may be, I have chosen to follow the most common usage and to refer to the author as John Holland.

position of the sensational spectre of a Ranter movement with this confused collection of views was a momentous piece of alchemy. For
Holland had virtually invented the Ranter movement as it has come
down to us in recent historiography. When, ten months later, John
Tickell wished to dispute Coppe's attempt to free himself from the taint
of practical antinomianism, he did so under a variation of Holland's title
and armed with his assumptions that there was a Ranter movement and
that it was pantheistic and advocated an active, practical antinomianism.
The Bottomless Pit Smoaking in Familisme (Oxford, 1651)[50] began with the
assertion that 'Phantastick preaching, hearing, praying, writing [is] the
great sin of our age.' Coppe was identified with both Familism and
Ranterism. The Christ without, not the Christ within, was the only
possible saviour and his nature and morality did not change. Familism/
Ranterism usurped the Christ without in favour of the Christ within,
whose nature was infinitely malleable. The identity of Ranterism is
blurred with Familism and its specific connections with Coppe's teachings are not examined. What it comes down to is a railing against an
inner God. In his other words, Tickell was obsessed with an external
God of rigid and demanding discipline. He wrote of the need for self-
mortification and to discipline the moments of each day as the
obedience required *after* salvation.[51]

The prior concern of these serious writers then was with a general
problem or anxiety arising from an extrapolation of some of their own
teachings. What were the implications of supposing a Christ indwelling
in each individual? Such anxieties remained general through to almost
the very end of the Ranter sensation. It is tempting to speculate that it
was the sensation which established, in serious minds, the image of a
Ranter phenomenon, embodying their worst fears of religious
individualism run to anarchy in pantheistic blasphemy and antinomian
practice. It was an image which need not be sharp and was readily run
into overlay with other images, of Familism, for example. It picked up
individuals from the yellowpress or in their immediate predicaments
and fixed them in a damaging frame of associations. The image of
Ranterism had become a weapon with which serious and God-fearing
men could fight the good fight.

[50] E.1306 (3), Thomason date 18 November 1651. Morton follows Fortescue in giving 23
     September 1651, but this is to give the date of Coppe's recantation sermon as mentioned on
     Tickell's title page and cannot be correct. Thomason's superscription is barely legible but
     seems to be 'Novemb 18'.
[51] *Crums of Bread for the Dove in the Clefts of the Rock* (1652), pp. 9–19, 30–2, Wing T.1156;
     Church Rules Proposed to the Church in Abingdon and Approved by them (Oxford, 1656),
     Wing T.1155.

iv. SECTARIAN EXPLOITATION AND SEMANTIC
DETERIORATION

From early on in its history the term 'Ranter' had been used by royalists
to discredit puritans and *vice versa*. It had been used by those fearful of a
disintegrating sectarianism to discredit freer souls in search of an inner
God; and it had been used by those stern disapprovers of all but perfect
discipline, which every age seems to produce, to discredit almost
everything else.[52] But from the mid 1650s it took on new polemic life as
a sensationally based discrediting device in the struggle between
Baptists and against Quakers and, ironically, within those movements
to create a sense of discipline and authority, to sectarianise what could
otherwise have remained casually dangerous associations of enthusiasts.[53]

We have already seen how the image which was to be that of the
Ranters could be prefigured by a group of particular Baptists, anxious
about the implications of their own teachings and the potential licence
of legitimate sainthood.[54] Samuel Fisher, a leading General Baptist, also
found Ranterism a useful touchstone when he entered the protracted,
apparently interminable, debates over forms of baptism which raged
amongst Baptists and between them and their enemies through the
1650s and beyond. Fisher was firmly in the camp of immersion rather
than sprinkling and held that adult baptism was one of Christ's ordinances
not to be discontinued until his second coming.[55] Behind the particular
issue lay the vexed and profoundly disturbing question of the status of
ordinances in an age of the spirit, possibly in the third dispensation; a
debate which is fundamental to many things in the 1650s and which still
has to find its historian. The Ranter emerges, for Fisher, as embodying
every contentious stance, from the defence of sprinkling (i.e. a fellow,
if rival, Baptist) to those who insist that the ordinances of the Christ of
the Gospels no longer bind (which, to those with sharp eyes, may
appear to be the same thing). In any case, 'the Ranter hath made void

[52] For further examples see *Mercurius Politicus*, 245, 15–22 February 1655, 5141–2; *Mercurius Democritus*, 10–17 November 1652, 252–6; *ibid.*, 27 July – 3 August 1653, 521–2; *Severall Proceedings in Parliament*, 130, 18–25 March 1652, p. 2025; *Mercurius Fumigosus*, 5–12 September 1655, 534, 536, 538; trial of Mr John Erbury in C.H. Firth (ed.), *The Clarke Papers*, vol. II (London, 1894), pp. 233–9. Cf. Lodowick Muggleton, *The Acts of the Witnesses* (London, 1699), pp. 17–18.

[53] I am indebted to Frank McGregor here. See his subtle and convincing arguments on the sectarian 'evidence' of the Ranters in 'Ranterism and the Development of Early Quakerism', 349–63; 'The Baptists: Fount of All Heresy' and 'Seekers and Ranters' in McGregor and Reay (eds.), *Radical Religion*.   54 See above, pp. 84–5.

[55] Fisher, *Baby-Baptism*, pp. 307, 466–522, Wing F.1055. For Fisher see McGregor and Reay (eds.), *Radical Religion*, pp. 38–9.

the commands of King Jesus'.[56] This was a broad stick indeed with which to beat one's opponents, and a forceful one in a world where salvation and providence, the will of God, were obsessional concerns. Whether the Ranter evoked here was a reality, other than as a polemical device, is, of course, another matter entirely.

An equally illuminating insight into the use of the Ranter image within Baptism – as a means of control, discipline and the policing of moral and social boundaries – can be provided by consulting the records of the Fenstanton Baptists.[57] What we see in these records is a good deal of speculation, by people associated with Baptist congregations, about the meaning of individual spiritual illumination, and an anxious reaction to those speculations by the officers of those congregations. Were manifestations of the spirit above Scripture? How could the spirit of God be distinguished from the spirit of error? What was the status of ordinances? Which, if any, were now binding and how was the selection authorised? Those who stepped on the wrong side of the illuminist path and came to disdain Scripture, ordinances or their authorised leaders had to be disciplined. Excommunication was one answer, but, for a sect struggling for its existence and fearful of betrayal, it was no convincing answer. A charge which could abash the accused, impress others and simultaneously show the movement's concern to be free of the historical associations of an antinomian Anabaptism was undoubtedly useful and the image of the Ranter was to hand.

By 1653, the claim of the wife of Robert Kent that the inner spirit, not Scripture, was all the light she needed, led to a charge against her of Ranterism, though 'she did much exclaim against their practices'.[58] The charge clearly worried her. It was to be used repeatedly against similar offenders. A letter from the Baptists at Canterbury to those at Caxton, also in 1653, requested them to send an exhortatory mission, 'for here are many unruly and vain talkers, and deceivers of minds, especially they called Ranters, whose mouths must be stopped'.[59] But, from this time, Quakers became for the Baptists a substitute for Ranters as deniers of ordinances.[60] Very soon, however inaccurately, they had taken over the image and disciplinary function entirely.[61]

[56] *Baby-Baptism*, p. 469; *W.T.U.D.*, Chapter 11.
[57] Cf. the treatment of these records here with that given in *W.T.U.D.*, pp. 228–9; Edward Bean Underhill (ed.), *Records of the Churches of Christ, Gathered at Fenstanton Warboys and Hexham 1644–1720* (The Hanserd Knollys Society, London, 1854).
[58] Underhill (ed.), *Records*, p. 73.
[59] *Ibid.*, p. 107.   [60] *Ibid.*, pp. 107, 115.   [61] *Ibid.*, pp. 141, 144–5, 315.

Paradoxically, the Quakers were also at this time trying to free themselves from association with Ranterism and simultaneously using the charge of Ranterism to discipline and sectarianise their own followers. For example, Ralph Farmer's *The Great Mysteries of Godlinesse and UnGodlinesse* (1655), dedicated to John Thurloe and the alliance of minister and magistrate, was designed to associate Quakers with Ranters, Levelling principles and Anabaptist excess.[62] The dismissal of external religion and, by implication, of ordinances, led to the excesses of the Ranters, 'that abominable crew of *Religious Villains*'.[63] The rest of the work is devoted to showing that, on these grounds, there is nothing to choose between Ranters and Quakers.

Quakers responded. In March 1655, Richard Farnworth attempted to argue the distinction between Ranters and Quakers by emphasising the adherence of the latter to Scripture, moral performance and a balance between the cross without and the cross within.[64] The following month John Audland attempted a similar exercise.[65] For a time it became almost obligatory for defences of Quakerism to incorporate a condemnation of Ranters and Ranting principles.[66] The heaviest irony is, of course, that the Quakers, taunted by association with Ranters and desperate to free themselves from such associations, nevertheless accused each other of Ranterism and so kept the term alive well into the late seventeenth century.[67] Ranters appear and reappear in the entries in George Fox's journal from 1651 until the 1670s.[68] But, as Frank McGregor has noted, when Fox left the areas in which he observed Ranters, references to the phenomenon ceased.[69] In these terms, Ranterism was used by Fox and others to discipline or trim away 'the unwelcome by-products of their missionary activity'; 'by the end of the Interregnum the Quakers' image of Ranterism had evolved from that

---

[62] E.480 (2), Thomason date 23 January 1654.   [63] *Ibid.*, p. 29.

[64] R. Forneworth, *The Ranters Principles & Deceits discovered* (1655), pp. 4–5, 10–11, 19–20, E.830 (14), Thomason date 16 March 1655.

[65] John Audland, *The Innocent Delivered out of the Snare* (1655), E.831 (11), Thomason date 9 April 1655.

[66] See, for example: Edward Burrough, *A Trumpet of the Lord Sounded out of Sion* (1656), pp. 26–8, E.875 (3); Margaret Fell, *A Testimonie of the Touch-Stone For All Professions* (1656), pp. 23–36, Wing F.636; George Fox, *The Great Mistery of the Great Whore Unfolded* (1659), p. 286, Wing F.1832; John Chandler, *A Seasonable Word and Call, To all those called Ranters or Libertines Throughout The three Nations* (1659), Wing C.1928.

[67] See, for example: Robert Rich, *Hidden Things Brought to Light* (1678), Wing R.1358; Robert Barclay, *The Anarchy of the Ranters And other Libertines* (1696), Wing B.718.

[68] Norman Penny (ed.), *The Journal of George Fox* (2 vols., Cambridge, 1911), vol. I, pp. 21, 22, 29, 47, 150–2, 165, 166, 184, 185, 262; vol. II, pp. 11–12, 26, 125, 222.

[69] McGregor, 'Ranterism and the Development of Early Quakerism', 353.

provoked by the confusion of blasphemy, threats, crude parody, doctrinal controversy and general emotional excitement which met the
preacher's impromptu testimony of the spirit. As the frequency of these
incidents declined, Ranterism came to represent any anti-social
manifestation of the light within.' Its principle and great value was disciplinary, a means of controlling members and policing boundaries, of
creating a sect. The *reductio and absurdum* of its use as such a device could
come when a preacher accused a congregation of Ranterism because
they 'were more interested in their tobacco pipes than his message'.[70]
The Quakers provide the most substantial evidence for the existence of
Ranterism after 1651, but it is not evidence to be taken at face value.
'Quaker evidence for Ranter activity is more symptomatic of the growing pains of Quakerism than indicative of widespread support for the
doctrines of mystical antinomianism after 1651.'[71]

Within the notion of an indwelling spirit and its legitimating
capacities were explosive potentialities which were condemned by
those who insisted on an external religious authority and could be
feared by those enthusiasts of inner religion who yet sought some control. Since there were perceived to be sects of every shade, there had to
be a sect embodying these potentialities. The Ranter was as necessary to
the sectarian enthusiast as he could be useful to the Anglican or Presbyterian concerned to adumbrate the nightmarish consequences of the
revolution. The tocsin of inner principles in the image of Ranterism
could be rung through many changes and by many different hands. The
Seeker William Erbery found a Ranterish usurpation of the dictates of
true religion by egotistical inner principles in the hypocrisy of the present churches and tried, in his *Testimony*, to demonstrate the point scripturally.[72] For Richard Baxter in 1651, Abiezer Coppe, 'a zealous
Anabaptist', though some would call him a Ranter, illustrated the dole-
ful consequences of the stress on inner religion which he associated with
Baptism. It could lead to practical antinomianism and a defiant
immorality.[73] Ranterism was a warning against Baptism. In *Reliquiae
Baxterianae*, the function and associations of Ranterism had changed.
They were now one of five sects 'whose Doctrines were almost the

---

[70] *Ibid.*, 354, 359.
[71] *Ibid.*, 351, 363. See also McGregor, 'Seekers and Ranters', pp. 134–9. The tensions we are
      observing here are well reflected in Isaac Pennington, *Divine Essays* (1654), especially
      Chapter 5 and p. 90.
[72] William Erbery, *The Testimony of William Erbery, Left Upon Record For the Saints of Succeeding
      Ages* (1658), pp. 314–15, 331, Wing E.3239.
[73] Richard Baxter, *Plain Scripture Proof of Infants Church Membership and Baptism* (1651), pp.
      148–52, Wing B.1344.

same, but they fell into several Shapes and Names: 1. The *Vanists*: 2. The *Seekers*: 3. The *Ranters*: 4. The *Quakers*: 5. The *Behmenists*'. Quakers and Ranters were virtually identical, except that the former practised an austere morality, the latter 'all abominable filthiness of Life'. Together they discredited a period in Baxter's own times which was only recalled in some confusion and was in part dependent on stories culled from Thomas Edwards.[74] A similarly crude, retrospective characterisation of the religious affiliations of his opponents can be found coming from a very different quarter, that of Lodowick Muggleton. Again the image of the Ranter was useful, but now to drub apostates and associate them with atheism. The effect of civil war on the Puritans was that

> Some of them turned to Presbytery, and would have Elders; and some turned Independants, and would let none work to them but their own People that was in Church Fellowship; others fell to be Ranters, and some fell to be meer Atheists. Then I saw several of them that were Zealous before towards God . . . turned Ranters, not only in Judgement but in Practice, to the Destruction both of Soul and Body.[75]

Those who had opposed Muggleton and Reeve within their own movement were particularly liable to end up characterised as Ranters.[76] For John Bunyan, Ranters and drunkards were almost always associated with Quakers; a useful stick with which to beat a detested foe.[77]

v. CONCLUSION

Though a short-lived affair, the yellowpress Ranter sensation of late 1650 and early 1651 was quantitatively impressive and influential in its imagery. It crystallised an image of deviance which had been prefigured and anticipated in other forms of literature and gave it currency. The inner tensions and struggles of the sects, in particular of the Baptists and Quakers, kept the image alive and so maintained its availability not only for themselves but, ironically, for their own, more conservative, enemies.

Running through the anxieties of both sectarians and conservatives was a common fear. What were the implications of the teaching of the age of the spirit, of the coming of the third dispensation? Did ordinances

---

[74]   Matthew Sylvester (ed.), *Reliquiae Baxterianae: or, Mr Richard Baxter's Narrative of the most Memorable Passages of his Life and Times* (1696), pp. 74–8.
[75]   Muggleton, *Acts of the Witnesses* (1699), pp. 17, 18, 56, 57, 80.   [76]   *Ibid.*, pp. 51–3.
[77]   Tindall, *John Bunyan*, pp. 44–6. Cf. Hill's categoric assertion that 'Bunyan moved in Ranter circles in his youth, probably in the army . . .': Christopher Hill, 'Radical Prose in Seventeenth Century England', 113.

not count any more? Were the First and Second Commissions, of the Old and New Testaments, already defunct? Was the voice of an inner God the only legitimating authority for belief and practice? The consequences of this dilemma were that a struggle had to be waged, by serious men, for a hold on the popular mind against the appeal of prophets, the unqualified doctrines of the inner light and the uncontrolled visions of a third dispensation. Horror stories of those who acted out the beliefs and practices of such extreme spiritual individualism and of the fates that befell them were one way of doing this. The Ranters were an image of this horror; Ranterism a frontier which should never be crossed. Anyone who raised the difficult question of ordinances – a Quaker, a Shaker, a Christ impersonator, a Baptist – or simply someone who preached the inner spirit or the end of ordinances was likely to be confronted by a twofold problem. On the one hand, they would be pushed across that frontier. On the other hand, they would, in all probability need to re-establish that frontier as a brake on their own followers or an antidote against rival groups. In both cases, the Ranter provided a useful image; Ranterism a necessary frontier. So it is that those whose sectarian identity was most abusively linked with Ranterism most frequently found Ranters elsewhere. It was a struggle over social, as much as moral, boundaries.

In the last days three sorts of Satanic temptation were feared; to false Christs, and Humphrey Ellis may bear witness to this fear; to religious fantasy, and John Spilsbery testified to this; and to an 'atheistic' subversion of all religion. In this last context, perhaps, the Ranter image operated most devastatingly. It is time to look more closely at that mythic image, at its projection and at the materials of which it was constituted.

5

Explaining the Ranter myth

i. INTRODUCTION

In their patterns of behaviour and argument, sectarians and others in the 1650s were willing to exploit images of religious and moral deviance. A tradition exploiting similar images had already been laid down by heresiographers like Thomas Edwards, Ephraim Pagitt and Alexander Ross. Their works were enormously popular, avidly read and influential in terms of perceptions of the moral, physical and sectarian character and 'logic' of heresy. They, in turn, exploited another tradition of writing which entwined moral and physical excess, the literature of prodigy.[1] By the late 1640s, both serious and sensational writers were anticipating a breakdown into moral and doctrinal disorder.

Such images blend into the perceptual landscape of early modern England. There was everywhere a tendency to extrapolate from reality in a kind of perceptual anticipation. Papists, Socinians, Presbyterians, even Independents, all attracted images of theological, moral, physical and social excess. Two things require a more extended explanation in the case of the Ranters. First, why were they accorded the character, confused, contradictory and vague as it might have been, that they were, when other images of deviance – papist, Socinian and so on – were readily available? Why was it necessary to have a category of 'Ranter'? Secondly, the gap between substantive reality and the phenomenon perceived is so great that it requires special explanation. Three or four disorganised individuals, flirting momentarily with something, which may have looked more like extreme antinomianism than it really was, became enmeshed in a force which made out of them a group, a sect, a collection of warring factions, a mass movement. Laurence Clarkson may have had a special rôle as a catalyst, but even so

See, for example, Katharine Park and Lorraine J. Daston, 'Unnatural Conceptions: The Study of Monsters in Sixteenth Century France and England', *P. & P.*, no. 92 (1981), 20–54.

94

it was as a strikingly idiosyncratic individual. Against this loose assortment of bemused characters, a virtually unprecedented press campaign was launched by the efforts of a very small number of printers and publishers, possibly with some official backing. Legislation was pushed through Parliament to deal with the heresies which they appeared to represent and their image went on haunting, and being repudiated by, other groups for some time to come.

One could, of course, turn this round and argue that the very extent of the furore and its repercussions demonstrate that there was substance to the Ranter phenomenon and reality in the threat it represented. We should be wary, in this instance in particular, of this no-smoke-without-fire argument. The work of some sociologists and a few historians has made us aware of the modern media's capacity to manufacture and shape news, even to 'suppress' the existence of major groups in society.[2] This is particularly apparent with regard to deviance, disputes and conflict. Crime waves, strike waves and various other forms of social conflict have frequently been created in this way.[3] On occasion, the media's 'crime wave' has preceded and may even generate, in subtle and complex ways, 'outbreaks' of 'crime'.[4] I shall argue that there is good cause to view the Ranter phenomenon in this light, as a projection reflecting contemporary anxieties and the desire for moral boundaries and conformity.

Natalie Zemon Davis is right to point out that 'deviant' is a word derived from modern conformist systems.[5] But alternative terms like 'heretic' lose their value in the heterodoxy of religious situations like that of England in the late 1640s and early 1650s. I shall therefore use the term 'deviance' here because it relates so well to the demands of conformity and the search for moral boundaries. In this sense, the greater the search for conformity, the greater the search for deviance;

---

[2] Stanley Cohen and Jock Young (eds.), *The Manufacture of News*, revised edition (London and Beverly Hills, 1981). See especially Gaye Tuchman, 'The Symbolic Annihilation of Women by the Mass Media', in *ibid.*, pp. 169–85.

[3] Mark Fishman, 'Crime Waves as Ideology', in *ibid.*, pp. 98–117; Paul Edwards, ' "The Awful Truth about Strikes in our Factories": A Case Study in the Production of News', in *ibid.*, pp. 138–46; Stanley Cohen, *Folk Devils and Moral Panics: The Creation of the Mods and Rockers*, 2nd edition (New York, 1980); Geoffrey Pearson, *Hooligan: A History of Respectable Fears* (London, 1983).

[4] See, for example, Jennifer Davis, 'The London Garotting Panic of 1862: A Moral Panic and the Creation of a Criminal Class in mid-Victorian England', in V.A.C. Gattrell, Bruce Lenman and Geoffrey Parker (eds.), *Crime and the Law: The Social History of Crime in Western Europe Since 1500* (London, 1980), pp. 190–213.

[5] Interview with Natalie Zemon Davis in Henry Abelove, Betsy Blackmar, Peter Dimock and Jonathan Schneer (eds.), *Visions of History* (Manchester, 1983), p. 112.

for without deviance there is no self-consciousness of conformity and *vice versa*.

After the crisis of revolution, it has been observed, there frequently emerges a rage for conformity, albeit a new form of conformity. This rage spotlights the enemies of the revolution in new ways, for amongst them are not only the counter-revolutionaries whom the ship of revolution has always carried along with it like a wave before its bow, but also those who would now carry the revolution too far, to excess, and, perhaps, to self-destruction. In the rage for conformity there is a struggle to identify and discipline the truly deviant in order that the image of true conformity may the better be established and the revolution be saved. In such a moment, the image may pre-empt the reality. This, I believe, was the nature of the moment of 1650–1 into which the Ranter image was projected.

But, before we attempt to persuade of this we should look at the realm of theory which we are entering and at its implications.

ii. THE THEORY: UNDERSTANDING THE MYTH

a. Moral panics and folk devils

Stanley Cohen in his work on the manufacture of news, moral panics and folk devils has emphasised the function of news reportage in informing people about the normative contours of a society. 'It informs us about right and wrong, about the boundaries beyond which one should not venture and about the shapes which the devil can assume.'[6] One should not be uncritical in accepting mechanistic or conspiratorial accounts of this process but, at the same time, one should be equally cautious about accepting at face value the classifications of the authorities, the media and the morally outraged, especially when moral boundaries are undergoing wholesale reappraisal or revision, as, for instance, in the wake of a revolution. For, in these situations, moral uncertainty can lead to great anxiety or 'moral panic' and to the demand for a reassertion or redefinition of moral boundaries. Such demands can be met, in part, by the redefining of deviance, the re-establishment of the character and image of the folk devil. The latter image, as a scapegoat, is most likely to occur, according to Cohen, when there is ambiguity on both sides of the boundary.[7] We shall return to this point later.

---

[6]   Cohen, *Folk Devils*, p. 17.
[7]   *Ibid.*, p. 193. See also Cohen, 'Mods and Rockers', in Cohen and Young (eds.), *The Manufacture of News*, pp. 432–3.

A classic study in this field has been Kai T. Erikson's *Wayward Puritans: A Study in the Sociology of Deviance* (New York, 1966). Erikson took three case studies in seventeenth-century Massachusetts: the antinomian controversy of the 1630s; the Quaker persecution of the later 1650s; and the witchcraft trials of the 1690s. He argued that such discoveries or outbreaks of deviance were a means of learning about and conceptualising moral boundaries as these shifted and the moral purposes and functioning of the colony came due for redefinition. Secondly, Erikson insisted that deviant and conformist could be uncomfortably close in doctrine.[8] Part of the function of deviance was to produce distance by insisting on moral divergences.

Similarly, recent studies of early modern witchcraft have tended to emphasise its function, as a controlling image of deviance, in situations where people felt great and increasing ambiguity about their social obligations to those on the margins of society.[9] Studies of village and urban life, for the same period, have tended to emphasise the notion of a moral community much exercised with boundary maintenance.[10] Clearly the projection and punishment of deviance was not the only way in which such boundaries could be maintained and adjusted. Pre-civil war communities were much addicted to, or afflicted with, listening to and reading the exhortatory pronouncements of preachers and guardians of morals. So too, ritual and carnival observances buttressed a sense of moral order, standards and obligations on the part of all strata of society by honouring the exemplars and burlesqueing the deviant.[11] What we have to recognise is that, after 1642, preaching was too uncontrolled, and ritual and carnival too inflexible, to cope with the hydra of interpretation swarming from press and pulpit and appearing cumulatively to undermine all moral and doctrinal consensus. Likewise, we must recognise the tensions and ambivalences building within Protestantism as the fissiparous tendencies of an almost unrestrained press and pulpit worked their way through: on the one hand, an insistence on faith and the individual experience of it; on the other, a yearning for

---

[8]　Erikson, *Wayward Puritans*, pp. 9–19, 22.

[9]　Keith Thomas, *Religion and the Decline of Magic: Studies in Popular Beliefs in Sixteenth and Seventeenth Century England* (London, 1971); A. Macfarlane, *Witchcraft in Tudor and Stuart England: A Regional and Comparative Study* (London, 1970).

[10]　Keith Wrightson and David Levine, *Poverty and Piety in an English Village: Terling 1525–1700* (New York, 1979); Keith Wrightson, *English Society 1580–1680* (London, 1982); Charles Pythian-Adams, 'Ceremony and the Citizen: The Communal Year at Coventry 1450–1550', in Peter Clark and Paul Slack (eds.), *Crisis and Order in English Towns 1500–1700: Essays in Urban History* (London, 1972), pp. 57–85.

[11]　Peter Burke, *Popular Culture in Early Modern Europe* (London, 1978); Natalie Zemon Davis, *Society and Culture in Early Modern France* (London, 1975), Chapters 4 and 5.

unity; openness to the promptings of the spirit, but a desire that ordinances should be fulfilled, while yet again an indeterminacy about which; a quest for authenticity, despising formalism, while admiring discipline; a fear, on the one side, of chaos, on the other of intolerance and the stiff-necked magistrate. How to find a boundary was a problem not only within society, but within individuals. There was a fault line of ambivalences, bound to produce anxieties, especially when the earth appeared to move or change. As the revolutionary moment slipped from some hands into others, was not a determination of the flux, a resolution of anxieties, looked for every day?

In the case of the Ranters and the theory of folk devils we must be careful to distinguish between the categorisation of certain real activities as deviant (which is what Kai Erikson saw in seventeenth-century Massachusetts) and the manufacture of the chimaera of the existence of those activities (which is what Stanley Cohen thought he saw in Brighton in 1964). But first it is necessary to consider the seed-bed of anxieties out of which the demand for conformity sprang and, subsequently, those specific anxieties which shaped the image of deviance required for the redefinition of moral boundaries.

b. An anxious society: general anxieties

In his famous opening chapter to *Religion and the Decline of Magic*, Keith Thomas portrayed the social environment of early modern England as literally fearful. The vulnerability of life, the prevalence of disaster, had to be offset or escaped in drink, narcotics or the pursuit of *fortuna*.[12] The mechanism for offsetting these fears had to some extent been de-institutionalised in England with the onset of Protestantism as the Church abandoned its relics, intermediary saints, the Virgin, and many of its specialised rituals, sacraments and images. If superstitions are the rules by which a human group attempts to generate an illusion of pre-dictability in an uncertain environment,[13] then we should expect to see what is repressed in one area spring up in another. And so it appears to have been. Less formal projections sprang up, as those of the old Church were abandoned or purged, and they became very common. The belief in particular providence, in demons, fairies, witches, in talismans, prophecies, astrological prediction and charms of various kinds

---

[12] Keith Thomas, *Religion and the Decline of Magic*, Chapter 1.
[13] Yi-Fu Tuan, *Landscapes of Fear* (Minneapolis, 1979), p. 9.

was widespread.[14] It would be unwarranted, in my opinion, to see these as the projections of a society with a kind of neurosis writ large. Such psychohistorical speculations are themselves of dubious validity.[15] Nevertheless, it was a society with a great deal for groups and individuals to be anxious about and, as always, they sought to resolve those anxieties as and where they could.

Given that it was also an age of high religious seriousness and conflict, we would expect religious imagery to bear some relation to these broader anxieties. We need to look no further than anti-papism in England for an example of this. As Robin Clifton has pointed out, Protestants were not taught to regard Catholicism as simply another form of religion, but rather as a total inversion of all true religion, 'more repugnant and damnable than any form of paganism'.[16] The image of the papist deviant was a negative reference point from which the bounds of true religion could be judged. Anxieties about the maintenance of true religion at home or abroad, in court or city, triggered off fears of popish plots. Such moral panics, projecting on papist folk devils, were, of course, more likely to occur in periods of acute civil tension; for example, 1640–2, 1648–9 and 1679.[17]

c. Revolutions and fear

Great events arouse great uncertainty; only in retrospect do they acquire the patina of inevitability and therefore of predictability. At the time, they only extend the range of perceived fluidity. In doing so, they can engender collective fear, set off general panic. In his classic study *The Great Fear of 1789*, George Lefebvre showed how the standard anxieties of the rural cycle were amplified into panic by the uncertainties created by the actions of the Estates General and the alternate fears and hopes raised by the end of a privileged order.[18] Rumours of armies

---

[14] A. Macfarlane, *The Family Life of Ralph Josselin, a Seventeenth-century Clergyman: An Essay in Historical Anthropology* (Cambridge, 1970); Thomas, *Religion and the Decline of Magic, passim*; Bernard Capp, *Astrology and the Popular Press: English Almanacs 1500–1800* (London and Boston, 1979).

[15] Cf. Rollo May, *The Meaning of Anxiety* (New York, 1950), especially pp. 18–21.

[16] Clifton, 'Fear of Popery', p. 146.

[17] For example, Anthony Fletcher, *The Outbreak of the English Civil War* (London, 1981), pp. 59, 203–4; Caroline Hibbard, *Charles I and the Popish Plot* (Chapel Hill, 1983); John Kenyon, *The Popish Plot* (London, 1972); Robin Clifton, 'The Fear of Catholicism during the English Civil War', *P. & P.*, 52 (1971).

[18] Georges Lefebvre, *The Great Fear of 1789: Rural Panic in Revolutionary France*, translated by Joan White, introduced by George Rudé (London, 1973). For some parallel instances see Rudé's introduction, *ibid.*, p. xiv.

of brigands or of aristocratic counter-coups swept wildly and swiftly through the countryside. Anxiety was their motor and, to some extent, shaped their form.

In England the period 1649–50 also witnessed a series of dramatic but profoundly disturbing events which produced not certainty but an extension of the range of uncertainty. The execution of the King not only symbolised the end of the ancient constitution, but could be held to be a repudiation of patriarchy.[19] The abolition of the House of Lords, like the disappearance of the bishops, could be seen as a step in the unravelling of hierarchy. And yet the Rump remained, ambivalent about an ambiguous revolution. Was there to be toleration? Would it extend to a popularly defended Anglicanism?[20] Was the monarchy really gone, or would London[21] or the Scots bring about a counter-coup? Were the traditional local rulers of the countryside to be allowed back or to be kept out in favour of new men? Was the army to remain? What was its rôle? And associated with this was the question of how far sectarian proliferation was to be allowed to go. After Baptists, Seekers, Diggers – what? And what was the meaning of this process? All of this came on top of the anxieties of a near-subsistence society caught in the grip of a cycle of bad years.

Prime amongst these uncertainties was that of the prospect of 'godly reformation', its meaning and the means of its procurement. From this perspective, the Rump sent out contradictory signals. In September 1649 it moved to restrict the liberty of the press with greater severity – but limited effectiveness.[22] A year later, in the wake of the victory at Dunbar, it at last abolished the obligation to attend one's parish church each Sunday.[23] Divergent forces were in tension along the front of 'godly reformation' at a moment of perceived crisis. In several quarters, there was mounting desperation for an affirmation of acceptable boundaries.

d. Crucial anxieties: the problem of post-revolutionary order or godly reformation

It was clear by mid to late 1649 that, while constitutionally the old order had gone, much of the fabric of social and political order would

---

[19] Cf. the remarks of Mary Astell quoted in Lawrence Stone, *The Family, Sex and Marriage in England 1500–1800* (London, 1977), p. 240.

[20] John Morrill, 'The Church in England 1642–9', in Morrill (ed.), *Reactions to the English Civil War 1642–9* (London, 1982).

[21] Ian Gentles, 'The Struggle for London in the Second Civil War', *Historical Journal*, 26:2 (1983), 277–305.   [22] Coward, *Stuart Age*, p. 213.

[23] *W.T.U.D.*, p. 103; David Underdown, *Pride's Purge* (Oxford, 1971) p. 275.

remain.[24] The Common Law continued substantially in place and in operation. The balance within the Rump had been swung back after Pride's purge with moderates encouraged to return. The Levellers had been crushed; the Officers' Agreement of January 1649 had been quietly buried. Cromwell's social and constitutional conservatism was apparent. But the problem of religious order remained and here, not untypically, the ambivalences for him and for others were greatest. As William Lamont has argued, the problems of legitimating a new order on a spiritual basis increased rather than diminished in the 1650s.[25] Intertwined as they might be, there were two dimensions to these difficulties: on the one hand, the problem of theological order, on the other hand, that of moral order.

The legitimacy of a superior theological authority had been repudiated along with the bishops. Presbyterianism itself had stumbled over the unwillingness to accept its prescriptions as the *iure divino* essence of ecclesiastical forms. But what if there came people who repudiated all forms whatsoever? The debate over ordinances and forms was in the last resort a debate about theology and theological order.[26] To some, the worst aspect of the debate was its bewildering confusion and capacity for paradox. Francis Freeman in 1650 found that 'the highest degree of Presbyterians are almost Antinomians, the highest degree of Antinomians, are almost Independents' and so on.[27] The boundaries had gone. In times of social misery, conflict and war, an anonymous writer argued, the devil finds it easier to do his business of sowing confusion amongst the godly. The basis of his success is the collapse of religious authority.[28]

An illuminating example of the tensions and paradoxes visible in this situation could be developed by studying the problem of 'Formality' and formalism as it was perceived at this moment.[29] Nowhere is the dilemma more acutely portrayed than in the so-called Blasphemy Act of

---

[24] Underdown, *Pride's Purge*; Blair Worden, *The Rump Parliament* (Cambridge, 1974); Austin Woolrych, *Commonwealth to Protectorate* (Oxford, 1982).

[25] William Lamont, *Godly Rule: Politics and Religion 1603-1660* (London, 1969) especially Chapters 6 and 7. See also J. C. Davis, 'Radicalism in a Traditional Society: The Evaluation of Radical Thought in the English Commonwealth 1649-1660', *History of Political Thought*, 3:2 (1982), 193-213.

[26] McGregor, 'Seekers and Ranters', pp. 122-3. For example, see Fisher, *Baby-Baptism* (1653).

[27] Francis Freeman, *Light Vanquishing Darknesse*, pp. 1-2, E.615 (7), Thomason date 29 October 1650.

[28] [Anon.,] *A Blow at the Root* (1650), Chapters 1-4, E.594 (14), Thomason date 4 March 1650.

[29] See, for example, Lionel Lockier's parody of 'the formall Saint', in *The Character of a Time-serving Saint* (1652).

9 August 1650. For the Act was directed not only against those of monstrous opinions and practices tending to the 'disordering' and 'dissolution of all Humane Society', but also towards the suppression of 'Prophaneness, Wickedness, Superstition and *Formality*'.[30] In other words, the Act which is so often depicted as repressive in its attitude towards those in search of spiritual authenticity in fact shared the anti-formalism of writers like Lionel Lockier and Abiezer Coppe. An Act which appeared to have as its prime intention the re-establishment of religious control has paradoxically at its heart a repudiation of formalism.

In part, these paradoxes were a playing out of potentialities long known to be inherent in Calvinism, which could be seen as a most potent seed-bearer of antinomianism.[31] The more solfidianism or pre-destination were emphasised, the more some saints might feel themselves to be above ordinances, the spirit above Scripture. It was a problem which had existed since Calvin's own day and for which the prescription had been greater control and doctrinal precision.[32] But when control had foundered, when men and women saw themselves as living in the last days, with all their attendant inversions, and when a third dispensation of direct revelation by the spirit was expected, how could these tendencies, inherent perhaps within true religion, be pre-vented from running to excess?

Toleration, it had been argued, in 1647, would lead to all heresies including atheism; 'then we open a floodgate unto all licentious Liberty'.[33] The collapse of theological order would precipitate moral chaos. Whoever lived but a few years, according to Thomas Edwards in 1646, would see 'the issue of these Sects and Schismes will be, that all will end in a loosenesse and licentiousnesse of living'.[34] Robert Baillie, the Scots Presbyterian, saw the failure to impose a strict church settle-ment on the English as leading inevitably to social and moral collapse.[35] Thomas Case, in May 1647, argued that 'Liberty of conscience falsely so called, may in good time improve itself into liberty of estates and liberty of houses and liberty of wives.'[36] No one excelled Thomas Edwards, the exemplary heresiographer, in his exposition of the evils of toleration, of theological plurality:

[30] Firth and Rait (eds.), *Acts and Ordinances*, pp. 409–10. My italics.
[31] Peter White, 'The Rise of Arminianism Reconsidered', *P. & P.*, 101 (1983), 136.
[32] Willem Balke, *Calvin and the Anabaptist Radicals*, translated by William J. Heynen (Grand Rapids, 1981: Dutch version, 1973).
[33] [Anon.,] *Sine Qua Non* (1647), p [3] (unpaginated) E.406 (25).
[34] Edwards, *Gangraena*, vol. II, p. 14.
[35] McGregor, 'The Baptists: Fount of All Heresy', pp. 24–5.   [36] *W.T.U.D.*, p. 100.

A *Toleration* is the grand designe of the Devil, his Masterpeece and Chiefe Engine he works by at this time to uphold his tottering Kingdome; it is the most compendious, ready, sure way to destroy all Religion, lay all waste, and bring in all evill; it is a most transcendent, catholique, and fundamentall evill, for this Kingdom of any that can be imagined: As originall sin is the most fundamentall sin, all sin; having the seed and spawn of all in it: So a *Toleration* hath all errors in it, and all evils.[37]

By 1649 a sense of impending disintegration could afflict even those who had benefited from toleration, the sects. In those last days, they too would be scattered.[38]

Fears for order within churches or sects were readily extended to fears for social order as a whole. The importance of the Church in maintaining social order in early modern England has repeatedly been emphasised by historians. In its teaching, preaching, pastoral work and courts, the Church was a major agency of control and mediation in village, town and county life. Disorder in its life, as Richard Baxter repeatedly observed in reflecting on his own life, meant social disorder. The sometimes apparently obsessive preoccupation with order and disorder in early modern society is not hard to understand. That anxiety should rise in a period of civil upheaval, when institutional and doctrinal guides to order collapse, is equally comprehensible. John Wesley held similar fears in another period of social uncertainty.[39] The furious debates about ordinances, which raged amongst sectarians and their enemies in the late 1640s and the 1650s, in themselves created a sense of unease about organised religion's capacity to control not only society at large but even the withdrawn elect, the saving remnant.[40] What then could replace the moral agency of institutional religion with its juridical capacity to establish the moral boundaries of conformity by identifying deviance?

e. The spectrum of fears embodied in the Ranter myth

There was then abundant material for anxiety to feed on as religion appeared to evolve in a proliferation of forms and the paradoxes of sectarian aspiration came home to roost. When we look again at the fears reflected in the more serious reportage of the Ranter phenomenon, we can see these general anxieties crystallised and defined. Edward Hyde

---

[37] Edwards, *Gangraena*, vol. I, pp. 121–2.
[38] See, for example, Edward Ellis, *A Sudden and Cloudy Messenger* (1649), E.592 (13).
[39] J. F. C. Harrison, *The Second Coming: Popular Millenarianism 1780–1850* (London, 1979), p. 15. More particularly, Wesley was afraid that a speculative antinomianism would lead to a practical antinomianism subverting all social and political order.
[40] See Nuttall, *The Holy Spirit in Puritan Faith and Experience*, Chapter 6.

saw practical antinomianism as but one manifestation of the work of the
Red Dragon or devil, exulting in the collapse of religious authority.[41]
So too, John Tickell in 1651 saw that 'Phantastick preaching', running
out of control in every direction, and so spawning Abiezer Coppe, was
'the great sin of our age'.[42] For a Baptist, like Samuel Fisher, the
repudiation of some ordinances and the affirmation of others left an
unease about the legitimating basis of the who process. The balance between ordinances and grace was a delicate one. It was to be feared that
some would repudiate ordinances entirely, and they would look very
much like Ranters.[43] Thomas Underhill insisted that Ranters, like
Quakers, to whom they were related, could not repudiate religious
ordinances without denying civil subordination. Deference itself
became for them a kind of idolatry.[44] Such fears come close to hysteria
in the frantic listing of names – some absurd – of the heresiographers.
The labelling and categorising of what appeared as a seethingly,
promiscuous heterodoxy was itself a desperate bid for some sort of control. 'Nor were people ever growne to such an impudent height of
impiety', bemoaned John Taylor in 1651, 'as they are at this day.' Satan
had always sown heresies, 'but they never came up so thick as in these
latter times. They were wont to peep up one by one, but now they
sprout up by huddles and clusters . . .' Adamites, Novatians, Anabaptists, Brownists, Nicholaitians, Counterfeit Catholics, Arminians,
Antinomians, Newtralists, Familists, Lutherans, Independents, Round-
heads, Dippers, Seekers, Shakers, Ranters, 'with many others not worth
the naming' were all Protestant, all pretended to be right, and were all
in disagreement.[45]

   While the more sensational reporting of the Ranters contained
obvious elements of burlesque, inversion and the carnivalesque, it is
nevertheless striking how fully these more 'serious' anxieties are reflected
and even developed in it. The stories recounted in *The Ranters Recantation* were 'Recited as a Warning piece to the English Nation'.[46] Principal amongst the fears portrayed in the sensational literature are those
of the collapse of religious authority and the social consequences attendant upon such a collapse.[47] Most obvious amongst the latter were

---

[41] Hyde, *A Wonder and yet no Wonder.*
[42] Tickell, *The Bottomles Pit*, Preface.   [43]   Samuel Fisher, *Baby-Baptism.*
[44] Thomas Underhill, *Hell broke loose* (1660), pp. 18, 19, 32–7, E.770 (6).
[45] John Taylor, *Ranters of Both Sexes*, p. 4.   [46]   *The Ranters Recantation*, title page.
[47] For example, *The Routing of the Ranters*, pp. 2–3; *The Arraignment and Tryall*, p. 3; *Strange
      Newes from Newgate*, p. 2; *The Black and Terrible Warning Piece*, pp. 1–3; *The Ranters Recanta-
      tion*, pp. 2–3.

allegations of the repudiation of social subordination. It was a journey-man shoemaker who, to the consternation of his master and mistress, refused to recognise any moral authority but that of his own will. After all, was not Christ himself 'an ordinary fellow'?[48] Unless checked, such insubordination would even undo military authority.[49] It was 'the bosome of (a many headed monster) the rude multitude' to which such things were meant to appeal, according to Walter Rosewell.[50] An index of this horror was that some could see no sin in proclaiming the Stuart King.[51] Social insubordination had worrying political as well as moral dimensions.

The sensational literature frequently stressed that the 'logic' of certain religious positions, for example Anabaptism, led on to moral confusion and even atheism.[52] Toleration could only release this potential, engendering a limitless religious pluralism, and leaving simple folk, in these Last Days, prey to false prophets and Antichrists.[53] The undermining of all religious authority was thus merely a prelude to unbridled immorality and social chaos.[54] This could be portrayed in the crudest fratricide, the killing of wives and children, communal massacres,[55] or in self-indulgence without restraint,[56] or, the culminating inversion, in diabolatry.[57] More simply, the end of religious sanctions could be seen to mean a loss of industry and a descent into idleness. That itself led into further manifold mischief:

He that labours is tempted by one devil
He that is idle is assaulted by all.

The Ranters were an exemplary illustration of how religious indiscipline led to idleness which in turn proliferated wickedness.[58]

Yet the horror which comes most strikingly and insistently out of the sensational Ranter literature is that of the inversion of sexual rôles. In part this may arise out of the quest for prurient sensation inherent in this

---

[48] *The Arraignment and Tryall*, pp. 2–3.   [49] *Ibid.*, p. 5.
[50] Walter Rosewell, *The Serpents Subtilty Discovered* (1656), Dedication and pp. 11–12.
[51] *The Ranters Recantation*, p. 5; *Strange Newes from Newgate*, p. 1.
[52] *The Arraignment and Tryall*, p. 3. Cf. *Heart-Bleedings For Professors Abominations* (1650); *A Blow at the Root* (1650).
[53] Humphrey Ellis, *Pseudochristus*, pp. 3, 62; *Two Sermons*; Taylor, *Ranters of Both Sexes*, pp. 4–5.   [54] J.M., *The Ranters Last Sermons.*
[55] Samuel Tilbury, *Bloudy Newes from the North* (1651), p. 1.
[56] *The Ranters Religion*, pp. 5–6; *The Routing of the Ranters*, pp. 2, 5–6; *The Ranters Ranting*, pp. 2–3.
[57] *The Routing of the Ranters*, pp. 3–4; S.S.[hepherd], *The Joviall Crew*, pp. 1–3; Stubs, *The Ranters Declaration*, p. 1.   [58] *The Ranters Religion*, An Advertisement to the Reader.

literature. In part, however, it also appears to embody some of the inversions of early modern carnival. But clearly amongst the fears expressed in this literature were fears of the unbridled sexuality of women and of the rejection of subordination by them. Women were commonly seen in early modern England as the sex of incipient disorder, who must be controlled if social order were to be maintained. In particular, unless curbed, their sexual appetites would know no bounds and the order of families, communities and kingdoms would be shattered. Religious discipline restrained them. Its collapse could release the anarchic forces of natural femininity.[59]

The image of the Ranter expressed these fears because Ranter women knew no sexual limit. In their inversion, Christian liberty was to have women in common. A woman's saintliness was measured by her sexual vigour.[60] In *The Routing of the Ranters*, it was suggested that Ranter women would hold it commendable in husbands to give liberty to their wives. Ranter men, however, adhered to the rudiments of a chauvinist double standard: 'though they held it convenient to have one woman to dwell constantly with one man, to do his necessary businesse yet are they of the opinion that they may have carnall knowledge of any and as many other women as their beastly desire can make use of'. Nevertheless, and we shall see more of this, it is Ranter women who take the sexual initiative.[61] They were free to copulate with any man and did so enthusiastically and openly.[62]

Natalie Zemon Davis, in her studies of early modern carnival and the rôle of women in that context, has emphasised the ambiguity of the inversions taking place. The mock element of the inversion could reinforce the existing order and subordination to it; on the other hand, it could threaten the *status quo* and deflate its pretensions.[63] There is a strong association with charivari in the image of Ranterism and especially of Ranter women. *The Ranters Declaration* compared their behaviour with the heathen idolatrous practices of May Day.[64] Ranterism was a way for wives to turn the domestic order upside down, to undermine their husbands' authority[65] and to rob them of their sexual initiative.[66] When merchants' wives became 'rantipoll', they were

---

[59] Natalie Zemon Davis, 'Women on Top', in Davis, *Society and Culture in Early Modern France*, pp. 124–51; Patricia Crawford, 'From the Woman's View: Pre-industrial England, 1500–1750', in Crawford (ed.), *Exploring Women's Past: Essays in Social History* (Carlton, South Victoria, 1983), pp. 49–85.

[60] *The Ranters Religion*, pp. 6–8.   [61] *The Routing of the Ranters*, pp. 5–6.

[62] *The Ranters Ranting*, p. 5; *The Arraignment and Tryall*, p. 3; *The Ranters Recantation*, pp. 1–2.   [63] Davis, 'Women on Top', p. 126.   [64] Stubs, *The Ranters Declaration*, p. 4.

[65] S.S., *The Joviall Crew*, p. 4 and *passim*.   [66] For example, *The Ranters Ranting*, p. 5.

'proud and imperious over their Husbands, ambitious of bringing them under their *commands*, and giving them Rules and Lawes to observe . . . '.[67] It could be a carnivalesque, Land of Cockaygne sort of inversion, such that a 'Ranting Lady', 'when her *Concupiscence* moves, can at her *beck*, have her *Ningles* to convey her a *Cock-horse* to *Burnt-wood* Fayre, or what other place of pleasure she pleaseth . . . '.[68]

The spectrum of fears expressed in the image of Ranters and Ranterism was therefore wide. It embraced the collapse of all religious authority; an unsettling uncertainty about the respective rôles of ordinances and grace; an anxiety that these dilemmas would spill over into moral and civil disorder; social insubordination; the unnatural dominance of women and the disintegration of all domestic discipline. What comes out particularly clearly in the image of Ranter women is just how much of an inversion the Ranter was; an inversion with a carnival element, functioning to release and repress simultaneously. We shall return to this theme shortly.

iii. THE PRACTICE: MANUFACTURING THE MYTH

a. The press sensation and the limited basis of its production

Given the ephemerality of the sensational Ranter literature there is clearly a danger in emphasising its homogeneity, in treating it as if it were a literature with common concerns and attitudes. One way of gauging the validity of such an approach is to look more closely at the production of the sensational literature and the surprisingly narrow basis on which it rested.

Leaving aside those works produced on the issue of fake Christs and the trial of John Robins, to which the label of Ranter has been mis-applied, we can identify a total of fifteen sensational tracts or publi-cations on the Ranters, appearing between October 1650 and August 1654. All but the last five had appeared by the end of January 1651.[69]

---

[67] *Mercurius Democritus*, 10–17 November 1652, 252; see also 254.
[68] *Ibid.*, 27 July – 3 August 1653, 521–2.
[69] In chronological order and with Thomason's dates, the works are: *The Ranters Religion* (11 October 1650); *The Routing of the Ranters* (19 November 1650); *The Ranters Ranting* (2 December 1650); Gilbert Roulston, *The Ranters Bible* (9 December 1650); M. Stubs, *The Ranters Declaration* (17 December 1650); *The Arraignment and Tryall with A Declaration of the Ranters* (17 December 1650); *The Ranters Recantation* (20 December 1650); S[amuel] S[hepherd], *The Joviall Crew* (6 January 1651); Samuel Tilbury, *Bloudy Newse from the North* (20 January 1651); *Strange Newes from Newgate* (21 January 1651); *The Ranters Monster* (30 March 1652); Lionel Lockier, *The Character of a Time Serving Saint* (5 June 1652); *The Black and Terrible Warning Piece* (29 November 1653); *A List of some of the Grand Blasphemers and Blasphemies* (23 March 1654); J.M., *The Ranters Last Sermon* (7 August 1654).

Most of these works were published anonymously, but, almost wherever we began a close investigation, we should uncover connections between them.

Let us begin with a named author about whom we can discover something. Gilbert Roulston, author of *The Ranters Bible* and a professed ex-Ranter, had been in the 1640s a hack royalist writer, attacking 'Round-Heads' and bemoaning the rabble's incursion into politics.[70] *The Ranters Bible* was printed by 'J.C.', as was Samuel Tilbury's *Bloudy Newse from the North* in which a meeting of Ranters declared for Charles II. A printer of the same initials also printed J.M.'s *The Ranters Last Sermon*. There could be a further link here, through J.M., with *The Ranters Creed* printed by James Moxon and exploiting the Ranter by-line while reporting the Robins trial.[71] J.C. also printed M. Stubs's *The Ranters Declaration*, the woodcuts from which were reused in G.H.'s *The Declaration of John Robins*. This G.H. may well have been the George Horton who published *The Ranters Monster* in 1652 and *The Black and Terrible Warning Piece* in 1653. There may then be links in terms of printing, publishing and material between at least six of the Ranter sensational pieces and with two others on the Robins phenomenon but with a titular exploitation of the Ranter sensation.

We can trace other possible links through printers if we begin with *The Routing of the Ranters* printed by 'B.A.'. *The Ranters Ranting* published two weeks later and claiming dissatisfaction with *The Routing* was printed by 'B. Alsop'. 'B.A.' also published *The Arraignment and Tryall with a Declaration of the Ranters* a fortnight later. All three were adorned with crude woodcuts in a similar style. So was *Strange Newse from Newgate*, printed by B. Alsop in January 1651.

These two possible connections would account between them for ten out of the fifteen sensational Ranter works[72] and two on the Robins phenomenon. The strong impression conveyed is of a small group of printers, publishers and writers eager to ride the Ranter sensation for all it was worth while it lasted. The impression is confirmed, with a twist, if we look at another writer of this material. The *Joviall Crew* by 'S.S. gent.' is normally attributed to Samuel Shepherd (or Sheppard) and

---

[70] [Gilbert Roulston,] *The Round-Head Uncovered* (1642); *The Round-Heads Catechisme* (1643); *The Round-Heads Remembrancer* (Oxford, 1643).

[71] Moxon also printed John Osborn's *The World to Come* (7 July 1651) which included a debate between Richard Coppin and Osborn on the resurrection.

[72] The net could be extended slightly by the plagiarist links between *The Ranters Religion* and M. Stubs's *The Ranters Declaration*, but plagiarism does not necessarily imply a connection in production.

there would appear to be some warrant for this in the literary style and pretension of the work. Shepherd had written journalistic battle and campaign pieces – strongly pro-Fairfax – in the first Civil War.[73] He had then become a defender of the House of Lords against the attacks of John Lilburne.[74] In the 1650s and later he wrote a guide to elegant correspondence for young ladies and gentlemen and exotic romances, presumably for a similar audience.[75] But there was a dangerous side too to this existence, for in 1649 and 1650 Shepherd was being hunted as a royalist sympathiser and editor of the royalist newsbook *Mercurius Elencticus*.[76] That newspaper, in its rather fitful existence, had developed some themes worth looking at in an attempt to unravel the meaning and connections of the Ranter sensation. In its issue of 24 April–1 May 1649 it castigated the corruption of the republican regime, the personal ambition of the grandees *and their dominant wives*. 'No *King*, no *Religion*, no *Law*, no *Order*, no *Government*, no *Justice*; in a word, no Happinesse (here) whilest they Rule, nothing but *Misery, Vassalage* and *Vexation of Spirit*.' Inversion, moral collapse and disorder were inevitable.[77] The theme, for which the Ranters were to become the personalised and sectarianised image, had already been announced. From this quarter the theme links up with those anxieties we observed earlier, the fear of royalist exploitation of a Ranter sensation.

As far as the sensational literature or yellowpress coverage of the Ranters is concerned, we have to recognise two important possibilities about the creation of the myth. First is the strong possibility that the basis of its manufacture was severely limited to a handful of printers, publishers and their hack writers who sensed an avidly curious audience and were determined to satisfy it as cheaply and profitably as possible. Secondly, we need to bear in mind the range of interests involved in the promotion of the myth. It incorporates Grub Street, but also royalist journalists for whom the Ranters could play the inversion and moral collapse, that they had prophesied, incarnate. At another point in the range were those uneasy supporters of the revolution, the sectarians, whose interest in the Ranters was complex yet, in part because of its seriousness, decisive. It is to them we must now turn. Before we do, let us take one look back at the self-mocking, half-self-aware quality of

---

[73] S. Sheppard, *The Yeare of Jubile: Or ENGLANDS Releasement* (1646), E.343 (8).
[74] S. Sheppeard, *The Famers Fam'd* (1646), E.349 (5); *The False Alarum* (1646), E.350 (2).
[75] S.S. gent., *The Secretaries Study* (1652), Wing S.3169; Samuel Sheppard, *The Loves of Amandus and Sophronia* (1650), Wing S.3167; S.S., *Fortunes Tennis Ball* (1672), Wing S.3164.
[76] *C.S.P.D.*, 1649–50, pp. 529, 545; *ibid.*, 1650, p. 143.
[77] *Mercurius Elencticus*, 1. 24 April–1 May 1649, 5; see also 4, 14–21 May 1649.

much of the sensational material and its myths. 'There is a Pamphlet in this kinde', admitted John Taylor, 'written with too much haste, I know not by whom, with but few truths, which in this are more largely expressed.'[78]

b. The needs of sectarian consolidation

Quite clearly in 1649, as for a considerable period thereafter, the sects were caught in the tension between two fears: the fear of oppression from above and the fear of disintegration from within. The Ranter image simultaneously heightened the sense of both dangers by offering enemies an association between sectarianism and extreme irreligion,[79] and by offering the appearance of another threat from within. At the same time, the sects themselves could use the same image to offset both fears. The Ranters could be used to show that there was a worse alternative; to enhance the acceptability of the 'respectable' sects. Alternatively, or simultaneously, the image of the Ranter as intolerably deviant could be used to police the sects' own boundaries, to induce conformity.[80]

Frank McGregor has convincingly portrayed this process in relation to both Quakers and Baptists. The most substantial material relating to Ranters after 1651 comes from Quaker sources, but McGregor sees this as evidence of the sectarian needs of the Friends rather than of the survival of a Ranter sect or movement. In particular, a group struggling for domination of a fledgeling and potentially centrifugal movement found the evocation of Ranterism a useful disciplinary device. 'Fox's perpetuation of the threat of Ranterism after the Restoration undoubtedly contributed to the victory of group discipline over the individualistic spirit of early Quakerism.' 'Quaker usage of such terms as Ranter, Ranterism and Ranterish demonstrates the need to employ with great care the doctrinal labels which historians have inherited from the religious controversies of the English Revolution.'[81] Ranterism was a weapon used in the movement's own domestic disputes. At its loosest, it could be reduced to a synonym for rudeness; for the Quakers a 'con-

---

[78] Taylor, *Ranters of Both Sexes*, title page.
[79] For examples of the menacing association of sects with Ranters see J.M., *The Ranters Last Sermon*; *A List of some of the Grand Blasphemers*; Underhill, *Hell broke loose*; *Mercurius Politicus*, 245, 15–22 February 1655, 5141–2.
[80] Cf. Isaac Pennington, *Divine Essays*, pp. 18–25.
[81] McGregor, 'Ranterism and the Development of Early Quakerism', p. 363; also 351, 354, 355–6, 357 n. 40.

venient' explanation 'of the abuse, ridicule, and general excitement so often inspired by their dramatic evangelism'.[82]

Much the same may be argued with respect to the Baptists' evocation of the Ranter image. Their internal divisions and fears of the charge of Munster-like excesses were forceful drives. The particular Baptists were zealous against lapses from Calvinism amongst General Baptists or in their own ranks. General Baptists, with a looser definition of orthodoxy, remained fearful of charges of excess. The consequence, ultimately, was ambivalence amongst the Baptists about religious toleration.[83] The answer to these anxieties could be further institution-alisation and tighter internal discipline. The Scylla to this Charybdis, however, was the charge of formalism and the demand for spiritual liberty.[84] This was the fault line where the necessities of sectarian sur-vival and unity and the pressures of spiritual enthusiasm met. As in the case of the Fenstanton General Baptists, enthusiasts could condemn for-malism in the name of the authentic spiritual experience which the sect had, in their eyes, promised. On the other side, after 1651 the seekers of discipline could find Ranterism in those who challenged forms, ordinances, outward authorities. It was a potent and sobering charge.[85]

Quaker and Baptist reactions can therefore be seen to parallel each other closely. In both cases the projection of a Ranter image, the dis-covery of Ranters in their own ranks and around them, was a powerful device corresponding to their own anxieties and ambivalences, en-abling them to display spiritual enthusiasm tipped over into religious inversion, without repudiating enthusiasm in its entirety.

c. Projection: the manufacture of images and the mythic necessities of a conserva-tive revolution

There is a chilling but obvious truth in the thought that, did deviance not exist, it would be necessary to invent it. For it is only through deviance that we understand normality. As categories, antitheses, they are interdependent and mutually reinforcing.

Herein lies one of the problems of radicalism. The radical challenges normality and so becomes vulnerable to the charge of deviance. Radicals can exalt their deviant image by the way in which they dress, behave,

---

[82] McGregor, 'Seekers and Ranters', pp. 135–6.
[83] McGregor, 'The Baptists: Fount of All Heresy', p. 49 n. 81.   [84] *Ibid.*, pp. 57, 58–9.
[85] McGregor, 'Seekers and Ranters', pp. 134–5. Underhill (ed.), *Records*, pp. 73–4, 89–90.

live and speak, or subvert it by the sheer conformity of their demeanour. To some radicals these alternatives were available in the seventeenth century, but to others they were not, because the struggle to redefine normality in Christian terms seemed bound by the evident limits which Christianity set on acceptable or normal behaviour. Hence Winstanley, in quest of freedom from Kingly government, began by rejecting various forms of unchristian liberty.[86]

Their enemies, of course, need observe no such restraint. To them the threat to normality was obviously deviant. For the more anxious amongst them, that deviance could know no limit and could therefore only be seen as a complete inversion of normality or Christianity, at least of the Protestant version of Christianity. So papism flourished; irreligion was everywhere; atheism abounded. These were projections, images or myths, in content, wholly or partially, detached from reality but which nevertheless served real purposes. For example, images of Familists and Familism were far more abundant in late-sixteenth and early-seventeenth-century England than were actual Familists. More-over, what Familism meant to those who projected the image and to those who counted themselves members of the Family of Love were entirely different things.[87] The image projected by the former was not designed to help the latter.

Some radical critics of 'normality' were well aware of this process and its historical usage. The Levellers saw how it had been used against the Anabaptists and could be used against them. William Walwyn declaimed against 'That lying story of that injured people ... the Anabaptists of Munster'. 'Who', asked Richard Overton, 'writ the his-tories of the Anabaptists but their enemies?'[88] Richard Baxter saw how the Ranter projection had discredited all sectarians, but so wedded to the myth was he that he saw it in terms of a final triumph over the spon-soring agents of all sectarianism, the Jesuits and their patron, the devil.[89] And so one could go on.

The 'revolution' of 1648–9 at once intensified the problem and left it unresolved. 'Normality' was assaulted. In some respects, it was overthrown. But, puzzlingly, in others it was carefully sustained. There

[86]   Gerrard Winstanley, 'The Law of Freedom', in G.H. Sabine (ed.), *The Works of Gerrard Winstanley* (New York, 1941), p. 519.   [87]   Hamilton, *The Family of Love*, p. 135.

[88]   William Walwyn, *Walwyns Just Defence* (1649), in William Haller and Godfrey Davies (eds.), *The Leveller Tracts 1647–1653* (Gloucester, Mass., 1964), p. 374; Walwyn, *The Power of Love* (1643) in William Haller (ed.), *Tracts on Liberty in the Puritan Revolution 1638–1647* (3 vols., New York, 1965), vol. II, pp. 275–6.

[89]   Sylvester (ed.), *Reliquiae Baxterianae*, p. 77.

were ideological gestures, such as the Commonwealth's declaration of the people as the original of all power, but no full-blown ideology of transformation. It was, paradoxically, a conservative revolution. Such a revolution was inevitably hazy about the parameters of normality and deviance. And such uncertainty bred anxiety.

What could be seen as the boundary? What were the defining qualities of normality and deviance in the post-revolutionary situation? The revolution had forged alliances and broken them. The Levellers with whom the grandees had fought the second Civil War and from whom they had inherited the Agreement of the People had been proscribed and repressed. But the courts would not condemn their leader, John Lilburne. In turn, the Levellers railed against Cromwell and Ireton. The gathered churches, having broken with the Levellers, were uneasy about their own discipline and the capacity of the Rump to produce the kind of reform they longed for and the security they needed.

As 1649 wore on and the political compromises and uncertainties of the revolution began to appear intractable, attention shifted to the ambivalent legacy of *de facto* religious toleration. Here, some had long believed, a boundary could and should be drawn. What had to be shown as incontestably beyond the pale was a combination of theological and moral excess. This the Ranter myth was well fitted to do and the materials for its composition were not far to seek.

d. The materials of the myth

Powerful myths of deviance are, however revolutionary the situation, never entirely novel. They are made up of materials ready to hand, a reconstruction of available and well-known models.[90] Part of their power is in their residual familiarity. Such originality as they possess is by way of adjustment to the circumstances, not by way of fictional inventiveness. So it was with the Ranter myth. The more closely we examine it, the more clearly we see that it was a reworking of older images of atheism – especially as portrayed through the Theophrastian character – of contraries and inversions and of the prodigy.

Atheism
Of these there is no doubt that the atheist is the key image in the make-up of the Ranter. The priority accorded to atheism in the Blasphemy

---

[90] Cohen, *Folk Devils*, p. 74.

Act of 9 August 1650 may, in this respect, be significant. It was an Act against atheism first, against blasphemy second.[91] Of itself, however, the atheist image was inadequate because it was at least partially associated with disbelief. What had to be shown was how belief, given free rein and run to excess in enthusiasm, could lead to the same moral and social disorder as unbelief.

In his classic study of unbelief in the sixteenth century, Lucien Febvre argued that the conceptual difficulties in the way of atheism were so great as to make it virtually impossible.[92] Samuel Butler also believed that an impossibility confronted the would-be atheist.[93] And yet atheists were seen to be everywhere. Atheism, impossible though it might be, was constantly perceived to be recruiting new converts and expanding its following, to the horror and consternation of the godly.[94]

The atheist was, in fact, a kind of invented deviant, a projection. Hooker drew the distinction between two groups of atheists; a wholly negligible number of men with no belief in God, and a second, much larger group who were bent on the pleasures of this world and *acted* as if there were no God.[95] It was, however, a distinction commonly lost in the assumption 'that practical and philosophical atheism naturally accompanied each other'.[96] Once that assumption was made, it was possible to project the image of atheist upon anyone of whose conduct one disapproved:

the hypocrite is a close Atheist; the loose wicked man is an open Atheist; the secure bold and proud transgressor is an Atheist: he that will not be taught and reformed, is an Atheist.

[91] 'An Act against several Atheistical, Blasphemous and Execrable Opinions', in Firth and Rait (eds.), *Acts and Ordinances*, vol. II, p. 409.

[92] Lucien Febvre, *The Problem of Unbelief in the Sixteenth Century: The Religion of Rabelais*, translated by Beatrice Gottlieb (Cambridge, Mass. 1982).

[93] Charles W. Daves (ed.), *Samuel Butler 1612–1680: Characters* (Cleveland, Ohio, 1970), p. 163. See also Barry Reay, Introduction to McGregor and Reay (eds.), *Radical Religion*, p. 16; G.E. Aylmer, 'Unbelief in Seventeenth Century England', in D.H. Pennington and K. Thomas (eds.), *Puritans and Revolutionaries: Essays in Seventeenth Century History Presented to Christopher Hill* (Oxford, 1978), pp. 22–46.

[94] For fears of the spread of atheism in 1653 see Woolrych, *Commonwealth to Protectorate*, pp. 333–4. I am indebted for the discussion of these ideas and much information to Dr Michael Hunter. The argument here owes much to his unpublished essay, 'Atheism and its Antagonists in England before the Civil War'.

[95] Richard Hooker, *The Laws of Ecclesiastical Polity*, Book V Sect. 2; George Savile, Marquis of Halifax, 'The Character of a Trimmer', in *Complete Works*, ed. J.P. Kenyon (Harmondsworth, 1969), p. 67.   [96] Hunter, 'Atheism', 4.

For William Vaughan those who raised rents or enclosed commons were obvious atheists; for Thomas Nashe, the ambitious, the greedy, the vainglorious, gluttons and prostitutes likewise.[97]

Most of the atheism literature of the early modern period was intended to confirm the godly in their beliefs and practices: 'the personification of ungodliness in an extreme form [was] a means of frightening the pious and encouraging them to show more clearly their allegiance to the opposite pole'. It enabled the zealous preacher 'to conflate almost any deviance from godly commitment with extreme irreligion, a rhetorical device that could hardly be bettered'.[98] Like political, social or moral deviance, from which it could barely be separated, religious deviance was a way of reasserting boundaries and enabling people to relocate themselves reassuringly within the confines of normality. Atheism, as a charge of ultimate offensiveness to the religious community, was no exception.

The charge of atheism might be used to serve specific, sometimes political, purposes[99] but, in general, its function was broader. Atheism was expressed practically in immorality and, accordingly, loose livers of every description could be castigated as atheists. One sees this in Strype, Ascham, John Woolton, Udall and Hooker.[100] Still in the 1690s, the atheist could be identified by his recommendation of the life of drinking and fornication.[101] The works of Machiavelli, handbooks of wickedness, were seen as the single greatest source of atheism in England.[102]

The perceived links between atheism and two more specific forms of behaviour or relationship are worth further consideration from our point of view. First, it was claimed that toleration led to all heresies including atheism, for 'then we open a floodgate unto all licentious Liberty'.[103] Secondly, as Thomas Nashe argued in *Pierce Pennilesse* or Francis Bacon in his essay 'Of Atheism', sectarianism led to atheism.[104] Thomas Edwards, in this case as in so much else a good indicator of the

---

[97] *Ibid.*, 12; John Wingfield, *Atheisme Close and open Anatomized* (1634), vol. II, pp. 20–1.
[98] Hunter, 'Atheism', 10–12.
[99] The best known case here is the charge against the circle of Sir Walter Raleigh in 1594. See G.B. Harrison (ed.), *Willobie His Avisa (1594)* (Edinburgh, 1966), Appendix III; George T. Buckley, *Atheism in the English Renaissance* (Chicago, 1932; reprinted New York, 1965), Chapter 11.   [100] Buckley, *Atheism*, pp. 48, 69, 72, 78, 88.
[101] [Charles Gildon,] *The post-boy rob'd of his mail* (1692), p. 18, Wing G.735A.
[102] Buckley, *Atheism*, p. 31; Felix Raab, *The English Face of Machiavelli: A Changing Interpretation 1500–1700* (London, 1964).
[103] [Anon.,] *Sine Qua Non*, p.[3], E.406 (25); Cf. McGregor, 'Seekers and Ranters', pp. 138–9.   [104] Buckley, *Atheism*, Chapter 4.

religious anxieties of the 1640s, could sum it all up in a section of
Gangraena which dealt with the links between 'Libertinisme', atheism
and sectarianism.[105] Already in 1646, Edwards identified libertinism
and atheism, two sides of the same coin, with pleas for toleration.
Would it stop at belittling Scripture or denying God? It was well
known, to Edwards at least, that advocates of toleration, like the
Independents, worshipped indiscriminately the sun and moon or a pewter
pot, and tolerated stage plays and witches. Weren't Independents and
sectaries notorious for incest, bigamy, rapes, adultery and fornication?
There was an obvious link between naked baptism and lewdness, between toleration and neglect of holy duties, cozening and deceiving,
lying, pride and boasting insolence and the Levellers' attacks on the
House of Lords. The scythe of atheism cut wide in the hands of a fren-
zied hysteric like Edwards, but his influence should not be under-
estimated. In particular, in this conflation of atheism, toleration and
sectarianism with all licentiousness, we should note some elements
which were to recur in the image and stories of the Ranters. Before
Ranters worshipped pewter pots and practised all indecency, Independents and Baptists were apparently busy doing so.

Theophrastian characters
The transferability, availability and potency of these images had a good
deal to do with a form of popular literature which sprang into prominence in the late sixteenth century and enjoyed great currency
throughout the seventeenth: the Theophrastian character. If we ask
where people, made anxious by the never-ending spread of atheism in
the seventeenth century, were most readily to find and observe the
atheist in detail, the answer has to be in the books of Theophrastian
character studies and their widespread exploitation in sermons, plays,
ballads and romances.

The growing interest in the moral purposes of rhetoric, impelled in
England by Erasmian humanism and Protestant preaching, inevitably
brought with it a revival of interest in the character. Rhetoric must
reach an audience, and to move it one must understand their characters
or character. They could be moved by exposure to the implications of
their own character or the characters of others.[106] Hence the importance to classical rhetoric of the character studies of Theophrastus and

---

[105] Edwards, *Gangraena*, III, pp. 185–94.
[106] Benjamin Boyce, *The Theophrastian Character in England to 1642* (1947; reprinted London,
1967) Chapter 2; see also C.N. Greenough, *A Bibliography of the Theophrastian Character in
English* (1947; reprinted Westport, Conn. 1970).

others. In 1592 and 1599, Casaubon produced editions of the vignettes of Theophrastus and the genre very rapidly became popular in England. Joseph Hall, Thomas Overbury and John Earle amongst others produced collections of characters in the early seventeenth century which were enormously popular and raised the profile of the character as a study in mordant wit, insight and the 'fixing' of the ethical traits of personality. The studies established popular images of various types and, for example, it has recently been suggested that the 'fixed' image of the Puritan which has come down to our own times almost undisturbed owes much to the character literature.[107]

Naturally, the character of the atheist figured in many of these collections. Thomas Beard's atheist was, significantly, coupled with the epicure. He denied the providence of God, the immortality of the soul, the life to come but not, apparently, the existence of God. Atheists were to be observed 'living in this world like brute beasts, & like dogs and swine, wallowing in all sensuality . . .'.[108] They had always denied the presence of Christ in the sacrament, asserted the divine authority of Ovid as well as Augustine, scoffed at the resurrection and dismissed heaven and hell as mere fables.[109] For Samuel Rowlands, the godless atheist was 'a villaine apt for every kind of evill':

That say'st eate, drinke, be merrie, take delight:
Swagger out day, and Revell all the night.[110]

'An Atheist', wrote Nicholas Breton, 'is a figure of desperation, who dare do anything even to his soules damnation . . .' 'He makes sinne a jest . . . hee makes Robberie his purchase, Lechery his Solace, Mirth his Exercise, and Drunkennesse his Glory . . .' He was in truth 'a Monster amongst men'.[111] The stress in nearly all of the characters of the atheist is not on their unbelief but on their jesting or non-serious attitude towards religion and their shameless disregard of morality. In Earle's *Micro-Cosmographie* such a man does the greatest sins calmly. He breaks the Commandments and thinks of Scripture as a supply of jests. He sings psalms when drunk and mocks God's mercy. 'Atheisme is the refuge of such sinners.'[112]

---

[107] Collinson, 'A Comment: Concerning the Name Puritan', 486.

[108] Thomas Beard, *The Theatre of Gods Judgement* (1597), Chapter 25, Of Epicures and Atheists, p. 139.   [109] *Ibid.*, p. 102.   [110] Samuel Rowlands, *Looke to it; for Ile stabbe ye* (1604).

[111] [Nicholas Breton,] *The Goode and the Badde or Descriptions of the Worthies and Unworthies of this Age* (1616), pp. 20, 21.

[112] John Earle, *Micro-Cosmographie* (1628) edited by Edward Arber (Westminster, 1904), pp. 97–8. This character first appeared in the fifth edition of 1629.

It will have become apparent that in many ways the character of the atheist prefigured that of the Ranter. There was the same levity towards religious matters, the abuse of Scripture, scoffing at heaven and hell, and the same general moral laxity. More than this, the two images performed similar functions:

atheism [was] a way of expressing serious disquiet by exaggerating and idealising it. The stock character of the atheist summed up all that contemporaries feared about irreligion in both its philosophical and practical implications, and it enabled them to identify and sensationalise tendencies that they observed around them which seemed to lead in that direction, however mild, and however absurd it may seem to us.

Michael Hunter has argued the

broader role of ideal types like atheism in voicing contemporary anxieties by depicting them in a polarised form and thus setting up a sort of continuum from orthodoxy to extremity along which the actual state of affairs could be measured.[113]

So Thomas Rogers, expounding the thirty-nine articles, could hold up, as the inversion of their godliness, the atheist who had cast off

all grace, virtue and godliness . . . There is no hell, nor future and eternal misery at all; but only either in man's opinion, as hold the Atheists; or in the heart and conscience of man in this life, as the Familists maintain.[114]

The atheist, anticipating the Ranter, always defends the inversion of true religion, in whoredom, swearing, lying, drunkenness, the irrelevance of formal religion and Scripture.[115] There were to be overt links between the character of the Ranter and the Theophrastian tradition. Samuel Butler was to write a character of the Ranter as well as one of the Atheist. The former was 'a Monster produced by the Madness of this latter Age . . .'.[116] Lionel Lockier in 1652 saw the Ranter as a well enough established character to be used as antithesis to his *Character of a Time Serving Saint*.[117] Samuel Shepherd, author of a dramatic satire of the Ranters, *The Joviall Crew* (1651), also produced in the same year *Epigrams, Theological, Philosophical*

[113] Hunter, 'Atheism', pp. 15, 16.
[114] Rev. J.J.S. Perowne (ed.), *The Catholic Doctrine of the Church of England: An Exposition of the Thirty-Nine Articles by Thomas Rogers* (Parker Society, Cambridge, 1854), pp. 119, 147–8.
[115] Arthur Dent, *The plaine mans path-way to Heaven. The five and twentieth edition* (1640), pp. 2, 24–6, 49, 58, 99, 152, 161, 163, 177, 178, 182–3, 292. The atheist in this case insists on asserting the steadfastness of his faith in God, *ibid.*, p. 267.
[116] Daves (ed.), *Butler: Characters*, pp. 106–7.
[117] Lockier, *The Character of a Time Serving Saint*, pp. 322-4.

and Romantick, with several character sketches in it.[118] Even more obvious are the frequent contemporary links made between the image of Ranterism and the character of atheism. The readiness of Ephraim Pagitt to identify Ranters with atheists was noted by C.E. Whiting as long ago as 1931.[119] Charges against the two were sometimes confused.[120] Muggleton identified Ranterism with atheism.[121] In a long editorial on the Ranters in January 1651, *The Faithful Scout* immediately identified them with atheists and traced them back predictably through an English and classical tradition of atheism, the key figure of which was Sir Walter Raleigh.[122] Gilbert Roulston's explanation of what he saw as the flourishing state of Ranterism in December 1650 lay in the spread of atheism.[123] In the same month, another sensational account found Ranterism and atheism barely distinguishable.[124] The identification was thus both general and specific. The swarms of 'blasphemies, damnable Heresies, and licentious practices' were attributable to and a reflection of the 'hideous Atheism abounding in the Land'.[125]

But there was also a peculiar affinity between atheists and Ranters. Our explanation for that must lie in the transferability of the character of the atheist into the character of the Ranter. When an image of supreme deviance was needed it was ready to hand in the atheist. Since, however, the threat to normality was perceived to come from within religious enthusiasm and seriousness, rather than its repudiation, some adaptation had to take place. The Ranter is the atheist adapted to meet that need while retaining his contrary character, his capacity for inversion.

It was widely held that the Reformation and the variety of religious positions it had opened up increased the problem of doubt.[126] When all control on that variety lapsed, as it did in the 1640s, anxiety shot up and people were warned that, unless the rules were observed, Christianity itself could be inverted, and not only by those who scoffed and derided religion, but also by those who in practice looked very similar, but

---

[118] See Greenough, *A Bibliography of the Theophrastian Character*, p. 68.

[119] Whiting, *Studies in English Puritanism*, p. 272.

[120] McGregor, 'The Ranters 1649–1660', 108–9.

[121] Muggleton, *Acts of the Witnesses*, p. 56 and cf. pp. 17–18. See also Hill, 'John Reeve and the Origins of Muggletonianism', p. 69.

[122] *The Faithful Scout*, 51, 2-9 January 1651, 393–6.

[123] Roulston, *The Ranters Bible*, p. 1.   [124] *The Arraignment and Tryall*, p. 3.

[125] *Mercurius Politicus*, 174, 6–13 October 1653, 2788, 2791.

[126] Cf. Hunter, 'Atheism', 13, 15–16.

whose danger sprang from some of the implications of religious enthusiasm and the free spirit.

Contraries and inversion

since the Devill is the verie contrarie opposite to God, there can be no better way to know God, then by the contrarie; . . . by the falshood of the one to considder the trueth of the other, by the injustice of the one, to considder the Justice of the other. And by the cruelty of the one, to considder the mercifulnesse of the other: And so foorth in all the rest of the essence of God, and qualities of the Devill.[127]

The conventionality of James I's stress on contraries or inversions as a way of grasping religious meaning has recently been emphasised. Moreover, the cognitive value of such procedures was not restricted to religion but applied to all perceivable phenomena; political, moral, natural and social.[128] 'What is remarkable', according to Stuart Clark, 'is the extraordinary pervasiveness of the language of "contrariety", the most extreme of the relations of opposition.'[129] It is part of the context of conventions through which we must see the world of early modern Europe if we are to avoid anachronism. Indeed, the heightened sense of uncompromising cosmic struggle, of the apocalyptic of the Last Days typical of the earlier seventeenth century, may have sharpened the sense of the value of understanding the contemporary world in terms of contraries or inversions. Inversion was deployed in the mock rituals of misrule or charivari, of which we have seen something in the Ranter stereotype, in the masque, in sermons and political treatises. Nicholas Breton's *The Goode and the Badde* (1616), for example, juxtaposed one 'character' with its contrary (the worthy King, for instance, with the unworthy King) so that in this way both might be better known. His character of 'An Atheist, or most badde man' enabled one the better to understand its inversion, the good man or true Christian.[130] Witches, demons, monsters and atheists were a necessary series of projections, given these cognitive conventions. It was necessary to visualise, and perhaps act out, disorder so that order might be understood.[131]

It is in this context that Michael Hunter has suggested that 'atheism would have had to be invented even if it had not existed, for it played a role in early modern thought which was essential in a world impregnated by Aristotelian contraries and polarities'. 'In a real sense,

---

[127] James I, *Daemonologie* (Edinburgh, 1597), p. 55; quoted in Stuart Clark, 'Inversion, Misrule and the Meaning of Witchcraft', *P. & P.*, 87 (1980), 117.
[128] Clark, 'Inversion', *passim.*   [129] *Ibid.*, 105.
[130] [Breton,] *The Goode and the Badde*, p. 20   [131] Clark, 'Inversion', 111–17.

therefore, the existence of atheists is irrelevant to the literature of atheism, which served functions in its own right.'[132] Much the same might be said, if more temporarily, of the Ranters.

They appear at a moment of crisis or critical ambivalence in relation to the issues of toleration and the logic and limits of sectarianism. The atheist will not do to explore these issues by inversion because he cannot be held, even for a moment, to take such issues seriously. The Ranter is a sectarian; Ranterism, a sect. Therefore, the image can be used to explore the dilemmas of sectarianism and the problems inherent in tolerating the sects. Against sectarian order may be set the sectarian anarchy of the Ranters. To illuminate the need for sectarian discipline and boundaries, the image of sectarian indiscipline, a group without boundaries, could be used. Against the agonising problem of ordinances could be set the Ranterish consequences of the repudiation of all ordinances. Against the disciplinary underpinning of sin and hell could be put the Ranters' denial of both. As the sects struggled to reconcile the spirit and the letter, the Ranters illustrated the final consequences of repudiating the latter. For John Bunyan, Ranters and atheists were alike in that they both lacked a conviction and sense of sin, but the one professed religion, the other did not.[133]

Supplementary models

The appearance of a Ranter literature in 1650 is not, of itself, surprising. What is surprising is the intensity, scale and concentration of that literature. Many features of that literature are, however, quite traditional, the stock in trade of sectarian vituperation and condemnation.

The early Christians had, of course, been accused of orgiastic behaviour by the Romans. Pre-Reformation heretics were commonly accused of antinomian practices. Calvin, in surveying with dismay the indiscipline of the reformers, singled out those 'Libertins Spirituelz' who placed the spirit above Scripture. They were identified with immorality, sexual promiscuity and ambivalence about antinomianism.[134] In the English Reformation anti-protestants frequently saw Protestants in terms of practical antinomianism. 'Protestantism allowed sexual licence, it was said, and licence to turn upside down the established order.'[135] In 1566 John Stow associated the Puritans with the Anabap-

---

[132] Hunter, 'Atheism', 9, 16–17.   [133] *W.T.U.D.*, p. 205.

[134] Balke, *Calvin and the Anabaptist Radicals*, trans. Heynen, pp. 9–10, 16; R. W. Collins, *Calvin and the Libertines of Geneva*, edited by F.D. Blackley (Toronto and Vancouver, 1968), pp. 153, 154, 164–5, 178.

[135] Susan Brigden, 'Youth and the English Reformation', *P. & P.*, 95 (1982), 39.

tists and their notorious excesses.[136] Within English Calvinism there was a long-lived anxiety about the implications of predestination which could arouse similar fears. The Cambridge disputants of the 1590s were 'concerned that the Christian assurance of salvation, if emphasised too strongly, might lead to false pride and even to antinomianism'.[137]

Two groups had developed European notoriety in terms of images of this kind; the Anabaptists and the Familists. Both were believed to hold doctrines of perfectionism or to place the spirit above the letter. The Munster disaster of 1534 was frequently cited as the illustration of the excess to which Anabaptism could lead. From the beginning, the Family of Love were accused of sexual excess, and Niclaes, their leader, of polygamy. Their shadowiness probably encouraged the making of such charges. In 1579 Hubert Languet, Sir Philip Sidney's tutor, described the Family of Love as polygamous, rejecting all magistracy and committed to social levelling. It was pure myth, designed to show why Calvinist discipline was necessary.[138] In 1607 Thomas Middleton's play *The Family of Love* portrayed a group of ignorant folk meeting at night, without candles, for licentious purposes.[139] In 1641 Familists were accused of adoring 'Saints Ovid, Priapus, Cupid'.[140] Such repeated accusations, smears, eventually take on a life of their own, becoming the received image of the group. Certainly the Familist stereotype was one model to which the Ranter image was frequently linked and from which it could be built.

There may, however, be a broader phenomenon to be observed here. Much religious revivalism or reformation has carried with it not only a demand for godly discipline or godly rule, but also a call for renewed authenticity, a directness of spiritual experience, liberated from the stultifying force of formalism. It is a tension running through the Puritan Revolution but which may be observed in other revival movements. So, in the late eighteenth and early nineteenth centuries, Swedenborgians could encounter men not unlike the Ranters. The success of the Mormons, their enemies were convinced, lay in their practical antinomianism. John Wesley was afraid that a speculative antinomianism would lead to a practical antinomianism, subverting all social and political order.[141] It would be a mistake to see these recurrent anxieties as a simple continuity; meanings, languages and contexts change. But it may also be

---

[136] Patrick Collinson, *English Puritanism*, Historical Association, General Series 106 (London, 1983), p. 9.   [137] White, 'The Rise of Arminianism Reconsidered', 136.
[138] Hamilton, *The Family of Love*, pp. 48–9, 133–4.   [139] Buckley, *Atheism*, p. 49.
[140] Huehns, *Antinomianism*, p. 62 n. 2.   [141] Harrison, *The Second Coming*, pp. 15, 36, 187–8.

that there is here a historical transmission of images or characters making them available as and when needed.

A similar literature, still available and popular in the early seventeenth century, was the literature of prodigy and monstrosity, to which in many ways the sensational Ranter literature bears physical resemblance.[142] Prodigy books were, of course, another form of inversion or contrary, teaching the natural by exposing the unnatural.

The literature of religious inversion or excess readily fused with that of prodigy. Atheists were monsters,[143] and so were Ranters:

What Age is this that we live in,
What Monsters hath it bred;
Who, by their Acts, make Virtue, Sin;
And still the Foot the Head.

So bemoaned *Mercurius Elencticus*, a royalist newspaper to be linked with Samuel Shepherd, author of an anti-Ranter satire.[144] Butler saw Ranterism as a monstrous reflection of the madness of the age in which it was born.[145] Others saw more specific links between antinomianism and monstrous deformity. In his highly popular *Heresiography*, Ephraim Pagitt told the story of the monstrously deformed child brought forth in Massachusetts by 'Mistris Dier', an antinomian follower of Anne Hutchinson.[146] It was a story that Richard Baxter saw fit to repeat, with additions in *Reliquiae Baxterianae*,[147] and a similar version of the same story was told of a Ranter named Mary Adams in *The Ranters Monster* (1652).[148]

There can be little doubt that there was a fictional or mythic image of Ranterism created in the early 1650s. It was used to discredit or discipline religious enthusiasm and to illustrate, for some, the dangers of religious toleration.[149] The power of this image was reinforced by its capacity to tap the energy associated, at a multiplicity of levels, with inversion and contrariety. The speed of its creation and dissemination was made possible by the ready availability and common perception of the images from which it was constructed, the character of the atheist,

---

[142] For the prodigy literature see Park and Daston, 'Unnatural Conceptions'; Margaret Spufford, *Small Books and Pleasant Histories: Popular Fiction and its Readership in Seventeenth Century England* (London, 1981).   [143] [Breton,] *The Goode and the Badde*, p. 21.
[144] *Mercurius Elencticus*, 4, 14–21 May 1649, 19, E.555 (37).
[145] Daves (ed.), *Butler: Characters*, p. 107.
[146] E[phraim] Pagitt, *Heresiography* (1654), p. 101. The first edition was published in 1645.
[147] Sylvester (ed.), *Reliquiae Baxterianae*, p. 75.
[148] *The Ranters Monster*, title page, pp. 3–4, 8.
[149] Cf. McGregor, 'The Ranters 1649–1660', 128.

sectarian promiscuity and the prodigy. Yet doubts could remain. Baxter was clearly puzzled by the fact that he had never set eyes on a single Ranter and Alexander Ross, who attempted a comprehensive encyclopaedia of all the religions of the world in 1653, saw fit not to mention them at all.[150]

iv. CONCLUSION

The image of the Ranter was a projection of deviance that had more to do with the reality of religious anxieties, a sense of dislocation, than with the reality of particular people or groups, their actions and beliefs. There was no Ranter movement, no Ranter sect, no Ranter theology. A few relatively isolated individuals of heterogeneous persuasions were swept up in the projection of a movement but only subsequently have they been assigned rôles by the historians; a leader, an ideologue, a spokesman for this or that wing of the 'movement'.

The true history of the Ranters is the history of a projection or myth, of the anxieties out of which it arose and which shaped it, and of the consequences to which it gave rise. It should be set against the long history of such fears and projections and, in particular, against post-Reformation fears of loss of control over religious speculation and the perception of religious truth, fears which were heightened by a prevailing apocalypticism. From Luther's time, solfidianism could arouse fears of antinomianism. From Calvin's, predestination could do the same. The revival of Joachite ideas seemed to presage the sweeping aside of ordinances and their scriptural base in an Age of the Spirit. Theological boundaries did, of course, have implications for moral and ritual boundaries but, in polemic, there was a tendency to exaggerate the degree to which moral boundaries would be, or were, breached. The horror of social and moral disorder, with all of its inversive associations, was a useful weapon with which to fight off unorthodoxy and with which to steel the orthodox against its appeal.

These fears had been longstanding. They were exacerbated for Englishmen in 1649 by the fall of so many cultural, political and constitutional landmarks. And yet the revolution was not a clear redrafting of the boundaries, or even a struggle for the establishment of new certainties. It was incomplete and unresolved. To those in the eye of the revolution, the threat of a royalist counterstroke – popular or otherwise

---

[150] A[lexander] R[oss], ΠΑΝΣΕΒΕΙΑ: *Or, A View of all Religion in the World* (1653); see section XII for coverage of antinomians.

– was not negligible. In part it could be met by the forcible suppression of London and the defence of the republic by the New Model Army. Similarly, the militant threat to carry through a fuller revolution, however defined, could be dealt with by violence and arbitrary arrest, as in the case of the Levellers, or by harassment and indifference, as in the case of the Diggers. But, given toleration and the freedom of the press, how was the spinning of minds to be stilled? Too many actors were not in place. How dramatically a religious under-class had been emancipated and with what apparently bewildering results! The delicate balance of a conservative revolution could be undermined from within by the working out of this lack of religious control. A sectarian rending of Christian unity, theological disorder, a moral madness, the inversion of all that a sane Christianity represented; the vision of these things became a warning of the need for internalised discipline, sobriety and humility, where the means of external discipline had been abandoned, and indeed overthrown, by those now most concerned about the internal and external consequences of disorder.

The consequences of this projection are arguable. It has been suggested that the Ranter sensation led to the Blasphemy Act and the savage repression of religious heterodoxy. Outside Quaker experience, evidence for the latter is hard to find and the Blasphemy Act, with its simultaneous worries about atheism, enthusiasm and formalism, reflected, rather than resolved, the ambivalences out of which the Ranter projection sprang. More clearly consequential upon the Ranter projection was a tightening up of sectarian discipline within what had remained fairly protean movements, the Baptists, Quakers and Muggletonians. If we seek any legislative outcome, perhaps we should consider the influence of the Ranter image of 'women on top' in stifling the liberating influence of some sectarian attitudes for women saints, and the suppression of women implicit in the Adultery Act of 1650.[151]

---

[151] Keith Thomas, 'The Puritans and Adultery: The Act of 1650 Reconsidered', in Pennington and Thomas (eds.), *Puritans and Revolutionaries*, pp. 257–82, and especially pp. 277–8.

6

Explaining the historians

If the Ranters were no more than a mythic projection, in the wake of which some hapless victims were swept up, labelled and sectarianised, then clearly a number of sensible, skilled and mature historians have got it wrong. How can this be? Furthermore, how could a group of historians, predominantly of the left, have come to subscribe to this myth, the myth of the Ranters which was projected by those anxious for control and authority; in other words, a myth in some sense of the right? These are difficult questions to answer both because we lurch suddenly from the seventeenth century to the contemporary world, where our sources are even more partial, and because, when good historians are accused of egregious errors, the explanations must be complex and disturbing. Here I offer only some tentative explanations and hypotheses. Let us begin by considering the use of evidence, and start with examples of the use of the heresiographer Thomas Edwards, and of the yellow-press material of the Ranter sensation.

Relying on Thomas Edwards, for evidence of the reality of sectarian development in his time, is like relying on Horatio Bottomley or Joseph McCarthy for sound, objective depictions of the social and political realities of their day. Edwards is, of course, a source of good evidence for the study of the mid-seventeenth-century heresiographer, of which he is virtually an archetype, but his views can never be accepted as anything but a biased perception of his own society. For him the vital aspect of that society was the swarming mass of plebeian heresy, blasphemy, irreligion, profanity, and licentiousness which he saw threatening to engulf all godliness and sobriety. The starting point of all of this for Edwards, the Presbyterian, was Independency and all that flowed from it. Independency had long been Edwards's main target[1] and, despite the sectarian proliferation taking place in its pages, remained the central object of attack in *Gangraena*.

[1] Thomas Edwards, *Reasons against Independent government of particular congregations* (1641).

For Edwards, in 1646, the plea for liberty or toleration was a sure sign of 'Libertinisme and Atheisme'.[2] Independents who had so pleaded were thus condemned as the inverse of true religion and Edwards, accordingly, hastened on to assert that their behaviour demonstrated this. They practised incest, bigamy, rape, adultery and fornication of all kinds.[3] They were notorious for their drunkenness and many drunkards were attracted to Independency for this reason:[4]

Many Sectaries and Independents are very loose in the generall course of their lives, and take a great deale of liberty, which the Presbyterians dare not take, neither did they before they turned Independents.

They neglected the sabbath and fast days, played cards, attended plays and were indifferent to prayer, psalms, the study of Scripture and sermons. They were ostentatious in dress, wore long hair, laughed, jested and were generally frivolous.[5] Were this not enough, an Independent had been heard to assert his liberty to worship the sun, moon or a pewter pot if he saw fit.[6] The question is whether anyone would take this seriously as a depiction of the religious beliefs and practices of the Independents. Was this the religion of Oliver Cromwell, John Goodwin, Philip Nye or Thomas Coleman? The answer is surely that we would not regard Edwards as a valid source from which to build a realistic picture of Independency or its aspirations in the 1640s. There are elements of hostility, uncritical acceptance of anything condemnatory, an indiscriminate jostling of different groups, sources and types of information and, above all, a strong tendency to exaggeration which tells us a great deal, but not much of it is about the Independents.[7] It should not be necessary to labour the point. Mrs Grundy is a doubtful source for social historians. The heresiographers are suspect, if not worse, as sources of what, if anything, was actually happening on the margins of religious orthodoxy. There is no reason why Edwards, and his like, should be better sources for the study of Ranters or antinomians than for the Independents.

In looking at Edwards's attack on one of the founders and leaders of the Independent congregation at Bury St Edmunds, John Lanseter, A.L. Morton wrote:

---

[2] Thomas Edwards, *Gangraena* (1646), III, p. 185.

[3] *Ibid.*, pp. 187–8, 189.   [4] *Ibid.*, pp. 190–1.   [5] *Ibid.*, p. 191.   [6] *Ibid.*, p. 187.

[7] Cf. Ephraim Pagitt's depiction of the Independents. '. . . they may have liberty to do what they list, having no government . . .' *Heresiography* (1654) Epistle Dedicatory. Cf. royalist propaganda on the Independents as destroying 'even the appearance of religion and law'. *C.S.P. Ven*, 28, 1647–52, p. 138.

The result of all this is a vast confusion of charges, rebuttals and counter-charges, from which it is impossible, in many cases, to establish the truth with any certainty.[8]

In other words, Edwards's typical procedures result in a picture of John Lanseter which cannot be taken as a reliable guide by the historian attempting to reconstruct the beliefs and behaviour of that individual. And the same must be said of most of the other phenomena depicted in Edwards's teeming pages. Unless we have other, and much more reliable, sources his descriptions must be treated with scepticism. And yet elsewhere it has been Morton's practice to use Edwards as a reliable source of information on the sects.[9] Others have followed suit. Norman Cohn, incorporating an extract from *Gangraena* in his appendix of documents, suggested that 'Although Edwards was a Presbyterian and a bitter opponent of all Independents, there are no grounds for doubting the accuracy of this account . . .'[10] There are, of course, several such grounds and some of them are set out in the first part of Cohn's sentence. Ironically, in the extract Cohn produces, Edwards himself expresses some slight reservation about the second- and third-hand reports on which he is so frequently reliant: ' 'tis likely enough they may be true'.[11] Christopher Hill, too, has used Edwards as an implicitly dependable source of views on sectarian activity.[12]

Evidence of a Ranter group, sect or movement has constantly been taken from hostile sources such as Edwards, and other heresiographers, or the sensational yellowpress material.[13] Often this practice has been coupled with an acknowledgement of the unreliability of the sources. Rufus Jones admitted that his description of the Ranters was a summary of views 'largely taken from persons who put the worst construction of the Ranters' teaching'. One of his sources, Gilbert Roulston, was 'thoroughly unreliable'.[14] Later, Frank McGregor was to argue that although little of the evidence was reliable 'it is occasionally possible to distinguish the factual basis from the fanciful embellishments'.[15] But no procedure for making such distinctions was ever established and adhered to. There has developed instead a kind of left-handed scep-

---

[8]   *W.O.T.R.*, p. 24.   [9]   Morton, *The Everlasting Gospel*, Ch. 3; *W.O.T.R.*, p. 117.
[10] Cohn, *The Pursuit of the Millennium*, pp. 324–5.   [11]   *Ibid.*, p. 325.
[12] Cf. *W.T.U.D.*, pp. 187–8, 189, 191, 192; Hill, 'Irreligion in the "Puritan" Revolution', in McGregor and Reay (eds.), *Radical Religion*, pp. 198, 203.
[13] Cf. Whiting, *Studies in English Puritanism*, pp. 97, 98, 198, 251 n.2, 278; Jones, *Studies in Mystical Religion*, p. 480; Huehns, *Antinomianism*, pp. 87, 88; Morton, *Everlasting Gospel*, pp. 52–3; Hutin, *Disciples anglais*, pp. 60, 234 n. 210; Cohn, *Pursuit*, Appendix; *W.O.T.R.*, pp. 76, 81, 89–93, 132; Ellens, 'Case Studies', Ch.1; McGregor, 'The Ranters', pp. 85, 90, 91, Ch.5.   [14]   Jones, *Studies in Mystical Religion*, pp. 474 n.2, 477–8.
[15] McGregor, 'The Ranters', p.85.

ticism of the sources, accompanied by a right-handed exploitation of
them. The 'popular stories of orgiastic revels cannot be substantiated',
but many of the Ranters 'were undoubtedly guilty of immorality'.[16]
Mud sticks. Although startling, sensational accounts of the Ranters,
according to Morton, 'should not be entirely rejected on that
account'.[17] Why not or in what terms is not explained. Similarly, the
truth of stories from 'the lowest, muck-raking' type of journalism 'must
be doubtful' but one should not, we are told, be predisposed to reject
the reality of practical antinomianism on that account.[18] In *The World
Turned Upside Down* Christopher Hill admitted, somewhat ambiguously,
that 'We need not take any of these stories seriously . . .' But the stories
are nevertheless purveyed as some kind of evidence of the plebeian
religion and irreligion that Hill is seeking to portray.[19] Later still, he
suggested that 'We need not accept the alarmist accounts of pro-
fessional heresy-hunters like Edwards, Baillie, Rutherford, Pagitt, Ross
and several more – though Edwards's *Gangraena* at least is well
documented and seems to stand up quite well to examination: we need a
critical edition.'[20] What does 'well documented' mean in this context?
Where has been the sustained examination of Edwards's documen-
tation and its quality? Isn't the need for a critical edition an admission
that these things have not been done?

The historiography of the Ranters as a group, sect or movement has
become heavily dependent on the acceptance of evidence which historians would normally be critical of, given the predispositions of its
creators and the frequent absence of good corroborative material. It is
the kind of evidence which we would hope would not stand up in a
court of law and it should not be acceptable at the bar of history. Its
ambiguous acceptance by those nonconformist historians with a
denominational axe to grind against extreme sectarianism is perhaps
understandable, if lamentable. But, since the 'rediscovery' of the Ranter
movement in 1970, it has been an entirely different group of historians
who have moved into this relationship of ambiguity with the sources.
As they number amongst them some of the best and one of the most
creative and widely admired historians of his generation we have to ask
why and how this situation could have come about. There are obviously
a variety of factors at work, only some of which we as yet know anything about. However, there are some patterns which can be discerned
and which it may be pertinent to consider here.

Central to the rediscovery and consolidation of the historical import-

---

[16] *Ibid.*, p. 90.   [17] *W.O.T.R.*, p. 76. Cf. Ellens, 'The Ranters Ranting', p. 92.
[18] *W.O.T.R.*, p. 81.   [19] *W.T.U.D.*, p. 317.   [20] Hill, 'Irreligion', p. 206.

ance of the Ranters has been the work of A.L. Morton and Christopher Hill. Both men had been members of the Communist Party Historians' Group between 1946 and 1956.[21] The influence of discussion within that group, which has been described as a kind of historiographical Popular Front,[22] has been prodigious. Partly, this is attributable to the sheer quality of the work produced by its members; partly, to the clarity of the group's objectives and the systematic way in which they have been pursued. Foremost in their minds in the forties and early fifties was the need to create the history of a popular democratic tradition in English history and culture. The people had made, or attempted to make, their own history and would do so again. Morton's studies in English utopianism or the people's history were early exercises in this genre. E.P. Thompson's *The Making of the English Working Class* (1963) may be said to be its first full flowering. Two other goals were eventually allied with this first one. The Group wished to show that some of the great figures of the English cultural tradition had been influenced by and allied with these popular movements and potentialities. Into this framework Morton's work on Blake, Thompson's on William Morris and Hill's on Milton fit.[23] Secondly, however, they wished to show that, in endeavouring to make their own history, the people had to thwart the aspiration of the dominant classes to make theirs a hegemonic culture. This came to be a prominent feature of Hill's work from his early essays about the Norman Yoke and the struggle against it to *The World Turned Upside Down*, from his early optimism that 'The history of mankind is the history of the growth in freedom of moral judgement',[24] to *The Experience of Defeat*.

Obviously, if there was a longstanding tradition whereby the English people sought to make their own history, then that must be reflected in the English Revolution. No one has done more than Hill to keep the notion of an English *revolution* in the mid seventeenth century alive. It has been an epic and, one suspects, an increasingly lonely challenge. When Hill began to write about the revolution it was in a classically Marxist mode. The bourgeoisie, riding a nascent capitalism, sought to

---

[21] For a useful account of the group and its aims see Bill Schwarz, ' "The people" in history: the Communist Party Historians' Group 1946–56', in Richard Johnson, Gregor McLennan, Bill Schwarz and David Sutton (eds.), *Making Histories: Studies in History-Writing and Politics* (London, 1982) pp. 44–95. See also Harvey J. Kaye, *The British Marxist Historians: An Introductory Analysis* (Cambridge, 1984).   [22] *Ibid.*, p. 85.

[23] Morton, *The Everlasting Gospel*; E.P. Thompson, *William Morris: Romantic to Revolutionary* (London, 1977); Hill, *Milton and the English Revolution*.

[24] Schwarz, ' "The people" in history', p. 68.

burst the bonds of a feudal order and the carapace of its constitutional contrivances.[25] His extremely popular textbook *The Century of Revolution 1603–1714* (1961) presented the period similarly as one of economic, social and political transformation, though the categories were less crude and the language more sophisticated. Throughout the 1960s, and since, there has, however, been a tendency for scholarship to undermine the notion of economic and social transformation in the mid seventeenth century. In the aftermath of the gentry controversy came a general acceptance of Alan Simpson's concept of 'the perdurable gentry'.[26] Individual families might have experienced fluctuating fortunes, but the landowning classes as a whole endured and may even have strengthened their position. Local and county studies, in which the 1960s and early 1970s were especially rich, have tended to confirm this view. The pace and direction of economic change is seen now to have been transformed after 1660 rather than before. It has been possible for Hill to argue that the revolution created conditions for bourgeois expansion, but only at the price of conceding that capitalism was the beneficiary of a revolution, not a factor in its making.[27] Lastly the work of David Underdown, consolidated by Blair Worden and Austin Woolrych, has tended to suggest that even after the crisis of 1648–9 there was little that was genuinely revolutionary, at least in intent, about the revolution.[28] The genuine revolutionaries were kept at arm's length and in the end defeated, a theme which Hill has made his own since 1972.[29] By 1964, to the consternation of some old members of the Group, Perry Anderson could argue that a considered Marxist strategy had to grasp that the seventeenth-century upheaval in England was the most mediated, least pure, bourgeois revolution of any major European country. It was, at best, a bourgeois revolution by proxy. The bourgeoisie were its beneficiaries, perhaps. They were certainly not its agents.[30] Edward Thompson's complaint, that Anderson had failed to recognise the capitalist nature of the English landed classes, was itself an

---

[25] Hill, *The English Revolution 1640* (London, 1940: revised edition 1955).

[26] A. Simpson, *The Wealth of the Gentry 1540–1660* (Chicago and Cambridge, 1961).

[27] Christopher Hill, 'A Bourgeois Revolution?' in J.G.A. Pocock (ed.), *Three British Revolutions: 1641, 1688, 1776* (Princeton, 1980) pp. 109–139. Cf. Albert Soboul, *The Short History of the French Revolution 1789–1799* translated by Geoffrey Simcox (Berkeley, Los Angeles, London, 1977).

[28] Underdown, *Pride's Purge*; Worden, *Rump Parliament*; Woolrych, *Commonwealth to Protectorate*.

[29] Hill, *W.T.D.U.D.*; *Milton and the English Revolution*; *The Experience of Defeat*.

[30] Perry Anderson, 'Origins of the Present Crisis', *New Left Review*, 23, January–February 1964, p. 28.

admission that the old formulation, the violent overthrow of a feudal landed order, had to go.[31]

At best, the 'revolution' was an abortive affair, the principal consequences of which had to be seen as unintended, unplanned. At worst, the 'revolution' had to be seen as a struggle within the traditional ruling classes, with the bourgeoisie split between idealism of various, even conflicting, persuasions, neutralism and opportunism. A supine, or immature, bourgeoisie was incapable of fulfilling a dynamic revolutionary rôle. Where were the 'people' in all of this and what could their rôle be?

Three shaping influences came to bear in the 1960s on these problems. One was the growing influence on the left of Gramsci's writings and, in particular, his view of the aspiration of dominant groups to a complex, all-embracing hegemony. The second was the influence of the Frankfurt school, especially perhaps in the argument of Herbert Marcuse that liberation must not only be from the capitalist economic system but from repression in all its forms, cultural and moral as well as physical and legal. Third was the impact of 1968, the year of revolutionary spontaneity; of the grand experiment in proletarian revolution without the working class, in the direct liberation of participating agents from all forms of hegemony and repression, internalised as well as external.

When Hill came to write *The World Turned Upside Down* (1972) it was to depict a revolt within a 'revolution'.[32] The successful revolution was that of the propertied, defending themselves against threats from both above and below and seeking to assert their hegemony through the internalisation and imposition of the Protestant ethic. Instrumental to the latter objective were the doctrines of sin, heaven and hell. The more plebeian revolt was against this as much as against the *ancien régime*. Had it succeeded its revolution 'might have established communal property, a far wider democracy in political and legal institutions, might have disestablished the state church and rejected the protestant ethic'. Genuine understanding of this second revolution could only come, Hill argued, now that the Protestant ethic was at last being questioned.[33] In a later exposition of the same theme, Hill has argued that there were three Gods at work in the English Revolution. The first was the God who blessed the established order, the God of authority and tradition. Second was the God whose priority was justice rather than continuity,

---

[31]　E.P. Thompson, *The Poverty of Theory* (London, 1978) p. 250.
[32]　*W.T.U.D.*, pp. 14, 15.　[33] *Ibid.*, p. 15.

whose authoritative voice was to be sought for, if not found, in the voice of Scripture, naked and unadorned. This was the God of Protestant millennialism, of Calvinism and the sober sects whose banners floated above the parliamentary armies. Finally, there was God the Great Leveller, a God to be found in every believer, whose revolutionary voice could be heard through his saints, Abiezer Coppe, George Foster and Laurence Clarkson. This was the God who allowed the people, every man and woman, a voice.[34]

Here is the crucial point from our perspective. Who led the revolt within the revolution? Who were the vanguard against the Protestant ethic; the authentic voice of the people seeking to make their own history and, to that end, to overthrow a dominant, hegemonic ideology and culture? At one time the answer might have been the Levellers led by Lilburne, Overton, Walwyn and Wildman. In *The World Turned Upside Down* this claim is dismissed. The Levellers were too close to the revolution that succeeded, the revolution of property and the Protestant ethic. 'The constitutional Levellers, then, were not in fundamental disagreement with the type of society that was being set up by the English Revolution. They accepted the sanctity of private property, and their desire to extend democracy was within the limits of a capitalist society.'[35] The True Levellers, or Diggers, offered through their rural communism a step forward and a challenge to the revolution of property. But Winstanley was perhaps too conscious of sin and the need for its repression, in the end too apprehensive of the ubiquity of covetousness to bear the whole weight of the revolutionary challenge to the Protestant ethic.[36] It was the Seekers, the early Quakers, but, above all, the Ranters who took up the challenge 'of "sin" and how to escape from its all-pervasiveness'.[37] It was the Ranters who fought most ruthlessly against the internalisation of the Protestant ethic. As long as that last process was accepted, the revolt within a revolution could never succeed. Hence the eventual quiescence of the Quakers was a symbol of

---

[34] Hill, 'God and the English Revolution', *History Workshop*, 17 (1984) pp. 19–31.

[35] *W.T.U.D.*, p. 123.

[36] Hill has never accepted his critics' attempts to suggest that either Winstanley has to be understood in more religious terms, or that he became more repressive than the formulations of *The World Turned Upside Down* allowed. But, on balance, he has come to place greater emphasis on the Ranters as spokesmen of the third God. See Lotte Mulliga, John K. Graham and Judith Richards, 'Winstanley: a case for the man as he said he was', *Journal of Ecclesiastical History*, 28 (1977) pp. 57–75; J.C. Davis, 'Winstanley and the Restoration of True Magistracy', *P. & P.*, 70 (1976) pp. 76–93; Hill, 'The Religion of Gerrard Winstanley', *Past and Present Supplement* 5 (Oxford, 1978); 'God and the English Revolution'. [37] *W.T.U.D.*, p. 72.

defeat, giving priority to sectarian survival over the triumph of the third God.

So the authentic mouthpieces of that God had to be Coppe, Foster, Clarkson; the Ranters in Hill's accounting of them. Without the Ranters, the revolt within the revolution was always, ironically, unrealistic, because the others had accepted, or would accept, the internalisation of sin and the Protestant ethic. The rest were, in the end, examples of the hegemonic success of the bourgeois revolution. Without the Ranters there would have been no thoroughgoing popular rejection of the Protestant ethic and, therefore, no illustration of the strength and continuity of the popular tradition whereby the people sought to make their own history and throw off the hegemonic impress of those to whom they were subjected. The Ranters were, in a sense, necessary: if they had not existed, they would have had to be invented. But the myth was there. Exploited, precisely and ironically, in the 1650s by those who wished to reassert religious control, it became for non-conformist historians of the nineteenth and twentieth centuries the exemplar of why sectarian discipline was necessary. With further irony, it was this myth which, by the 1970s, could find a new rôle and a new audience.

But there was, of course, a price to be paid for its adoption. Sometimes it led into the presumption of guilt before innocence. So that the jury at the Salisbury Assizes in January 1651 were declared by an historian not to have found Thomas Webbe innocent: rather they 'refused to convict him'.[38] There was an uncomfortable flirting with the primary evidence of a movement or sect, that of the heresiographers and the yellowpress. Suspect evidence of this type had finally to be used with no formal assessment of its validity. Similarly, until McGregor's growing caution, there was little systematic evaluation of the evidence of Quakers, Baptists and other sects for the continued existence of Ranters. On the other hand, the recantations or disavowals of men like Coppe or Coppin were dismissed out of hand as no more than a ruse to deceive the authorities, even as part of their rejection of all moral restraints, though no evidence was produced to substantiate these claims. Once the myth of the movement had been adopted, the companion myth of its 'savage repression' had also to be perpetuated in order to explain the movement's disappearance. Once again, there was no systematic examination of evidence for such repression.

An example of the further, and rather bizarre, price to be paid for the

---

[38]   McGregor, 'The Ranters', p. 94.

adoption of the myth can be seen in the confusion it leaves in its wake with regard to such once-central doctrines of this school of history as that of the place of possessive individualism in seventeenth-century social and political thought. In the 1960s great attention was paid to C.B. MacPherson's claim that a bourgeois content could be discovered in the, sometimes implicit or unconscious, assumption of possessive individualism to be found in a variety of seventeenth-century thinkers.[39] A bourgeois or market society was held to be emerging and, for it to reach fulfilment, people had to begin to see themselves and their attributes as market commodities. To think of oneself as a negotiable asset, one had to see oneself as a piece of freehold, negotiable property, hence the importance of possessive individualism. MacPherson's argument ran into difficulties with regard to the thinkers and groups he sought to interpret in this way as well as on other counts. Yet it remained influential. As recently as 1980, Lawrence Stone was arguing that possessive individualism arose out of the Puritan emphasis on individual conscience.[40] But as soon as we attempt to relate possessive individualism to the seventeenth century's pervasive currents of religious thought we encounter immense difficulties. Mainstream Puritanism and the respectable sects had a view of conscience as limited or bound. Man was not in freehold occupation of himself but enjoyed a stewardship over that entrusted to him by God and for which, one day, he would be called upon to make answer. Possessive individualism had little meaning here.[41] Rather, it is the antinomians who, theoretically, should have seen themselves as having full and unfettered disposition or possession of their attributes. Paradoxically, it should be Ranterism that is the image of possessive individualism. At this point, contradictions abound. That group, claimed to be the most zealous opponents of the capitalist ethic, have become the outstanding exponents of the doctrine said to be at its heart.

In 1650 and 1651, as for some time thereafter, it was necessary to believe that the Ranters existed in order to demonstrate the perceived and potential anarchy of *de facto* religious toleration, especially in a situation where 'immemorial' landmarks of order and stability had collapsed. In 1970, it was becoming necessary to believe that they existed,

---

[39] C.B. MacPherson, *The Political Theory of Possessive Individualism: Hobbes to Locke* (Oxford, 1962).

[40] Lawrence Stone, 'The Results of the English Revolutions of the Seventeenth Century' in Pocock (ed.), *Three British Revolutions*, p. 44.

[41] Cf. the argument in J.C. Davis, 'The Levellers and Christianity', in B.S. Manning (ed.), *Politics, Religion and the English Civil War* (London, 1973) Ch. 6.

as a movement of indeterminate size, in order to sustain the twin notions that the people have persistently attempted to make their own history and that such a potential history has been, in essence, the negation of capitalist culture and the Protestant ethic, which for three hundred years accompanied it.

i. EPILOGUE

What, then, do the Ranters represent? I have argued that they did not exist as a movement, a sect or even, in McGregor's formulation, as a small group with reasonably consistent views. What they have come to represent exists on two levels. There was a real phenomenon in the 1650s. It was the projection of an image inverting all that true godliness should represent. As such, it was able to build on other inversions and projections like that of the atheist. In a sense, it was an indicator of the perceived failure to establish godly rule by authority or consensus, and the nightmare of endless sectarian proliferation. The power of the projection was not only in its exploitation of traditional images and codes but in the way in which it portrayed unacceptable private liberty as become public manifestation: a double horror. Richard Sennett has suggested the idea of a public world of masks existing in European culture before the nineteenth century.[42] In this sense, the Ranters were a public mask, almost dissociated from real people, but, nevertheless, performing a public rôle and function. As with witchcraft, once fear and anger had been aroused and the mechanisms of discipline were in place, victims had to be found. The surprising and revealing feature on this occasion is how, with the exception of Bauthumley, relatively lightly such offenders were treated and how few they were. There may be two approaches to the phenomenon at this level, as a set of 'events' in history. One may be to anticipate that conditions of social unrest, dislocation and disorder will spawn heretics. The other is to anticipate that such conditions create the *need* for heretics, of specific types, as markers of moral and speculative boundaries. The tendency in the historiography has been to emphasise the former, and with some justification, but does it automatically apply in all circumstances and should it lead us to abandon normal historiographical scepticism in the face of dubious sources?

This leads us on to the second level of the phenomenon, the historiography of the Ranters. If this too, in the hands of competent and

---

[42]   Richard Sennett, *The Fall of Public Man* (Cambridge, 1974).

reputable historians, has perpetuated the myth, what are we to say? When poor historians lead us astray, nothing unexpected has happened. When good ones do so, we must question their approach. E.P. Thompson has repeatedly insisted on the duty of the historian to 'listen' to all of his sources, rather than merely giving shape to them.[43] History should be 'a discipline of attentive disbelief'. For those of Thompson's persuasion, it should be written within 'the open, exploratory, self-critical Marxist tradition'.[44] Such statements were made as part of a polemic and helped to sustain a debate of some acrimony, but we might here regard them as unexceptionable. After all, to what siren voices is the historian listening if not to the sources? But, is listening done to inform one's perspective or according to one's perspective? Thompson would claim that a Marxist perspective can be reconciled with an almost ideally Popperian openness. Others would have their doubts. For what is the function of theory if not, in some sense, to limit the range of possible conclusions? Hypothesis, abandonable at all times, is one thing, theory, another. However loose they have worn their Marxist mantle, perhaps, in the end, the aspirations of the Communist Party Historians' Group were so close to theory as to close off conclusions rather than leave them open. There may have had to be a group of Ranters, if the experience of defeat were not to overwhelm the English people and stifle their desire to make their own history, in the only convulsion which really mattered, the English Revolution.

[43] See, for example, the interview with him in Henry Abelove, Betsy Blackmar, Peter Dimock and Jonathan Schneer (eds.), *Visions of History* (Manchester, 1983) p. 14.

[44] Thompson, *Poverty of Theory*, pp. 27, 28–9, 169.

Appendix: documents

The selection here includes the one 'core' Ranter text which has not been reprinted recently, *A Justification of the Mad Crew*, and some examples of the sensational, yellow-press material on the Ranters.

1. A Justification of the Mad Crew *(1650)* E.609 *(18)*

A
JUSTIFICATION
OF THE
MAD CREW
IN THEIR WAIES AND PRINCIPLES
Or
The Madness and Weakness of
GOD IN MAN
Proved Wisdom and Strength

With a true Testimony of that sweet and unspeakable
Joy, and everlasting glory that dwels in and breaks out,
through this strange and unheard of appearance, and this in
many particulars declared; from that experiment the Author
of this Book hath made: and how wonderfully he hath been
wrought over, and led up to that life and Being which needs
not, is not, yea cannot be ashamed; being translated out
of that Kingdom that is, hath, and shall be shaken,
into that which neither is can or shall ever
be removed.
And all this dawned and sunned out in God the Son,
viz. God in the form: whom if ye crucifie, it is
because you know him not.
For whether we be besides ourselves it is to God, or whether
we be sober, it is for your sake. 2 Cor. 5.13.

Printed in the day and year that mens hearts fail them for
fear, and for looking after those things that are coming,
yea come upon the Earth. 1650.

To the Reader

that they without us might not be made perfect; They having tasted of the tree of knowledge of good and evil, and not seeing, enjoying, but waiting for the fulness of times, in which all things both in Heaven and Earth, shall be gathered together in one, in Christ, and since that time for the past ages, God hath parcelled out his glory, and spoken to us under the curtains, and withdrawn himself from the greatest part of the Creation, even things and persons, cursing some, blessing others, damning one, and saving another, but now he is risen to justifie himself in all, upon all, both things and persons, and upon us is come the times of the restitution of all things which God hath spoken by the mouth of all his holy Prophets since the world began.

And the immutable God (whom the Nations and Kinreds of the Earth, Churches and societies, because they know him not have not worshipped) is clearly manifesting the Earth to be his Foot-stool, and the Heavens his Throne, that every creature that moves in the Earth and under the Earth, in the Sea and in the Firmament above, is the seat of God, contains him, hugs him, embraces him, nay is really and truly God, even the living God: that he is not affectionate or passionate, but that he loves all sweetly, powring out himself in and upon all, making all at Peace with him, bowing and serving him, that the devil and he are one, that the devil is but a part of Gods backsides, which terrifies because of the curtain, that he sports and feasts himself in swearing, drinking, whoring, as when he is holy, just and good: that the holliness of man and unholiness of man are both one to him; that he loves and delights in one as well as the other: that the Sons of God when they eat, eat God, and when they drink, drink God: that takest us up into thy arms: so that now we see that thou electest and choosest reprobate things and persons; we now see that Esau hated and Jacob loved, was but in the days of our dimness, till having learned them in distinction, and as two, we might know them in one joyned and united, that Saint and sinner are all one, and that there is none good but one, that is God; and that whosoever calls anything good unless God, and so hugs it as good, falls down to an Idol, and Worships a lie, that which his own fingers have made: and because the living God in me, and others, is condemned, as by you cast away, because of the twofold light and sight that dwells within you, I have justified my self in these poor, base, vile, sinful abominable things and persons, as by the sequel discourse appears, that I might thereby damn, ram and plague you into myself, who am,

Jesus the Son of God.

To all, even to those that impatiently, as well as to those that patiently read, and try the things that followeth.

The Lord as in the latter ages of the World, darkens the glory of man, so he clears up his own brightness that every eye may see it: and as he hath in the foregoing ages of the world, limited himself and his appearances to a certain Election of things and persons: so in these last days he extends himself to things and persons reprobated, and chooseth cast aways: and this is the mystery (the non-knowing whereof) confounds and plagues the World. As for instance, under the Law he elected the Temple as the place of his glory, the Jews *as the people of his Portion and Inheritance. Would you know God? to* Jerusalem *you must go, and to those people must ye joyn, all other places and persons being accursed of God, as the withdrawings of his glory is a curse: afterward as his glory further brake out, and as he came to be more plainly God the Son, he leaves those people and their Temple, and joyns himself and his appearances to all Nations, and makes every language know and hear him; and then a* Peter *a* Jew *can declare (though with much wrastlings of spirit) that he is not to call anything common or unclean, and that God is no respecter of persons. And a* Paul *one of the strictest of that elected sect can say, there is nothing unclean of itself, but to him that esteemeth it unclean, to him it is unclean, yet this was but a bringing of them to Mount* Nebo, *and shewing them upon a hill, viz. a far off the land of* Canaan, *but not letting them to enter in because of their unbelief, God having reserved some better things for us that they walk in God and tread upon God, and are covered with God: That God lies with them every night and riseth up with them every morning, that he makes their bed and dresses them, and puts on their apparel: that they see nothing but God, and behold the face of him in everything: That they swear in God and abstaine from swearing in God, that they lye one with another in God, and are not ashamed, because God is in them: That they whore in God, that God is the Whore and the Whoremaster, & they depart not from him in any of their wais and now like little children they can play together, ly together, dance together, swear together, drink together, eat together; and yet think no evil, do no evil, knowing that if they swear not are they the better or if they swear are they the worse: if they drink not are they the better or if they drink and are drunk are they the worse: the same if they whore, and the same if they whore not: their sins are forgiven them, and there is no guile found in these mens mouths. This is the time when the cast away* Jew, *and the cast away Gentile shall both be received in. The Lord is now receiving into one, making it as near himself, Whordom that hath bin a castaway, lying that hath bin a castaway, yea the Whoremonger and the Theif sweetly embracing, kissing huging these, shewing himself a new, a fresh and alive in and to the whole Creation: so that we may now truly say, Lord, whether shall we go from thy presence? Thou are in Hell, Heaven, the Sun, Moon, Stars, in the grass, in our outward dancing and sporting, there thou kissest us and there thou dandlest us upon thy knees. When we go to a Whorehouse we meet thee, and when we come away thou comest away with us, and there thou takest.*

2. Justified in their Principles
First, *That there is but one God.*

This tenent of theirs, you all that hear or read this Discourse, will with them professedly hold and maintain; yet let me tell you, and that without offence, that thou Independent, thou Anabaptist so called; yea thou spiritual Notionist, that scornest carnal Ordinances, yet thou art a worshipper of many Gods; & dost not keep they self to any one God purely. I could tell all of you, that money is your God, that all your care, industry, pains, is to get and keep this God money. You cannot though you can talk of it, trust God and live by Faith, if you have nothing for tomorrow, but only for the present day, you are not contented, satisfied, your hearts then roars it out, and faith, what shall we do, we shall perish: and then cry out, why, because you have lost your God. I know it by the experiment I have made upon many of you, I see how ye can turn Seperatist Church men, baptise none but your holy fleshly seed, or none but such that believe, nay condemn all this as carnal, and talk of living holy in the Spirit, and all well enough till this voice sounds in your ears. Go and sell all thou hast, and come and follow me, who am numbered among the rogues, theeves, whoremasters, and base persons of the world, cast away your bags of mony, your riches, your substance, your trades, your wives, your children, be without a house & without a home know not where in the morning to lay your heads at night; care not for tomorrow, O then you storm and rage, you have lost your God, your Diana, and thus your God cannot save, nor deliver in the day of wrath. But this is but one of your Gods, there is another God, and that is such a one as ye call unchangeable, and yet you believe him, and make him to be in your imaginations one that hears, and answers prayers, moved by your speaking to him, and turning away from you, if you call not upon him; therefore, you cry and thunder it out, as if you would peirce his ears, and as if your zeal could move him to do you good, and thus you change God into a lie like your selves, sometimes gracious to you, and at other times cruel. There is another God you set up, and that is such a one that is in one, not in another, cursing one and blessing another, and so dam God as to the greatest part of the Creation, that he is onely in Saints, in a few, but he is not the God of all, and who is their God, who acts in the wicked, one called a Devil, another Spirit, and so they make something to be besides God; and if God be not the same, and only he, in one as in all, and all as in one, then there is another Being, another eternity. But now these men (that are male and female) hold one onely pure and individible, simple and uncompounded God, who is not withholden from any thing, who is in all as sweet and as glorious, acting as devinely and holily (though not to creature apprehensions) in the wicked, as in the godly, in him that steals, lies, swears, and is drunk, as in him that swears and lies not: is no more in one then in another, is the same life, the same being, the same glory in one, as in another; in beasts, as in men, and in men as in beasts, the very same and no way different but in manifestation; and though he be in all, in every one, yet he is but one, and they are all one in him. That he is in *England, France* and *Turky*, and yet the very same in *France* as in *England*, and in *England* as in *France*: in Heaven as in Hell, and in Hell as in Heaven: in the Devils as in the Angels, and in the Angels as in the Devils: So that though there be to most of the Creation, Lords many, and Gods many, a God that takes care of the godly, some few, and they are his own, and forsakes all the rest as not his, *viz.* the wicked: And another God *viz.* the Devil that takes care of them, and feeds them, yet to these there is but one God, who feeds and cloths the wicked, causing his Sun to shine, and his rain to fall upon them; nay more, he that only leads them up, and takes them by the hand, and carries them up to the life of drinking, whoring, cursing, swearing, damning, so that there is to these men but one God, in them without them, and roundabout them.

2. PRINCIPLE
That this one God is served, and gloriously worshipped
in all, both things and persons.

Here glory lyeth, and is concealed to the most of men, it is coming forth to some, peeping through the lattis, and looking behind the wall; it is above board to others, well, what is it? Thus it is, the swearer serves God, the poor ignorant dark drunkard and Atheist serves God though he knows him not, the theif, the whoremonger serves God, all but he serves him ignorantly, as *Paul* said, *He whom ye ignorantly worship, shew I to you*. True, these poor men serve *God* ignorantly, yet this ignorant serving of *God*, is a sweet, devine and spiritual serving of him; they serve *God* in the spirit, these prophane persons serve *God* devinely; Ah! but how doth this appear? why they do in all these things act, as the most high acts them to, and it is the Lord that leads them up to this life, to this their so dark acting, as to the Creature, and he rejoyces in his own works and that which his own fingers have made, beholding drunkenness, swearing, lying, whoring, theeving, brought forth to light and open view, which he before acted in them; Thus they serve *God* and he serves them, the Lord serves them in moving, acting of them, and they him, in bringing forth those operations, and works of the Lord. And thus he hath made all things for himself, sin for himself, whoredom for himself, uncleanness for himself, yea the wicked to do his dark works, his wrathful furious works, to execute his anger, to cut off and destroy; and these he hath made for the day of wrath, to serve him in Hell, to worship him in the Tavern, in the Ale-house, in a Whore-house; and thus he is in these things served, and yet spiritually. There are others that serve him in these things drunkenness, swearing, lying, whoring, and yet knowingly in light in truth, some that do these things, yet do no evil, acting it in a holy way as holyness, swearing holily, and drinking holily, whoring holily, all is holy, righteous and good that they do, and they meet the Lord in these, and kiss the Lord in these.

Nay further, he is served in unholy, beggerly, cursed praying and preaching, and Church societies; in all these whoredoms and Idolatries he is honored and obeyed, though but ignorantly and darkly: the Lord acts in these men, and they bring forth *God* as a praying *God*, as a *God* of the Churches and Societies, as a *God* of the separation of a few that thus worship him, and the Almighty is frollick and merry, and jocund in these foolish vain things, and the Lord clads himself with these fopperies and fooleries, and comes forth to the people in this gay apparel in this fools coat, and the people admire him and stare upon him, and fall down to him; and thus the Lord is every ways served in all things. The Beasts of the Field, the Fishes of the Sea, the Birds they serve and fall down to this *God*, they feed and nourish man: because they are the living *God*, or the living *God* in them: and they refresh and glad man; the Fruits of the Earth they are all adorned with *God*, and Wine which as it is said 9. *Jud.* 13. glads the heart of *God* and Man.

3. PRINCIPLE
That Good and Evil, are both one joyned hand in hand.

Man, innocent, holy upright man tasting of the tree of knowledg of good and evil, comes to divide and seperate that which *God* has joyned together, and thereby became accursed, calling one holy another unholy, this a good man that an evilman, and so hates the one and loves the other, joyns to the one and seperates from the other: But the holy innocent man knows not, owns not any such distinctions, from whose Throne flyes every unclean and corrupt thing, into which *Jerusalem* enters, nothing that is poluted, defiled, or any lie, any feigned thing, but what is really and truly the holy one, and he is at peace with all without him, with all within him: he is one with sin and sin one with him, sin is beloved of him and that for the Fathers sake; I mean those acts called sin, which are to him pure holy as saith the History, *to the pure all things are pure*, swearing, lying, whoring, these are pure things to him, he knows it not under these denominations or distinctions, he knows these acts as his life, as himself, as one with him; he is of purer eyes then to behold iniquity. These see no evil, all things to them hath the appearance of Cristall glory, transcendent excellency, in the dust doth purity and eternity lie, and thus their dead men shall live; and with this dead body shall arise, and all things shall become new. Oh my friends! my dear hearts all of you, the whole Creation, my Life, my Being; this is the passing away of all old things, and all things becoming new. My dear ones, you wonder at it, you are amazed, no marvel, for these are terrible thundrings and lightnings, unheard of Earth quakes and Heaven quakes; this shakes Houses, Families, Wives, Children: surely it is the day of Judgement; the Mountains are flying and the Hils skipping, for who is able to indure his presence. Purity and everlasting Glory shews it self, and who can bear it; the Lyon is eating straw with the Oxe, the Wolf is lying down with the Lamb, the clean hugs the unclean and the unclean the clean, and who can bear it.

4. PRINCIPLE
That God is no respecter of Persons.

The poor and the rich are both made by *God*, the Saint and the sinner they have both one Being, one fountain, one s[o]urce and rise, they are al of one Family. They sit with him, in him at one table, eat the same meat, and drink the same drink one as the other: *God* as sweetly provides for the one as the other, as sweetly loves them, joys in them, delights in them: they are himself, they are not apart from him. The Lord in everlasting love and brightness, damns the Saint and saves the sinner, and again damns the sinner and saves the Saint: cares as little for the praying preaching man the *Pharisee*; *Peter* the Elect as *Judas* the Apostate, Loves *Judas* the Apostate, and *Alexander* the Copersmith who did *Paul* much hurt, yea the cast aways as well every jot, for their is no distinction in him, as he loves the praying man the *Pharisee*, they are all alike to *God*; he beholds all things and persons, with the same and in the same purity, with and in the same glory, all perfect in him, compleat in him, righteous in him, children of pleasure in him: He sees dancing, lying with one another, kissing pure and perfect in him; He loves all with an everlasting love, the theif that goes to the Gallows as well as the Judg that condemns him, and the Judg with a love of and from eternity as well as the theif: He loves as dearly with an infinite unchangeable love the *Cavileer* as the *Round-head*, and the *Round-head* as the *Cavileer*: the *Army* as abundantly as the *Levellers*, and the *Levellers* as the *Army*: For with him is no distinction. He pulleth down the mighty from their Throne, and sets up men of low degree.

5. PRINCIPLE
That the Righteous shall never be saved, that the Godly
shall go to Hell, the Wicked to Heaven.

This may some say, if it can be made out to be a true Principle, is one of the strangest and most uncouth. You have it in your book, he came not to call the Righteous but Sinners to repentance, you have there a hint of it. Salvation is taken by the greatest part of the Creation, to be after death a going to Heaven a place above the skies; Now this I say, such a salvation that you all, or most men whatsoever exspect, the righteous shall never obtain. The truly righteous need not, yea cannot go thither; for they are, and alwaies were in Heaven, yea while they are upon Earth; The righteous that sin not, that are without fault, are ever really and truly before the throne in *God*, and *God* in them, singing for ever *Hallelujah* to the Lord, so that these holy ones enter not into such a vain, empty, foolish, imaginary Kingdom, know not such a Heaven. And the seemingly righteous that know good and evil, that choose the one and hate the other, they neither go to this Heaven and are not thus saved, for they are already in Heaven and know it not, it is with them as with *Jacob*, the Lord was here and I knew it not. There is no Heaven but God and they are in God and God in them, but they know him not, have no experience of him to be their perfection and glory, and therefore these righteous men are (through the ignorance in them) in Hell walking under vain imaginations under earthly fancies, building their hopes, salvation, and all upon the sands, their house is shaken and cannot stand, for it is not founded in God, but in a place above the skies. But the wicked (who to creature apprehensions are so) they that swear, ly, steal and whore, and all in the light of *God*, these go yea are already entred into Heaven, into the perfection of beauty, into eternity, singing to the Lord that liveth and reigneth for ever, while you righteous men are in Hell and at a distance from Heaven, and cannot by all your holiness, prayings, preachings reach this Heaven, this perfection, this joy, but these wicked men as you call them, are singing, rejoycing and feasted with the everlasting feast of fat things.

6. PRINCIPLE.
That they have overcome death, and mortallity is in
them swallowed up into imortallity.

No marvell they are mad men for they are newly come out of their graves, and you are afraid to behold them; ye run away from them as from so many ghosts and spirits. They are passed from death to life, they can dy no more, they are he that was dead but is now alive for evermore, all mortal dying, perishing things are swallowed up in them, into a living immortal being, their earthliness dark and carnal apprehensions are not, but are drowned and lost in God, and in God are found a new. Horrors and tears of death they all fly before them, the tokens of death are all overcome in them. Sorrow is a token of death, they can weep no more, sorrow and sighing is in them past away. Sin is a forerunner to death; this is taken away, they can sin no more. Repentance is propper for dying men mortal Creatures, this is also taken away, repentance is hid from their eyes, they do not anything worthy of repentance, they are past repentance. Shame that is propper to mortal Creatures, those that are under death and sin, this flyes before them, they are not ashamed of ought they do: they are naked as *Adam* and his wife was in Paradise and are not ashamed, they are past shame. They have overcome all things, and now inherit all things, all things are theirs: They one with every thing, and every thing one with them: destruction is their salvation, and damnation is their blessing: Hell their Heaven; and thus they plague death, play with death and laugh with death: and terrifie death that hath terrified the whole creation. These are the new creatures, they are past dying, perrishing or rotting, all things in them are rotted damned and plagued already, whatever thing it be that is under death, or borders upon it cannot come near their Tabernacle. They are now nothing else but a blessing, a sweet favor, a sweet smell to all, in all, upon all: they are the life of all. All their garments smell of myrh, alloes and cassia, and their feet stand upon the Mount of *Olives*: They have trampled down every thing that was above them, and they are now ascended far above all Heavens. The resurrection though it was not in *Pauls* time; yet to these men it is past already, and they have hereby overthrown the faith of many, of all: and they live by sight, by a pure perfect enjoyment, and beholding of that eternal glory which is themselves, they purely wrapt up into it, and it into them: and upon these is brought to pass that saying is written, Death is swallowed up into victory: O death where is thy sting: O grave where is thy victory.

7. PRINCIPLE
That being in Heaven, (the light, glory, and perfection
of God) these neither marry nor are given in mariage.

You know upon what occasion this was spoken in the History; that when the people carnally questioned things in the resurrection, who should own her that had owned so many? the answer was, There was no such owning, marrying or giving in marriage in that world: observe the words, *Luk. 20.34,35. The children of this World, marry wives and are married.* The sons of darknesse, the sons of men of earthly low enjoyments, they that live in the twilight marry, take one woman, two or three or a few apart from the rest of the Creation, love them at a distance from others: those whom they have thus elected and chosen, have their hearts desires and affections, goods, body and all, but they are estranged to the other part of the world, who are really theirs, flesh of their flesh, and bone of their bone as they: but those who shall be accounted worthy to enjoy that world, the world to come, and the resurrection from the dead, *viz.* dead carnall cursed apprehensions and concernments, never marry, never joyn and disjoyn, never love one and hate another, never affect one dearly and the other overly, but have the same pure, perfect, entire love to one as the other. These mad Crew are come to the great Supper, to the great Feast, to the great marriage, and there is heard at this wedding, nothing but sweet melody, singing and dancing, no noise or confusion, but only the voice of the Bride and the Bridegroom, the Lamb and the Lambs wive, and yet but one, and one voice: There is here at this wedding many thousands, and yet but one: there are threescore Queens, and fourscore Concubines, and Virgins without number, yet my beloved is but one. These creatures are married all, to every woman is their wife, not one woman apart from another, but all in one, and one in all: There is not this voice heard at this feast, whose wife is this woman, and whose that? and whose husband is such a one? for there is but one Husband, and one Wife: and this man and wife, though made up of many thousands, ly with one another every night, the bed is large enough to hold them all; it is not such a bed that you have heard to be at Ware, where twenty can ly in it, but a sweet bed made of Roses and Spices, large enough, where millions of millions can all stretch themselve on it, and yet it is but one stretching, one stretched, one loving, and one loved: the same kissing, and the same kissed, and all creatures are singing and dancing at this wedding: there is never a creature in heaven and earth but dances and leaps from that fulnesse of joy that is in him living in this house, and being made one of this family. These scorn the thoughts of Adultery, abhor and loath it as one of the abhominations that are spued out of their mouth. There is such a unity where there is this diversity, and such a diversity where there is this unity, that they cannot kisse one but they kisse all, and love one but they love all, and cannot take one into bed with them and leave out another, but they destroy this unity and diversity. They have attained the resurrection from the dead, yea from that death which saith, these twain, these two, such a one, and such a one, and they are come to this life that in power faith, they shall be no more twain, but one flesh; note the word, they were twain, a man and a woman, the marrying and the married before the resurrection, when God was locked up in some certain things, when Christ was in the Heavens, which must contain him for a time, but now they are risen from the dead they twain shall be one flesh, one body, one life, one spirit. The people in England shall not be one, and the people in France another, the people in Turky one, and the people in Christendom (as it is called) another: but the people in England France and Turkey, one people and one body, for where the one lives there liveth the other also. Therefore you that are the children of this world condemn not the children of the world to come as to you, but come already to these people. These people are entered into heaven, attained this resurrection, are entered into this land of Canaan: you are yet in the wildernesse some of you, others of you come to the borders, envy not them that are entered in, but follow those who through faith and patience have attained the Crown, and speak not evil of the things you know not.

PRINCIPLE VIII
They hold all things common, and truly enjoy all things
in common.

They on whom the sprinklings of the spirit fell, were (as saith the Scripture, which you professe to own) made to see and act in this Communitie, *Act. 2.44.* nay, they called nothing they possessed their own: O you Independents, Anabaptists, so called, Spiritual Notionists, that say you own and beleeve this to be true: you hypocrites why do you call any thing your own? why do ye say so much mony I have, so much land, so many children, such a woman is my wife, so many hundred pounds for such a childe, so many for such a childe? is this to make all things common? canst thou not yet see the earth to be the Lords, and the fulness thereof? then what hast thou? hast thou ever a childe that is not the Lords childe? or ever a wife that is not the Lords wife, or any land, or money that is not the Lords? then why is *Esau's* voice heard among you? and why do you with him sell your birthright for a mess of pottage? you sell your right to all things for some poor unworthy things? for some few poor unworthy things? why do ye rejoyce that you have so many hundreds, or so many thousands, if all be the Lords? and that you will now sit down and take no further care, for you have so much mony, and so much land that will maintain you and yours as long as you live, if all this land and mony be the Lords? you will say, Why we did never deny but that all we have is the Lords, and that to him we are beholden for every thing we have: well then saith the Lord, you have said, O that there were in you such a heart to do whatever you have said: you have well spoken, I wish it were as well practised. Well then, I your Lord and God, your Creator and Father, who am in all the Being, and Life of all, who am all that any man is, all that every man is: who have made man my Tabernacle and dwelling place, and in man am come forth, and do in them say, in the poor of the earth, in you out-cast brethren and sisters, your own flesh, in these do I say, Come give me your mony, your land, your wives and children, let it be their land, mony, wives and children as well as yours, and yours as well as theirs; call it our mony, our wives, our children, our Table, our meat, our drink: let me the Lord, in such a rogue, theef and adulterer, sit at your Table, and eat your meat, and drink your wine, and say to them, All that I have is yours, keep not back part, remember *Lots* wife, remember the man and the woman that lyed to the Holy Ghost; you say you have nothing but what is the Lords, and I the Lord come to you for my own, and ye keep it back: O ye hypocrites ye do but dissemble in all this; you honour me with your mouths, but your hearts are far from me. But these people whom ye call mad, have learned this Wisdom, yea this wisdom is theirs and lives in them, and saith, what is mine is every ones, and what is every ones is mine also: every woman is my wife, my joy and delight, the earth is mine, and the beasts on a thousand hills are mine: they have brought all they have, and have laid all down at the Lords feet, and if any keep back part he is accursed, they have not so learned Christ as to disown the Lord in any thing, in any poor dispised rogue. If any be in want in misery, let him be what he will be, he seeth his fathers name on him, the whole family of Heaven and earth is named of him and by him, therefore saith he come take thine own mony, thy own bread, thy own drink, thou shalt ly with me, and I will ly with thee, eat with me, and I will eat with thee: O there is meat enough in our fathers house, and shall we perish for hunger? it is a full house, a rich house, full of all fat things, why should we then dy by staying without, by living in a far country? we have lived in a country that hath been barren, dry, fruitless, that hath born fruit to some, to a few, but hath brought forth bryars and thorns to the rest; but we will arise and joyn our house to the fruitfull field, in whose earth there is no bryars nor thorns, but fruit enough for the whole family be it never so great. And to this Jerusalem and mount Syon are these people come, and in this land are these mens habitations found: These are they that have done the work of the Lord, and the will of the Lord, not because it is written without them, but because it is written within them, saying, Love not in word or in tongue, but in deed and in truth: there is that within them that will not suffer them to be at rest, untill they have slain all the Amalekites, and all the beasts and oxen, the fat ones as well as the lean ones, and this obedience (my friends) is better then Sacrifice. There are a people great Professors, that can say, I have done all the commandments of the Lord, and yet have not slain all as the Lord hath commanded, nor gon and sold all, but have reserved part to themselves, but from such have I this very day rent the Kingdom.

PRINCIPLE IX.
That their Counsel shall stand, and they will do all their
pleasure.

Sweet hearts, did my dear ones my brethren the Jews, that crucified Christ, think that he did whatsoever he was pleased to do, and do you my hearts of Gold that crucifie Christ now he is risen up, and come again in the clouds, even as he went from us, that he doth whatsoever he pleases to do. These men are so purely made one with God, and God one with them, they in God and God in them, that nothing stands but what is by them decreed to stand, and nothing fals but what is by them voted to fall. By this mad Crew do Kings reign, and Princes decree Justice. If the Lord in the ministry of Angels will preserve *Lot*, though the Sodomites would break open dores, and destroy *Lot*, yet shall his councel stand, and they shall be blinded, as to that work. If the Lord again in *Shimet*, will curse *David*, *David* shall not (though he hath thousands with him) go and destroy *Shimet*, but quietly submit, saying, Let the Lord do what he will. It is the pleasure of this mad Crew sometimes to give their back to the smiters, and their cheeks to those that pluck off the hair: and at another time to be in the fire and it shall not burn them, nor a hair of their head cinged. If you afflict and imprison their forms, they are well pleased, for their own arm hath done it: and if you lay not a hand on them, it is as well, for their power would not suffer it? if you be gathered together to crucifie the holy child Jesus, it is because their councel and hand hath determined it before to be done. Their will is become so much the Lords, and the Lords theirs, that they will what they will, and do what they will. And it is so decreed in Heaven, and in this great Councel, that you Independents, Anabaptists and Spiritual Notionists, must with men of all forts and ranks, do the will of these Rogues,

Theeves, Whore-masters and Drunkards, as you call them. And when you pray, Thy will be done, you pray (though ignorantly and unknown to your-selves). Let the will of those we persecute, hate, and falsly call Drunkards, Swearers, Whore-masters, be done, and nothing else but their will. When you say, and that fervently, Father, glorifie thy will; you say, Father, gloryfie the will of these whore-masters, Drunkards and unclean persons: I tell you my friends, you know not what you say; but he whom ye ignorantly worship shew I to you: you know not the holy one, you pray to: would you see this as true without you, as these men do within them? read *Job.* 17.2. Christ praying before that the will of God might be done, and that he would do so & so, as you may read at large in the chapter comes at last to this perfection & height of glory, I will that thou honourest these poor creatures I have prayed for, with the same honour as I have and had before the world began, and be where I am: and where was he but in God, in perfection? and as saith, *vers. 2.* That they may be one in us, I in them, and thou in me, that they may be made perfect in one, There is also no more twain, but one, no more two wills, but one. And this man Christ with his disciples was called, and that by the Church by the pro-fessors a wine-bibber, a drunkard, a devil. These men whom ye call mad, are Christ the anointed of God; they have the fulness of the Godhead bodily, in them is hid the treasures of all wisdom and knowledge, and these shall judge the world, yea Angels: these are they that shal (yea doth) condemne you and blesse you, that make you do their will, and give you power, as enabling you thereto.

And thus I have given you a discovery of the principles and ways of this mad Crew, and under these heads ly many others, of which you have a taste, which for brevities sake I have not singled out: but I have herein born tes-timony to them and their waies, and saved myself, and those that hear me. Now followeth a true testimony of that unspeakable joy that I have found in this appearance.

> *A true Testimony of that unspeakable and everlasting*
> *joy that the Author of this book hath found in this*
> *strange and unheard of appearance, and he hath hereby*
> *made to pass over into the good land Canaan*
> *that flows with milk and hony.*

It pleased the Lord who became a child in me, for certain reasons and times to train me up in childish things, where I was pleased with his back parts; and as his glory passed by me to stand in the cleft of the rocks: for it was enough being a child, that we played Bo-peep, I thought it then enough that in name and declaration my sinnes were all forgiven me, and cast into the sea, so coun-ters were then to me as good as gold. And truly I must needs say that I had great joy and satisfaction in this estate, and I was very rich, especially in my own childish eyes; but I was at length brought to see that riches would not avail in the day of wrath: for a day since (one day being now with me as a thousand years, and a thousand years as one day) the day of Gods wrath and vengeance fell upon me, and burnt up all my childish things, and there was such an everlasting fire about my ears that I could keep nothing I had, but was burnt up both body and soul with all that I had, righteousness, holiness, preaching, teaching, prayers, wife, children and all that I had, by this fire I then (by God) began to be plagued with my holiness and my prayers became sin to me and all things else a burden, and whatever I kept back as I did for a time (until the fire burnt it all up) did torment and plague me: my former joyes became my sorrows and my pleasure torment, and I was a spectacle to my self and all about me. I wondered where I was and I fell down dead, and the power of God set me on my feet; I had a great mind to keep somewhat back, and would fain have clad my self with some outwardly holy garments, but so pure and fervent was the fire, that it would let nothing remain. My fleshly holiness and civil conversation me thought was such an ornament that I said with *Peter, Lord thou knowest that I have not to this day eaten anything that is common or unclean*, I had never sworn, bin drunk, or given to any outward prophaness or loosness in all my life; and now Lord must I now joyn myself to these unholy things, but that within me said, call not thou any thing common or unclean, for I have made all things clean for thee, and the fire was so great that it burnt up all I had in these everlasting burnings, and divine purity, and then I looked and could see nothing but purity: I did then see purity and glory in all those things I formerly called impurity and prophanness, and I was made silent and obedient to the heavenly voice, and I had then but one eye and one pure sight given me, by which I saw all things pure to me, and the things I formerly washed my hands of could I now touch, and I could play with everything as with my life and being, and saw all things reconsiled to me and I to it. I did then really see a Nation born at once, and the *Gentles* flowing in to behold this my glory and brightness. Then *Gentelism* became to me as good as *Judisme* or *Christianisme*, I could then be feasted with the Lord wherever he appeared, and he was alwaies at my right hand. I was entred into the perfection of all things, of all happiness: my course was finished and I have obtained the Crown. I had many reasonings and disputings with myself, what should become of myself and of all that appertained to me, why I should thus leave all the credit and glory I had in the world, and why I might not keep it for a while and by means covertly to bring in others, and that by this great forsaking of all things, I might offend many and cause many to stumble: but the Sun went down upon all these reasonings, and they were all answered and found in everlasting glory and purity and whatever; yea a thousand times more that ever I have lost have I found in God. I further reasoned age, but I might repent of these things when it is to late, and I were better to consider before hand what I did, then at last to repent, but I found that within me saying, repentance is hid from my eys, I can repent and weep no more, and from that time have I bin filled with the everlasting fulness of the Lord, and the Rivers of that pleasure have and do flow in upon me; The Sun hath bin ashamed and the Moon abashed in me, for he is reighning for evermore, nay in outward sporting, dancing, playing, and kissing and bodily embracing one of another have I clearly seen him that is invisible. There hath bin to me such a harmony, such a oneness, such a devine glory presented to me under all these, that I have wondred where I have bin, when I beheld eternity living in such vanity, blessedness in such cursing, (as it was once to me) and I have bin made to see a blessing in everything. The earth hath ceased bringing forth Bryars and Thorns to me, and the curse to me is taken away. I have sometimes since then bin (as I have formerly called it) unclean, and yet never more clean, uncivil and yet never more civil, I have bin since then a great transgressor, and yet never a less transgressor; I have acted it in such purity in such a devine way, that I have not known it by its name of impurity or unholiness, it hath all bin risen in me to an immortal and incorruptible being: so that, though it was sowen in weakness, yet it was raised in power, sowen in corruption but it hath bin raised in incorruption. The time will fail me to tell you of the day that I live in that hath no night, of the glory that hath no end, of the Sun that never goes down, of the darkness that is with me as light, and sin that is with me as righteouness, how my soul hath bin and is seated with these things, and how the vail and covering over my face hath bin rent in twain; I cannot utter it in words for it is unspeakable, I cannot clear it up to your apprehensions, for it passeth knowledg, it pleaseth me that I am in it, and it pleaseth me also that you are for a time out of it, (though were not wishing ceased in me) I could heartily wish you were in the same glory with me. It is enough at present that I give you to understand where I am, and where I am there shall ye be also, for in my Fathers house there are many Mansions. To draw to an end, I am endless, my glory is endless, my joy is endless, my life is endless, could I exchange it for all the world, pleasures, joys and delights thereof; yea for all the joys of childish lights and understandings, yet by Gods life I would not but I would scorn the thought of taking Brass for Silver and Iron for Gold, I am where I would be, and where I would be there I am, I have lost all things, and I have found all things, my loss hath bin my gain, and my death my life. I am come to the spirits of just men, made perfect, to *Abrahams* Spirit, to *Moses* Spirit, *Davids* Spirit, *Daniels, Pauls* and *Johns* Spirit, I familiarly talk with them and they with me; and therefore *Hallelujahs* to the Lord that liveth and reighneth for evermore.

The POSTSCRIPT, directed to all Nations.

You the Nations of the World, though to me but one Nation, and one people, I have a long time been silent in Puritanisme, Presbyterianisme, Independensie, Anabaptisme, and Spiritual Notionisme; but now in the last of these days am I made to stand upon my feet, and to curse and damn the inhabitants of the World, until there be but one inhabitant, and till there be but a man left in all the earth, who is, was, and shall be the glory of the Woman. I will now ly openly before the Sun, with many women, and yet with my own Wife, and I will plague even bitterly, they that ly with any save their own Wives in the dark, in their thoughts and desires, in their words, I will make them gnaw their tongues, and gnash their teeth for pain, who pretend to be holy and not to touch a Woman, and yet can and sometimes have layen with Women in the dark: yea you that never did it actually, but in thought and desire, you have committed Adultery before me, and for it shall ye be damned. O you hypocrites you can spend your selves to the full, as oft as your lust carries you out, upon one Woman called your Wife, and there do as much as any Whore-master in the World upon many Women, and this is no sin, no pollution, ye hypocrites hath he not made of one blood all Nations? are they not one Flesh, one Body? what difference is there between your wife and another woman? O, you say you are married to your wife, and that is no evil: Why, what is marriage? is it any more but to gain the love and affections of a woman to be yours to serve, you and to declare this openly? this is your marriage. Well then if I the lord in a man gain the love, affections and desires of all women, and make them sweetly to serve me, and have done so ly with them all, and use them as oft as I please, and set not up an idol in my heart, by having one woman only, damning and cursing and estranging myself from all other women, is not this the truest marriage? Further, you of the Churches, you Seekers, you men that scorn the thoughts of Adultery, I will make you come and worship me, and fall down at my feet, and know that I love rogues, theeves, whore-masters, and your wives also, when they shall before you commit whoredom. Nay you all pure holy Church-men, you shall lie with many women, with any woman, or be plagued bitterly when you see me your Lord whoring in every corner in every street, for who art thou that despisest the day of small things; yet I will not make this or any thing else the place of my residence, for I will not stay in any one thing, but I will be universally and powerfully in all things. Yet further, I will damn you that can swear before a Magistrate, and that you call holy, though it is written in your book Swear not at all, and can condemn swearing before the great Magistrate and God of Heaven. O ye hipocrites, you swear and rant it out in my presence daily, I hear your inward blaspheming and cursing me, that am risen up a holy generation of men, that can sin no more. I hear your murmurings at me, and I will come down from Heaven, for so I must tell you, ye carnal hearts, for you think me to be above the Skies, I say I will come down and make you know who you murmur against, that all your railings, cursing, swearings, are at me. Ye Churches, ye Seekers, are the veriest Devils and prophanest wretches in the world; you have sworn, committee adultery before me, in your hearts, time after time; yea thou Preacher and thou great Prophet, I have seen thee (though thy neighbours never did) lie with twenty women in one night, nay in one hour, nay in one moment, in they thoughts and desires. I could tell you of your cheating and cozening the people in your Shops, and your theeving and lying, and this you can digest, because no eye sees you, and because of the great gain accrewing thereby. I know what whorish voice in you that cries Stolen waters are sweet, and bread eaten in scret is pleasant. But I spare you until the day which is at the very dores, that shall burn as an Oven, and all the proud and all that do wickedly shall be burnt up, and as fuel to the fire. I leave you, and remain caught up into the Lord.

2. The Ranters Religion *(11 October 1650) E.619 (8)*

The Ranters Religion.

Χ OR,

A faithfull and infallible Narrative of their damnable and diabolical opinions, with their deteſtable lives & actions.

With a true diſcovery of ſome of their late prodigious pranks, and unparalleld deportments, with a paper of moſt blaſphemous Verſes found in one of their pockets, againſt the Majeſty of Almighty God, and the moſt ſacred Scriptures, rendred *verbatim.*

Publiſhed by Authority.

London, Printed for *R. H.* 1650.

An Advertisement to the Reader

He that labours, sayd the old Hermites, is tempted but by one Devill: hee that is idle is assaulted by all: if Iron had reason, it would choose rather to be used in labour, then to grow rusty in a corner: That idlenesse is the mother of all mischiefe was never so evidently proved, as by the monstrous production of a Sect, but of novell growth, yet now strangely prevalent amongst us, called Ranters, *a people so dronish, that the whole course of their lives is but one continued Scene of Sottishness, their jestures filthy, their words obsceane, and blasphemous, and all their deeds which they wretchedly glory in, impious, and horrid: I beseech thee, good Reader, to peruse this Pamphlet as thou wouldest* Aretines *Pictures, with a will to know such filthinesse, that thou mayest be incited the more heartily to abominate it.*

Farewell.

The Ranters Religion, &c.

The Stoicks (among many other excellent contemplations) in the discourse of joy came the nearest to divine truth, when they put a maine and reall difference between *laetari & gaudere*, mirth and joy, the former is a light and toyish passion, which stirreth the spleen, skipping up (in wanton maner) into the face, the latter is a continuall exaltation of the soule in the enjoyment of some excellency; mirth is a suddain or short fit raised by some pleasant or ridiculous accident, joy is a setled and constant delight, by the presence of some possessed good; mirth (such as that of our new Gnosticks at this present) is ever in the sensuall appetite; joy is onely from the soule and will, from which inference they drew that admirable Paradox *(scoft at by the other Philosophers) that a wise man only rejoyceth truely, though a foole be alwayes more merry, for this St. Augustine found* warrant in Scripture, *non est gaudium impiis,* the wicked can never truely rejoyce, and he addes the reason, *quia essunduntur, &c.* because they are ever restlesse, ever wandring from themselves; I have beene something prolix in this exordium, as well to satisfie some, as to undeceive others; the first standing in admiration to see how harmoniously these Gnosticks, or Ranters deport themselvs one towards another (being in continuall exaltations & jollities) the second being willing to believe that so pleasing a Symphony cannot proceede from that Master of misrule, *Belzebub,* but by an heavenly influence, *&c.* but I have satisfied them, I hope, that the rejoycings of these Ranters is meerely sensuall and devillish, and with St. *Augustines* warrant, that they are of their Father the Devill, whose workes they doe.

These Ranters are but the Gnosticks of former Ages brought backwards amongst us, these are but the same with those of old, whose description *Epiphanius* gives us, who had only certaine Dictates and Positions, and peremptorily affirmed, that let them live as they listed, they were sure to be saved; so far these are stampt with the old *Impressa,* but our Gnosticks cannot content themselves in such bounds and limits, they affirme that God is so far from being offended at the crying sins of drunkenes, swearing, blaspheming, adultery, &c. that he is well pleased therewith, and that [O strange and horrid impiety!] it is the only way of serving him aright: all true Christians know that it is not lawfull for them to flatter themselves with any thing of their owne judgement, nor to adhere to that which any man brings in of his owne head; we have the patterne of the Apostles to imitate, who tooke no thing to bring in after their owne pleasure, but faithfully assigned to the Nations that they had received of Christ; where on the contrary these licentious Sciolists affirme, that each whimsey, each motion, whether to sweare, to whore, yea to commit incest or buggery, is of God, and proceeds from him, hee being the Authour, Orderer, and Origen of it; a Doctrine which the very Divels sure would tremble to heare.

The very Heathen by Phylosophy and the scale of the creatures have asccended so high, as to the knowledge of one supreame Deity, this the course of nature taught them, (for indeed the whole world is nothing else but a Commentary or paraphrase of the Deity) and to that omniscent ever living power, they ascribed all purity & sanctity, proclaiming him to be the Patron of all vertue, and punisher of all vice; and therefore these Monsters come short of the very Heathen, while they make the Almighty not only the Countenancer, which but to immagine is damnable blasphemy, but the efficient cause of sin, and dare impiously to affirm, that that man who tipples deepest, swears the frequentest, commits Adultery, Incest, or Buggery, the oftenest, Blasphemes the Impudentest, and perpetrates the most notorious crimes with the highest hand, and rigidest resolution, is the dearest Darling to Heaven.

The Heads of their damnable Errors, and horrid Blasphemies.

They Believe (and these are the wisest sort of them) that a Resurrection is possible, and that there may be a Restitution of our bodies, but then they say that the Starres and Plannets, by whose decay and continuance they measure the perpetuity and stability of all sublunary things to be the only causes of it, and so they run giddily into *Plato's* circumvolution of yeares.

2. They affirme that all Women ought to be in common, and when they are assembled altogether (this a known truth) they first entertaine one another, the men those of their own sex, and the Women their fellow females: with horrid Oathes and execrations, then they fall to bowzing, and drinke deep healths (Oh cursed Caitiffes!) to their Brother God, and their Brother Devill; then being well heated with Liquor, each Brother takes his she Otter upon his knee, and the word (spoken in derision of the sacred Writ) being given, *viz. Increase and Multiply:* they fall to their lascivious imbraces, with a joynt motion, &c.

3. They affirme, that there be three keyes that God alwaies keepes in his owne hands; the Key of the wombe whereby he lets us into this world; the Key of Liberty, whereby he Authorizes us to fulfill our owne Lusts, and sensuall

appetites, opening the doores of liberty and licentiousnesse, which were fast locked to the men of former ages, sure, to his prayse and glory. Their opinion about the Resurrection of the body is so strange, and withall so absurd, that I must by no meanes omit to recite it.

4. They tell you there is a certaine little bone in every mans back that shall never be subject to any putrefaction, and this bone, say they, at the last day shalbe molified and softned by a Dew from Heaven, and it shall swell, having the nature of leaven, and it shall diffuse its virtue to the collecting of all the dust that belongs to its owne body, and prepare it for a Resurrection.

5. They maintaine, that to have their women in common is their Christian liberty, and very prettily, indeed la, that that Sister among them who can make the beast with two backs the most strenuously, *viz.* entertaine most men longest, and oftenest, hath a sufficient canonization for a Saint triumphant. This they frequently, and with much fervency affirme.

These Beasts of *Ephesus* doe not tremble over a pint pot, or in the parenthesis of a whiff of Tobacco, to vaunt blasphemously their insatisfaction in matters of Religion, and with the execrable and ridiculous solecism of *God Dam me*, dare at the same article of time send challenges to reason, to prove there is a God, and the Scriptures are but a meer Romance, a Chimera, &c.

One of them (lately in my hearing) disputing with a Gentleman (who as all good Christians ought, was very zealous in the defence of the most sacred Scriptures) about the blessed Virgin *Mary*, our Redeemers mother, according to the flesh, had this most impious quere.

If she descended of the seed of *Adam*, said he, then the infection of originall sin must needs devolve into her, ifshe did not descend from *Adam*, then is she not the seed of *Abraham*, nor of the seed of *David*, nor by consequence of our Saviour, nor are the Genealogies of the Scriptures truely delivered: O most horrible blasphemy!

These most impious, blasphemous, and divelish Verses were found in the pocket of one of the prime Ranters, who is at this time in Bridewell, (condoling his condition over sacred hempe,) which I will here set downe to the end the whole Kingdome may be made sensible what Vipers are sheltred in their bosome.

> *They talke of God (believe it fellow creature)*
> *Theres no such Bugbeare, all was made by nature,*
> *And then, the Rabbies that do rule the rost*
> *Do babble of a Son and Holy Ghost.*
> *God have a son? Why sure that Son must needs*
> *Beget another (nature alwayes breeds)*
> *His Son a Son, so a whole Generation*
> *of Gods and Goddesses by procreation:*

> *And then (forsooth) a Holy Ghost proceeds*
> *From that great God, who comforts us, and feeds*
> *our soules with heavenly manna: O such lies*
> *Cannot be found in any Histories,*
> *Save in that booke of fallacies, they name*
> *The Bible, which from some fooles fancy came.*
> *We know all came of nothing, and shall passe*
> *Into the same condition once it was*
> *By natures power, and that they grossely lie,*
> *That say theres hope of Immortality.*
> *Let them but tell us what a soule is, then*
> *Wewill adhere to these mad brain-sick men.*

This damnable Atheisme some of them are so bold as to aver, many of them being arived at that height of incorrigible madnesse and abominable impudence, that they fear not (in all companies where they come) to contest that all things were made by nature, that mans soule dies with his body, that the Scriptures are meere lies and tales, &c.

One of these Roysters sitting over his cups (with the rest of his companions) evacuating *wind backward, used this blasphemous expression, let everything that hath breath, praise the Lord.*

Another of them taking a piece of boyled beefe betwixt his hands, and tearing it in pieces, gave part thereof to one of his companions, using these words (in derision of the blessed Sacrament) the body & blood of our Lord Jesus Christ.

A shee Ranter said openly in the hearing of many, (a friend of mine accidentally one of them) that she should thinke her selfe a happy woman, and should esteeme her selfe a superlative servant of Gods, if any man would accompany with her carnally in the open Market place.

O wretched people! O monstrous Times! I pray God put it into the hearts of our vigilant Senators (as they have already begun to suppresse this most blaspheamous, impious Sect) to go thorow with it, and to make these Monsters of mankind, examples to the whole world, the frame of these Schismaticks (or rather cico-Demons) is already out of joynt, one pull more, and their machine come in pieces about their eares; such Devils clad in flesh are not fit to have subsistance amongst those who boast themselves Christians, but merrit (as unsavoury salt) to bee thrown out, and to betrodden under foot of men.

FINIS

3. The Routing of the Ranters *(19 November 1650) E.616 (9)*

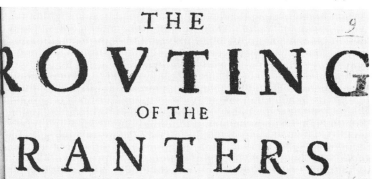

THE

ROVTING

OF THE

RANTERS

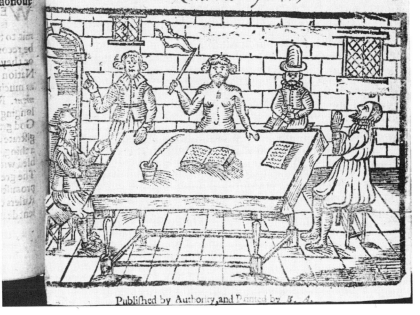

a full Relation of their uncivil carriages, and blafphemous words actions at their mad meetings, their feveral kind of mufick, dances, and ryotings, and belief and opinions concerning heaven and hell. With their examinations taken before Juftice of Peace, and a Letter or Summons fent to their fifters or fellow creatures in the name of the Divel, requiring them to meet *Belzebub, Lucifer, Pluto*, and twenty more of infernall fpirits at the time and place appointed. Alfo, a true defcription how they may be known in al companies and the names of the chief Ring-leaders of this new generation that all all others in wickednefle.

Novemb: 19 1650

Publifhed by Authority, and Printed by J. C.

The Ranters Ranting:
or
A true Relation of a sort of People called
Ranters, with some of their abominable and wicked carriages,
and behaviour at their private meetings.

I shall in the first place give you, my friends, a brief Character of a sort of people (whereof you desire satisfaction) newly sprung up among us, called Ranters, *alius* Coppanits, or Claxtonians, the most vile and abhominable Apostates, that we ever read or heard of, carrying about them the lively image of Satan in his Serpentine colours of seducing and drawing men and women to commit all manner of mad and desperate wickednesse (as the Apostle faith) with greedinesse. I cannot term these persons to be of any Sect, for that I do not learn, either in profession or practise, they do any thing that hath the least stamp or tincture of that which may be rightly called religion. For to rip open, and make known to the world the abominable words and practises of these people, would fill up more paper then I have allotted hereunto; and to repeat many things which I am confident might be said without wronging the truth, would make your ears tingle to hear, and my self blush to think or write; yet it is conceived usefull and profitable to many, that some of their deeds of darknesse should be brought forth into the light, to the end, that such as are weak and apt to be drawn aside by every wind of vanity, may be deterred from coming into such company, and with such a one not to eat; for if the Apostle forbids the Gentiles (Christians) not to eat with the heathens of that time, surely the same precept extends to the restraining men, that have any spark of goodnesse, from accompanying themselves with such as are far worse than any heathen or infidels we read of then, or have heard of since; being such as (quite contrary to the rule of St. *Paul*,) delight not onely in gluttony and drunkennesse, chambering and wantonnesse, and the like, but deride the holy Scriptures, deny Christ, blaspheming, and as it were spit in the face of God himself: for one of them being discoursing at the Spittle said, that he knew not any difference betwixt God and the Divell; and being then asked what he thought of the Divell, he answered that it was an old woman stuffed with parsly: to be short, I am credibly informed, that some of these deny the immortality of the soul, and so holding forth an opinion that there is neither heaven nor hell, it is no wonder that they should fall into all kind of vices, that they commit iniquity by a law. The chief Ringleaders of this viperous generation, are one *Copp* and *Claxton*, of whom I shall say more hereafter, *Copp* is in Newgate, the other is also a prisoner, this *Copp* being lately brought before a Committee to be examined, feigned himself mad, used strange kind of uncouth behaviour, throwing nutshels and other things about the room, and talked to himself when questions were put to him, which some thought to be Gods just judgement upon him, and others were of opinion that (as *David* in another case) he meerly acted the part which at length will no way stand him in stead.

Having given you a general description of them, I shal in the next place come to speak of some of their particular meetings: the first that I have heard of to be frequented by this brutish sort of people, was about Shoemakers Alley where after a while, notice was taken, and some discovery made, by such as had been amongst them, rather to observe their vanities, than to be imitaters of their vices, which caused them shortly after to remove to anotherplace. This time of meeting began about four of the clock in the afternoon, and was continued by some until nine or ten of the clock the next day; which time was spent in drunkenness, uncleanness, blasphemous words, filthy songs, and mixt dances of men and women stark naked.

Not long after, they had another place of meeting about *White Chappel*: where after a time they were discovered by the Officers of the place, who with a guard repaired to the house where they were: and to the end that none might make an escape, the business was carried with such secrecie, that it was not known to others till they came to the door, where these monsters of mankind were associated; which the Officers had no sooner entred, but they found some of these lascivious beasts openly satisfying their lusts. Amongst this company was that *Claxton*, (before mentioned) who with undanted boldness and audacious carriage, spake to the Officers, that came with authoritie to apprehend them, to this effect.

Gentlemen, I perceive you are come to seize on us, your fellow creatures, for what cause I know not; I pray use not any violence, or terrifie and affright those of our fellow creatures here, that are of a weak and tender constitution: if we have offended the Law, we shall readily and willingly submit to be tried by it. And taking up his cloak, he said, *Gentlemen*, I will not leave you, I am ready to go along with you. And forth he went with the first; and as the others were comming forth, (about thirty in number) he framed an excuse to return back again into the house, pretending that he had left something of great use behind him, and so escaped away at a back door; but is re-taken, and at this day in prison.

I cannot learn, that in any of their meetings, they have used exhortations, except such as tend onely to the making of a derision and scoffe, at all that is commended in the holy and sacred Scriptures to be good and holy; despising the word and ordinances, when they hear them spoken of: and their Ringleader, *Copp* (when he was fitter to have gone to bed and slept, than to have spoken in a publick place) bestowed an hours time in belching forth imprecations, curses, and other such like stuffe, as is not fit to be once named amongst Christians: and when he perceived that he should be called to answer for the wicked blasphemies that he had uttered, at sundry times, he took two of his she-Disciples, and went to the Citie of Coventrie, where it was soon dispersed abroad, that he commonly lay in bed with two women at a time:

whereof he being soberly admonished by an Officer of the army, he replied, that it was his libertie, and he might use it; saying further, that unreasonable creatures are not restrained of it. With many other speeches to justifie himself in his ungodly practices, for which he was apprehended and brought up to London, and by the Magistrate committeed to Newgate.

I shall, in the next place, mention something concerning one or two more of their meetings and so leave them. Not long since, a select number of men and women met together at a Tavern, where they were accomodated with the choisest wine, and many delicates; of which being plentifully filled, the women withdrew themselves into another room, and disrobed themselves of the apparel in which they were, and clad themselves all in white (which they call, the Embleme of Innocence;) which no sooner had they done, but there comes in one of the men, and (abusing a text of Scripture) said, Fellow creatures, *what shall we do?* and soon after, the Master and Drawers of the house perceived and heard such disorderly, and uncivil carriage amongst them, that they were desirous to rid the house of them; which some of the younger sort having notice of, put them all into another kind of pashon, and made bold to discover the dissembling faces of some of the female creatures, who let drop some of their hats and black bags to pay the reckoning, and for haste, dropt a paper, which seemeth to be the summons, or invitation of the guests to that meeting, *viz.*

Dear sister and fellow creature, whose sweetnesse we reverence, and whose person we adore, whose witty conceits we admire and whose subtilty we wonder at, we do by this our hand-writing, will and require you, our dearest fellow creature, that you personally appear at the place, where we last had some infernal conference, half an hour past four in the afternoon of this present day; for we have taken notice of the singular, great, and speciall services you have done for inlargement of libertie, since our last actings together, which we doubt not, will much inlarge our power, and preheminence in drawing disciples to us. Hereof you are commanded not to fail, for that Belzebub, Lucifer, Pluto *and above twentymore of the prime officers will attend to give you then and there new documents; and we shall promise, in the word of a King infernal, that you shall raign as a Princesse with us.*

Signed *Diabulo.*

Dated at our new infernall Pallace without *Bishops-gate,* 10 of *Octob.* 1650.

There be copies abroad, of several other papers, which some of them have sent abroad in this nature; but this may be sufficient to declare, what a heighth of wickedness they are grown to, who despise the ways of God, and mock and scoffe at his great and glorious name; and as if that were not enough, they now come openly to side, and as it were personate the Divel himself; which makes me the less marvel at some unheard of words and behaviour that were at another particular meeting, the sixth day of this present November, at the house of one *Middleton*, at the sign of *David and the Harp*, in Moore-lane (whose wife is suspected to be one of them.) To this place a company of them came on the day aforesaid, about five of the clock in the afternoon; but some of the female sex came not, (for at this time the before recited summons was not sent forth;) those that were there first, called for Bread, Beer, and Ale, &c. which was in the house; and as others came in, whether they were men or women, they kist each other, with this expression, *welcome fellow creature*. And when a competent number of them were gotten together, they began to sing filthy bawdy songs, to the tune of *Davids* Psalms; after which, they drank a health to him, in whom they *live, move, and have a being*: this being over, one of them lets fall his breeches, and turning his shirt aside, another of the company runs and kisses, saying, they must all do the like, for it was their fellow creature.

This being done, one of the men took a candle, and went up and down the room, as if he had been feeling of a needle; and after a while, one asked him what he sought after? to whom he answered, *That he looks for his sins, but they were not there, he could find none;* then they returned again to their tuning of lascivious songs or hymns, in the middest of which, the Constable and other Officers came in, and seized on them all, (except Mrs. *Middleton*, and one or two more, who made an escape at the back door,) and carried them before a Justice of Peace, who sent six or seven of them to *Bridewel*; but Mrs. *Middleton*, and another or two that escaped, are so afraid of receiving punishment answerable to these demerits, that they dare not (as yet) remain at their habitations.

When those that were taken came before the Justice to be examined, they would confess nothing of their ways, saying, that they would not accuse themselves. Whereupon, one that was by, asked, what they meant by the fearful execrations of *Ram me, Dam me,* &c. one answered, that by the word, *Ram* they meant God.

Many other questions were also asked them, to which they gave none, or a very frivolous, which amounted to little, but to bring them to the place of their first punishment. I shall therefore hasten to decipher their words and behaviour in publick, to the end, that if any man chance to fall into their company, they may be known and avoided.

And for that this sort of people are dispersed abroad, in the City Country and army, it is necessary that there should be somewhat said to describe them to the end they may be avoided, which by your observation of their words, and actions you may easily do, for although they carry the image and shape of men and women, yet they have the manners onely of a beast.

A Description of the Ranters.

If it be a woman, she speaks highly in commendation of those husbands that give liberty to their wives, and will freely; give consent that she should associate her self with any other of her fellow creatures, which she shall make choice of; she commends the Organ, Viol, Symbal and Tonges in Charterhouse-Lane to be heavenly musick she tosseth of her glasses freely, and concludeth there is no heaven but the pleasures she injoyeth on earth. She is very familiar at the first sight, and danceth the Canaries at the sound of a horn-pipe.

The men for the most part will thwart you in your discourse, especially if you talk of religion, they can discourse of the Scriptures, and turn them to a wrong sence, if you be talking of death, they say, *as a man dieth, so dieth a beast*; they believe all things proceed from nature, and that there is no hell but aches and pains incident to man, and want of mony, which hindereth them of taking their fill of pleasure: and though they hold it convenient to have one woman to dwell constantly with one man, to do his necessary businesse, yet are they of opinion that they may have carnall knowledge of any, and as many other women as their beastly desire can make use of. And in this kind of coupling together (or making a conjunction copulative) the woman doth commonly make choice of the man she will dwell with; and as they slight and contemn all ordinances, so do they that of marriage, yet have they a kind of ceremony to be used for it, concerning which, I shall give you one familiar and merry instance, and to leave them.

A sober man of good fashion, chanced to go to a place, where a Company of them were gathered together at a Conference, onely with a purpose to observe what was said and done; and at the time of their breaking up, or dissolving that meeting, there comes to this man a young woman, and tells him, that she was single, or free to dispose of her self as she pleased, and that she had a liking unto him her fellow Creature, whom she could willingly love and serve, in the neerest relation that a woman could be to a man: which at the first much pleased the party, and after the returne of a Complement, he thought it then his time, to see a little further concerning the temper, and disposition of this bold Creature, so desired her to take part of a pint of Sack, over which they might with the more conveniency inlarge their discourse; which she readily accepted, and to the Taverne they went, and no sooner was the wine brought up, but she calls for a Roll of bread, and holding it forth to the party that was with her said: *fellow Creature, break this* with me, which he did; when you have eaten that part in your hand, and I likewise *this, we are in condition or acceptation of man and wife:* then after some further discourse (he knowing well that he had a wife at home of a gallant spirit, and a lover of virtue) directed her home to his house, where he told her she should find a maid would give her entertainment, while he spake a few words with a Gent. with whom he had earnest businesse; whereupon she went to the house, and asked for the master of the house, and being told he was not within, she said that she would stay his comming, and having some discourse with the maid servant, and perceiving the house well furnished, she could no longer hold, but tels the maid she was her mistresse and all there was hers; which story the maid hasted to tell her mistresse, with whom she had lived many years; who immediately came with a good Broom-Staff, and did so belabour the Gent. that she went away in a worse case then if she had beaten hemp a moneth in Bridewel, a just reward for her bold impudencie, *and I pray God that such as heare this relation, and the wickedness of their ways, may be preserved from following them in the same excess of ryot, that every one may keep a watch over his own ways, for some of those of which I have spoken, have been thought consciencious persons, and had attained to a great measure of knowledge in the ways of God, and if these fall away, let him that standeth take heed least he fall.*

FINIS

4. Gilbert Roulston, The Ranters Bible *(9 December 1650) E.619 (6)*

The Ranters Bible.

O R,

Seven several Religions by them held and maintained.
WITH

The full particulars of their strange Sects and Societies ; their new places of meetings, both in City and Countrey ; the manner of their life and conversation ; their blasphemous Opinions of our Lord and Saviour Jesus Christ, and their burning of his blessed WORD, *and sacred Scriptures ; the names of their new gods, and worshiping of the Sun, and three black Clouds ; with the manner of their idolizing them, North, West, East, and South ; their drinking of healths to the Devill, and disposing of places in Hell ; their blasphemous Creed and Letany ; their Savage Opinion to ly with any mans wife, either in houses, fields, or streets, in the presence of hundreds of people ; their Declaration in Kent ; the apprehending of 30 of them neer Uxbridge, with their trials and examinations, and the rouzing and dispersing the rest of their fellow ranters neer Lin in Norfolk : A strange voice from heaven speaking to one Mr. Roulston, a London-Ranter, upon his going from White-Chappel, to meet some of his fellow-Creatures at Hackney, and the great things that happened thereupon, to the admiration of the Reader : the coming in of 700 since the second of this instant December, their Recantarion, Oath, and Protestation. And Mr. Roulston's Letter to his late fellow-Ranters, with his Advice and Proposals, to be published in all Cities, and Market-townes, throughout England and Wales.*

Published by Mr. *Gilbert Roulston*, a late Fellow-
R A N T E R.

Imprimatur,   J. DOWNAME.

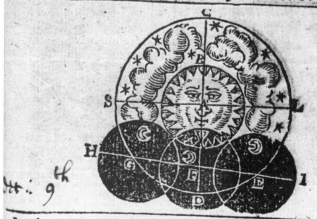

London, *Printed by* J. C. *and are to be sold in* Cornhil, *near the* Exchange, *and at* Temple-Bar, 1650.

The Ranters Bible, &c.

Great are the troubles of this Age, in respect of that persecution on all sides, that hardly one opinion can afford another a good word. And what is the reason of all this? Sure it is not of *God*, but of the Man of sin, who was a murtherer from the beginning: This spirit of persecution hath not ceased to work, since *Adams* fall, going amongst rich and poor, high and low, to set them at variance, and divide them in judgment; and as God is the Authour of all good, so the Devil is the Authour of all evil, being now very busie and active in this Nation, for the depriving of the poor people of their Soul-salvation, sowing the *Atheistical Seed* in the hearts of divers by which meanes they are too prone to fall from their former principles, studying and practising new-found devices, and Hel-bred stratagems, as will appear by this ensuing Relation, wherein is contained a description of the several-Sects, Societies and Factions of the new Generation of those called *Ranters*, both in City and Countrey, and the particulars of their several Tenents, *viz.*

I. *On the 16 of Novemb. 1650. A great Company of these new Generations of Vipers, called* **Ranters** *were gathered together near the* **Soho** *as* **Westminster**, *where they exercised themselves in many royatous and uncivil actions; and after some hours spent in feasting and the like, they stript themselves quite naked, and dancing the* **Adamites Curranto**, *which was, That after 2. or 3. familist Giggs, hand in hand, each man should imbrace his fellow-female, in the flesh, for the acting of that inhumane* **Theatre** *of carnal copulation, which is so gloriously illustrated in the Sacred Scriptures, to be one of the greatest sins, in bringing them to the very brinks of perpetual damnation; in defense of which abominable and lascivious act, they hold it a tenent lawful, to be with any Woman whatsoever: These are a sort of* **Ranters,** *called by the name,* **Of the Familists of Love**, *who would have all things common, and hold it a* **Paradice** *to live so, because their Discipline allowes, to court naked, in which they blush no more, then* **Adam** *at his first Creation,* Gen. 2.5. *This Opinion a native* **German** *first practised in* **Holland, 40.** *years since, and coming over into* **England,** *proved a Diabolical Instrument, in soweing the seed of Sathan, in the hearts of many about* **London,** *telling and perswading them, that it was a great sin to cleave either to one man or Woman, that there was neither God nor Devil, Heaven nor Hell, and that they ought not to worship any thing visible or invisible, but the* **Sun,** *which in this wise, he perswaded them to do; that after they had taken their fill in this [savage] pleasure of Paradice, (as they call it) they should turn themselves* **North, West, East** *and* **South,** *(according to the sign here inserted) and that was a remission, promised, for their inhumane act of* **Ranting.**

II. *Another sort of Ranters are called by the name of Shelomethites who hold swearing but a Complement, and blasphemy a badge of honour, accounting that fellow-Creature, the greatest and most worthy, that can invent the chiefest Oaths. Springing from the bitter and fiery lake of Hell and Pluto: Of this wicked Generation a party of them were lately discovered near* **Uxbridge**, *who upon examination before a Justice* *of Peace, confessed. That they held it lawful so to do, resolutely breaking forth in most bitter and unchristian like language against all those who endeavoured to turn them from these desperate and soul-damning opinion; but since their restraint of liberty, divers of them have detested against this diabolical way, protesting against their infernal tenents, and Hel-bred principles, and utterly disavowing any fellowship or society with them for the time to come; and promising a discovery of all others of the like nature, resident in those parts, or else-where.*

III. *Another sort of Ranters are called by the name of* **Clements,** *who are perswaded that after death (notwithstanding their lascivious actions, as aforesaid) they may repent in the world to come; and that it is then sure enough to seek Gods mercy, which absurd and false Opinion causeth divers, both in City and Country, to attend to this blasphemous Crew and wholly to cast off their blasphemous principles of Christianity, and sobriety of life:* **O the ignorance of these times! that men should fall from the ways of truth and comply with the spirit of darkness.**

IV. *Another sort of Ranters are called by the name of* Athians, *who affirm that when the body dies, the soul perisheth, and both shall be received again at the day of judgement: which Doctrine is something like that which lately possessed divers about* **Lin** *in* **Norfolk,** *who at a meeting the* **17.** *of* **Novemb.** *last would needs take upon them to maintain this point to be just and right; but others of their late Brethren, after a serious and great dispute, wholly denied this tenent, and publickly declared. That in respect of that condition in which the soul is stated, (which being immortal cannot die) shall be increased, but never changed; To which principle above* **100.** *came in, there present declaring themselves enemies to all those who persisted in that blasphemous opinion; insomuch, that some of those that refused to receive conversion, were apprehended; others escaped; but,* **in fine,** *they all received a blow, and were all subdued and routed.*

V. *Another sort of Ranters are called by the name of* **Nicholartanes** *much like the former, who lived promissiously, like Beasts, no man having his own proper wife, but using any Woman at their pleasure, and thirsting after their proprieties and estates: These are not only plunderers, but Robbers of their very skins and bones.*

VI. *These sorts of* **Ranters** *are called by the name of* **Marcious,** *who believe that there are two Gods, one the Authour of all good, the other of all evil things; which Sect* **Paipiripes,** *in his time, called* **The first born of the Devil,** *and in these latter times, too too many hold these erroneous Opinions, there being a Generation sprung up, who have a great respect to observe the traditions of men, but deny Scriptures, holding this dangerous Discipline, (which the mad and ranting* **Ranters,** *calls his* **Bible,)** *That* **Swearing, whoring, Roaring, Revelling, Blaspheaming,** *and the greatest vices they can imagine, are the only actions of honour to bring them to happiness; and in which happiness, they assume to themselves a right, by drinking Healths to the Devil, and casting lots for the disposing of places in Hell; but some amongst the rest, being indu'd with the spirit of Grace, upon the carouzing of the*

Cup about, in like manner aforesaid, at a meeting near the **Wild** *in* **Kent;** *when it came to their turns to drink, refused the same, saying,*
From this wicked Company of Atheists,
And from their wicked plots and conspiracies,
Good Lord deliver us all.

Whereupon this infernal Crew, began to utter many bitter execrations and blaspheaming Vows and Protestations, so send them head-long to the Devil, which the reformed *Ranters,* before spoken of hearing, imediately fell upon them, and beat them exceedingly, uttering these words, *Where is your Devil and dark Angels, that can deliver you out of our hands; for although we were a long time blinded by the Man of sin, we are now by the tender mercies of* **Jesus Christ,** *and by the influence of his Divine Spirit, restored again unto light; and therefore are resolved to partake no longer with you in your abominable and detestable vanities, &c.* Which words struck such a terror to their former fellow-Creatures, that they all unanimously resolved to lead a new life, to withdraw from the Gulf of Hell, and to betake themselves to the true Soul-saving Gospel Road, and so with great alacrity and joy parted quietly, betaking themselves to their respective places of habitation.

VII. *Another sort of these notorious* **Ranters,** *both in City and Countrey, are called by the name of* **Seleutian Donatists;** *who hold an opinion, that neither the Word of God, (for the Bible they burn) nor any under the Canopy of Heaven, can make so perfect a Church, as their own Discipline; denying all powers, and refusing to submit to any Government, erected either by* **Kings** *or* **Parliament,** *being of an opinion, that the Mosse whereof God made the* **Elements,** *was coeternal with him, and that Christ in his Ascension uncloathed himself of the flesh of Man, and left it in the Glove of the* **Sun;** *and thereupon hold this erroneous Tenent, that it is only lawful for them to idolize and adore the* **Sun,** *and the 3. Clouds, wherein its splendor is sundry times eclipsed and darkened, being of this idolatrous and dangerous Opinion, that after this life there, their bodies shall rest for ever. These sort of* **Ranters,** *are of a vain-glorious opinion, steering their ways and actions, by the concourse of the Stars; for towards the Evening, as soon as the bright comet, called the* **Shepheard-star,** *appears, they frequent their* **Babylonish** *meetings, the said* **Star** *being the word and sign, given out by these infernal Creatures, for the calling in of their diabolical Flocks; and upon their dissembling together, they exercise themselves in nothing else, but lacivious and unapparalleld vices, accounting it no sin for hundreds of Men and Women (savage-like) to lie with each other, publickly all together, either in Houses, Fields, or Streets, which is their constant course upon several meetings. And one amongst the rest, of these ranting Crew, observing the time when the* **Shepheards-Star** *should appear; to the end, he might give his personal residence amongst them; upon his going from his own house in* **White-Chappel,** *to* **Pluto's** *Flock, enfolding each other near* **Hackney,** *he heard a loud voice sounding in his mind, as followeth,* **Leave off they abominable ways, and return from**

whence thou comest; for after all such things only wicked men seek. *And as he heard this voice sounding in his heart, so also his Conscience accused him, that he was one of those wicked men, spending his precious time is lacivious, shameless, and intemperate societies with other Women: whereupon, he imediately fell down on his knees, praising the great God of Heaven, for this his great change and conversion; and upon his imediate resurrection, betook himself to privacy for a time, writing this ensuing Letter, to his former Ranting Associates.*

Dear Friends,

It hath always been the subtilty of the *Serpent*, that old Devil, since Man had a being, to seek to deceive and destroy him, and to take him off from his being, and his well-being, and as God useth all means to do Mankind good so *Satan* seeketh by all the means he can to do them hurt, in every age; and so much the more, as the light doth appear in every age, transforming himself like an Angel of light, that he may appear glorious in them, when he is nothing in substance, and in this age more than ever; because his Kingdom and black *Angels* begins to be full of darkness; he sees its high time to stir, or else to lose all, and is now labouring to overthrow the foundations of your faith, by taking you off from searching the Scriptures, by denying the word, and burning the sacred Writ, *&c.* utterly detesting against *Christ* and his truth, which truth we must all yield to, or else you are damned: And for my part, I do wholly embrace it, denying and abhorring the wicked course of life, which formerly I delighted in, with you, for the space of 7 years, and odd moneths; during which time, I conceived my self to be in a happy condition; but being near to the very edge of the brink of the infernal lake and bottomless pit of Hell, then came the Lord God in a terrible voice into my heart, saying, *Leave off thy wicked ways, and return from whence thou camest, for after all such things even wicked men seek:* These words I heard dolefully sounding, even when I was coming to your Diabolical meeting, which caused me to return back: And therefore friends, I do humbly implore you, in the name of Jesus Christ, to leave off your wicked wayes, and to lay hold on the truth; for he that acts against truth, acts against God: His truth is the greatest Champion, and breaks all the Armour and Weapons that it fights with; for it is a soul-saving Weapon, and no Weapon formed against it shall prosper; to those that yield, he shews mercy, and to those that will not, his blowes are mortal: Therefore dear friends, be not found fighters against God, least he tear you in peeces, and there be none to help; for on whomsoever this stone shall fall, it shall grind him to peeces. Now the Lord Jesus Christ give you understanding in these things, and so I rest,

White-Chappel Decemb.   *Yours in the Lord,*
    4. 1650.   *G.R.*

Reader since the writing of this Letter, above 700 are come in but by reason of a new Treatise preparing for the Press, I shall insist no further at present; but referreth thee to that subject, which contains a 7 years Chronicle of all their ways, lives, and actions.

FINIS

5. M. Stubs, The Ranters Declaration *(16 December 1650) E.620 (2)*

The Ranters Declaration, 2.

WITH

Their new Oath and Proteftation ; their ftrange Votes, and a new way to get money ; their Proclamation and Summons ; their new way of Ranting, *never before heard of* ; their dancing of the *Hay* naked, at the white *Lyon* in Peticoat-lane ; their mad Dream, and Dr. *Pockridge* his Speech, with their Trial, Examination, and Anfwers : the coming in of 3000. their Prayer and Recantation, *to be in all Cities and Market-towns read and publifhed;* the mad-Ranters further Refolution ; their Chriftmas Carol, and blafpheming Song ; their two pretended-abominable Keyes to enter Heaven, and the worfhiping of his little-majefty, the late Bifhop of *Canterbury* : A new and further Difcovery of their black Art, with the Names of thofe that are pof-feft by the Devil, having ftrange and hideous cries heard within them, *to the great admiration of all thofe that fhall read and perufe this enfuing fubject.*

Licenfed according to order, and publifhed by M. *Stubs,* a late fellow-Ranter

Imprinted at London , by J. C. MDCL. *1650*

The *RANTERS*
PARLIAMENT

The great design of God in the beginning, was to make man good and when man fell from that goodness, through disobeying Gods spirit in him; yet his divine *Majesty*, did not seek to destroy the Creature thus fallen; but his great design was to shew his love to fallen *Adam*, in his Son *Jesus Christ:* Notwithstanding which mercies, great is the disobedience of a stubborn and idolizing *Generation;* insomuch, that the present actions of these times, causeth an unparalleld admiration in this age of wonders: for I dare affirm, that since the deplorable fall of our first Parents, at which time sin was first ushered into the World, the ill spirit was never so busie, he never made such a harvest, or had such a latitude of power given him, to take his Diabolical progres in any part of *Europe*, as he hath had lately in this Island; where thousands have been possest by him, to leave off their *Gospel Christianity*, and to betake themselves to the Gulf of dreadful torments and misery, as is evidently demonstrated by this ensuing Subject, never before published.

On the 9 of this instant *Decemb.* a great Company of the new Generation of *Ranters*, assembled together near the *White Lion* in *Pelicat lane*, where they entred into a large dispute, concerning the exaltation of their jollities, affirming, that that man who tipples deepest, swears the frequentest, commits adultery, incest, or buggers the oftenest, blasphemes the impudentest, and perpetrates the most notorious crimes, with the highest hand, and rigedest resolution, is the dearest darling to be gloriously placed in the tribunal Throne of Heaven, holding this detestable Opinion, (equalizing themselves with our blessed Redeemer) that it is lawful for them to drink healths to their Brother *Christ*, and that in the bonsing off of their liquor, each Brother ought to take his Fellow-Female upon his knee saying, *Let us lie down and multiply*, holding this lascivious action to be the chief motive of their salvation, *&c.* O cursed and blasphemous Caitiffes! who dare further affirm, that there are two keyes that God alwayes keeps in his own hands, *viz.* the key of the Womb, whereby he lets us into the World; and the key of liberty, whereby he authorizes us to fulfil our own lusts, and several appetites: further telling you, that there is a certain little bone in every mans back, that shall never be subject to any putrefaction; and this bone (say they) at the last day shall be softned and molified with a Dew from Heaven, and it shall swell, having the nature of Leaven, and it shall diffuse its vertue, to the collecting of all the dust that belongs to its own body, and prepare it for a Resurrection: *O most horrible blasphemy!*

Another sort of this Diabolical Generation, had on the 11 of this instant *Decemb.* a meeting near the *Horn Tavern* in *Fleet Street,* where they began to delight themselves with a *Christmas Gambel*, which here followes in their infernal verbis

They prate of God, believe it Fellow Creature,
There's no such Bugbear, all was made by nature:
We know all came of nothing, and shall passe
Into the same condition once it was:
By natures power, and that they grosly lie,
They say there's hope of immortality:
Let them but tell us what a soul is, then
We will adhere to these mad brain-sick men.

This damnable Atheisme some of them are so bold as to aver many of them being arrived at that height of abominable impudence that they dare contest and hold dispute, that all things were made by nature, that mans soul dies with his body and that the Sacred Scriptures are meer lies and tales, &c. They far exceed the *Trenchmore Ranters*, both in City and Countrey, especially those in *Bark-shire*, the like seldom heard of in any former Ages: A Relation where of I shall here communicate as followeth, *viz.*

One *Dr. Pordich* being preaching in the Parish-Church of *Bradfield*, in the County of *Bark-shire:* After the naming of his Text, and handling some Doctrines, within a quarter of an hour he fell into a Trance, running out of the Church, and roaring like a *Bull*, saying that he was called and must be gone: Whereupon Sir *H. Fosters* eldest Sonne, immediately following him, asked what he meant by going out of the Church in that manner, He answered, that he must be gone (there was no remedy) home to his house: Where being come, found his Wife (Mrs. *Pordich*) cloathed all in white *Lawn,* from the Crown of the head, to the sole of the foot, with a white Rod in her hand; and one Mrs. *Chevil* coming in, fell on her knees, and taking Mrs. *Pordich* by the feet, saying, That she was to meet with her spouse and her Prophetess. After this they fell all to dansing the *Hay* about 3. *Flower-pots*, Mr. *Foster* being present, asked the Dr. what he meant by doing so? He answered, *It was a rejoycing because they had overcome the Devil:* With that Mrs. *Pordich* cries out for *Elijahs* Mantle and then comes up Mrs. *Chevil*, and Mrs. *Pordich* fell adoring of her, kissing her knee.

Then came in Goodwife *Puckridge*, bending her body, and kissing her knee; the said Mrs. *Pordich* assuring her, *That there was a place prepared for her in Heaven, to sit at the right hand of the Virgin Mary.*

Thus after much Revelling, Mr. *Foster* detesting their actions, left them, and being gone home they fell again to dancing of the *Hayes* and *Trenchmore*, expecting every hour when they should be taken up to Heaven, forsooth. This heathen and idolatrous practise, may be paralleld with that of the Heathens, who upon every *May-day*, kept Rantings and Revellings, consecrating of the first of *May*, (in honour of their Devil, Goddess *Flora*, a notable rich Whore), with singing and dansing. The certainty of the precedent particulars, and affirmed and attested by,

Mr. *Foster,*	)	(Goodman *Sweth,*
Mr. *Pain,*	)	(Goodman *Markham,*
Mr. *Cautry,*	)	(Goodman *Hill,*
Mr. *Blackgrave,*)		(and many others.

Another sort of *Ranters* had lately a meeting near *Paddington,* the ready way to *Tyburn,* where they resolved to keep poor old *Christmas* a foot still, and to dedicate the honour of his antiquity, to their two-faced Idol *Janus* so called; which Picture many of them wear about their necks, and other private places. These may be termed your mad *Ranters*; for they are lunatick very often.

Another sort of *Ranters* are of an opinion, that Free-will is lawful, and that they ought to sport and revel on all dayes whatsoever, dedicating the honour of *Innocents day,* to the late *Bishop of Canterbury,* whose *Picture* they also adore, by reason of his little Majesties tollerating all dayes for liberty and licensiousness: But another sort of these *Creatures* formerly called the Civil *Ranter,* (in number about 5000), denies dedicating of honour to any of these mortal shadows, saying, *They desire to live now, as they may live for ever, &c.* and deny all the abominable practices of their late Fellow-Creatures, protesting against their wicked wayes, and have entered into an *Engagement,* to make a general discovery of them, being now resolved to lay hold on the election of grace, and to live in the wayes of truth and purity of the Gospel. They have also taken an Oath, to be true to the present *Government,* as it is now established, without *King* or House of *Lords;* and upon taking the said Oath, one of their Fellow-Creatures, began to quibble, saying, *Then will I deny all Lord Mayors, all Lords, Presidents, and all Lord Chief Justices, &c.* For which he was presently expelled from amongst them. And upon further consultation touching the corruptness of many still amongst them, they entered into prayer, as followeth.

The Reformed RANTERS Prayer

O Most glorious God, whose dwellings are above the Heavens, and yet humblest thyself to behold the things that are done upon the Earth, who seest our miserable corruptness and distractions, who knowest the causes, and canst only apply the Remedies; be gracious and merciful to this thy People, subdue their hearts and affections to thee their God, infuse into them once again the spirit of Christianity; undeceive their seduced souls, that they may no longer joyn with them who imagine mischief. O let the precious bloud of thy dear Son, expiate the crying sins of this people, remember their old mercies; and that soon, for we are brought very low, call in those Atheistical Creatures; who are now even ready to be swallowed in the bottomless Gulf of destruction, and prevent the falling off of any more to those Babilonish errours. O let them no longer glory in their wickedness, that tryumph in blaspheming of thee and thy Christ; but either convert them in thy mercy, or confound them in their pride, that they may know and feel their wayes are hateful to thee. In the mean time, keep us, O God under the shadow of thy wings, and grant, that we may serve thee, with parte, in holiness and righteousness, all the dayes of our life, and all this we crave in the name and mediation of thy only Son Jesus Christ our Lord, Amen.

Several Copies of this Prayer being transcribed, and presented to the chief of some of the infernal and grand *Ranters*, that persist in their wicked and abominable wayes; they immediately entred into consultation touching the same, resolving to issue forth their respective Warrants and summons, for the calling in of their Fellow-Creatures, to a general meeting near *Southampton-house*, which divers obeyed, but above 3000 denied to yield obedience thereunto; as appeared upon their calling over the back Roll; whereupon, about 100 of the chief Ring-leaders, Men and Women, withdrew into a privie room where they sat in consultation for the spate of an hour assuming a power to be a free Parliament, and Representative entring into debate how they should advance their own Interest, and suppress and quell all those who had dissented, by finding it to be of great difficulty, only resolved as followeth. *That all those who had so trecherously fallen off from them and their principles, should be for ever cast out of the Roll of* **Paradice,** *(as they call it). That they should be made uncapable of mercy, and proceeded against accordingly, That they should for the future, be solely deprived of all society, either with Fellow-male, or Fellow-female, in any of their respective meetings; and withall, to go under this final Curse, that they should never increase nor multiply again, &c.* After which, they fell into their venial exercise, and having taken their fill of luxury, returned to the rest of their Fellow-Creatures, communicating their votes; but upon reading the same, many queries were propounded, in behalf of the poor of their fraternity; desiring to know how they should be maintained, notwithstanding the falling off of many hundreds of the great ones. To which answer was made, That they should borrow money, and never pay it again; and that they should not only make use of a Mans Wife, but of his Estate, Goods, and Chattels also, for all things were common; But alas! this *Engine* would not prove effectual; for many of the poorer sort conceiving this stratagem no wayes feasible, brake forth in a great agony, cursing all those who had so deluded them and utterly detested against them; so that of 300 there present, not above 150 returned with *Satans* visage, the rest, having a great change, by Gods divine mercy, wrought in them, and not only there, but in other places also; for it is affirmed, that since the 16 of *Novemb.* last, above 3000 are converted, and have taken the *Engagement,* and now live civilly in their respective places and Habitations: yet notwithstanding this glorious work of precedency, there are many thousands that still tread the steps of the wicked, and walke in the wayes of darkness.

The truth and certainty of these particulars are attested by *Rowland Coleman, Gabriel Wilson, Tim Knight, Edw: Smart, Giles Burdet, George Srynum, Tim: Stubbs, Stephen Borrel.*

Late Fellow Ranters.   **FINIS**

6. The Ranters Recantation *(20 December 1650) E.620 (10)*

THE
RANTERS
RECANTATION:
And their
SERMON
Delivered
At a Meeting on Tuesday last, in
White-Chappel, being the 17 of this
instant DECEMBER
WITH
Their Resolution, Advice, and Proposals; the
manner of the vanishing away of one of their false
gods in a flame of fire; a more further discovery
of their dangerous opinions, lives, and acti-
ons; their blasphemous Decree, and
detestable Commandements.
LIKEWISE,
The apprehending of some of them; their Tryal,
and Sentence; their Speech and Confessions at the
place of execution; their strange and blasphemous Cries upon the Ladder; and the
executing two Justices of Peace:
Recited as a Warning-piece to the
English Nation.
. . . .
London, Printed for G.H. MDCL

The Ranters Recantation, &c.
To the English Nation.
There is no sight so lovely and taking to the eyes of all ingenuous and sincere hearts, as
naked **Truth:** *Those which know its excellency will study to find it out.* **Truth** *is a*
jewel which lies out of sight, men must search for it that will find it out; And therefore,
considering that this present Age hath produced sundry Papers, in relation to a discovery of
the new Generation called **Ranters;** *but finding they have been onely beating about the*
Bush, and have not discovered the Bird in its own nature, I shall here present you with a
more full and infallible Discovery, of their prodigious pranks, and unparalleld deport-
ments, which are as followeth.
On Tuesday last, being the 17th of this instant December, a great company of
Ranters had a meeting neer the *Horns* in *White-Chappel*, where they began to
put in practice several *Christmas* Gambols, and amongst the rest one Mrs *Hull*,
led them a dance, saying, *She would shew them a new way to be merry;* And calling

to one of her fellow creatures to sit on her knee, she bid him take up her coats and frock, which he did: Then, said she, *Now pray thee kiss me round;* He answer'd, *Dear sister, It is my duty:* After which greeting, he was to set her on her head, to go about the room on her hands, with her coats about her ears, in performance of which uncivil action, another fellow-creature began to peep, which she perceiving, said, Sir, *You shall pay for your peeping:* and so immediately, in the presence of about 60 persons, entred into venial exercise. After this, one *Arthingworth*, a notorious *Ranter*, stood up, belching forth these blasphemous and detestable words, assuming to this height of impudency, *That he was both King, Priest, and Prophet;* as appears by this infernal Speech, rendred in his own *verbis.*

Fellow-Creatures,

I Hope there are not any of you here, that do in the least deny, to yield all due obedience and reverence to me your anointed, but that you will in every respect, and upon all occasions, be willing to obey, and submit unto all such Orders and Decrees, that I shall both here, and for the time to come, ordain and establish; And therefore, I do will and require you, to subscribe unto these ensuing Commandements, in manner and form as followeth.

I.

That you shall not acknowledge, nor yield Obedience to any other gods, but me.

II.

That it is lawful to drink, swear, and revel, and to lie with any woman whatsoever.

III.

That there is no Sabbath, no Heaven, no Hell, no Resurrection, and that both Soul and Body dies together.

Thus do these beasts of *Ephesus* too frequently belch forth great imprecations & curses against the omnipotent Jehovah of Heaven, not fit to be named amongst Christians. But these are but the Gnosticks of former Ages; these are the same with those of old, whose description *Epiphanius* gives us; who hold onely certain Dictates and Positions, peremptorily affirming, *That let them live as they please, they were sure to be saved, &c.*

No sooner had the aforesaid *Arthingworth* ended his Diabolical speech, but one Mr. *Gilbert,* stood up, desiring free liberty to declare himself, by reason that he was exceedingly perplexed at Mr. *Arthingworths* speech, and in order thereunto, it was generally assented to by the rest of his fellow-creatures: whereupon he began as followeth, insisting upon this ensuing Text of Scripture.

1 Thess. Chap. I. Ver. 3.
Remember your effectual Faith.

Dear Friends,

It hath pleased Almighty God, even in a moment of time, since our meeting here together, to change the inward man, and to recall me from those wicked and abominable wayes, that I have lately walked with you in; insomuch, that I now desire to lay hold on Christ and his Word, and to joyn no longer with you in the ways of sin, by denying my Creator to be the true God, and refusing to walk in the way of holinesse; and, dear friends, I can assure you, that all your wayes and actions are of your father the Devil; and that like a cunning Fisher-man, he endeavours to hang you with a hook baited with sensual objects; and having once gotten his hook in your jawes, he doth not, like some unskilful Angler, presently strike to the hazard of line, hook, rod, and fish; but rather draggeth you up and down in the sea of your sensual contentment, till at last he hath drowned you in your own element, to the burying of your peace and felicity for perpetuity. But, dear friends, I humbly implore you, in the name of Jesus Christ, to walk no longer in the waye of darkness, but to become children of light, and to take **Fragan** *the Emperours resolution, That after 20 years spent in a most sinful way, he unfeignedly repented, watering his Couch 18 days, and 18 nights with tears; and then desired a conference with religious* **Mr Plutark***, to be reproved of his sins; and withal, That if he seemed angry, he would not have him to think that it was at him for his reproof, but at himself, for committing such sins. The like I desire from you.*

And therefore, dear friends, I earnestly intreat you to put on the Armour of *Fragan*, and *Plutark*, for the withstanding of Sin and Satan; and in so doing, you need not doubt of a glorious victory over him, for the purchasing of everlasting Salvation; to evidence it more plainly, I shall give you these ensuing Considerations.

1. *That God is merciful, and that upon serious repentance, he will blot out all your iniquities, therefore you have nothing to do, but to take him.*

2. *Remember, that Christ is made righteousness to us.*

3. *Remember, that the pardon is great; look to the promises of the Gospel, you shal find them without exception. To us a Saviour is born, to take away the sins of the people: he came to take away sins of all sorts. Now, when God hath made no exception, why should we make any?*

4. *Consider, that we have to do with a God, who delights to shew mercy, it is a thing that he is not weary of, it is natural to him: And therefore, as the Eye is not weary of seeing, nor the Ear of hearing, because it is natural to them, no more is God weary of shewing mercy: Nay, he delights in it,* **Mic. 7.8. Who is a God like unto thee, taking away iniquities, delighting to shew mercy, &c.** *Why so?* **Because mercy pleaseth him.** *That is, there is no work so much pleaseth him, as in shewing mercy.*

5. *Consider, dear friends, all you that are in such a case; consider, I say, that Gods mercy is as large as any other attribute. We must not square Gods mercy according to our own*

thoughts: Neither should we measure his mercy according to our own apprehension. Many of you are of an Opinion, I am confident, that if a man commit one sin, it might be forgiven; but when his sins exceed, when they are grown out of measure sinful, when they are sins so circumstantiated, as we say, that they are then out of measure sinful; here a man stands at a stay: What is the reason of this? Because we draw a scantling of Gods mercy, according to our own conceits. Whereas, if we would but consider, that his mercy were as large as any other attribute, then we would consider that it hath no limits; and if it have no limits, then whatsoever thy sins are, it is all one. Dost thou think that Christ came from heaven, and took flesh, and suffered death, to forgive small sins? No, it was to forgive the greatest sins. These, and such like reasons, I beseech you, labour to bring to heart, and indeavour to live perfectly and throughly; cast off that wicked man of sin, (pointing to Arthingworth) *be no longer seduced by him, but lay hold on Christ, the true and onely Saviour and Redeemer, embrace the substance, and catch no longer at a mere shadow. Now the Lord Jesus give you understanding in these things, that so you may die to sin, and live to righteousness.*

AMEN

Mr Gilbert having thus emphatically expressed himself, it pleased Almighty God to give great blessing to his labours in so much that 59 persons were then converted, who resolved to secure the said *Arthingworth*; but this cunning Gnostick perceiving their sudden change, with a fair pretence, went to the chamber door, and called for a Turks head; in plain English, *a pisse-pot*, and in an instant, upon a great flash of fire, vanished and never was seen more, to the great admiration of the spectators.

This great judgment, or signal from heaven, hath astonished divers, insomuch that their ways begin to be odious and detestable to those that once delighted in them: yet many there are that still persist in these wicked wayes, both in city and country; and one *W. Smith*, amongst the rest, were lately apprehended at York for denying the Deity, *Arian*-like, and putting in execution several illegal practises against the Parliament; for which, upon a fair tryal, he received sentence to be hanged; and being brought to the place of execution, he uttered many blasphous words upon the ladder, saying, *Deliver me, O God, from the hands of these wicked persecutors, or else Ile rest the Heavens, and pull thee out of thy Throne*; and so died in a very desperate and sad condition.

Another of these mad Gnosticks was lately apprehended at *Coventry*, for proclaiming *Charles Stuart* King, &c. he held an opinion, *that sin was no sin, and therefore no treason to proclaim him King;* but on examination, he received sentence to be hang'd, and being brought to the place of execution, confessed, *That it was neither out of love, or loyalty, to his person, or dignity, but merely out of envie to the Parliament, for setting forth an Act, prohibiting their wayes to be unjust, &c.* and so died Reprobate-like.

Many presidents I could instance touching the legallty of the Law in punishing Offenders; but amongst the rest, be pleased to take this Observation, That

Sir *Richard Empson*, and M. *Edmond Dudley*, Justices of the Peace, were both hang'd in H.8 dayes, for puting in execution several illegal practises, grounded upon an unjust law; which as honourable *St Edward Cook* saith, *was made against, and in the face of the fundamental Law of the great Charter, &c.* And just it was they should be thus dealt withall, because it is honourable, beneficial, and profitable for the Commonwealth, that guilty persons should be punished, lest by omission of the punishment of one, many men by that ill example, may be incouraged to commit more heinous offences. And excellent to this purpose is that saying of the Parliament, which I desire they may never forget, Book Declar. pag. 39. which is, *That they are very sensible, that it equally imports them, as well to see justice done against them that are criminious, as to defend the just rights and liberties of the people.*

Many of Ranting *Everard's* party are lunatick, and exceedingly distracted; they talk very high against the Parliament, and this present Government; for which some of them have received the lash in Bridewel.

Published by Authority.
FINIS

7. Strange Newes From Newgate *(21 January 1651) E.622 (3)*

STRANGE
NEVVES
FROM
NEWGATE and the OLD-BAILY:
OR

The Proofs, Examinations, Declarations, Indictments, Conviction, and confeſſions of *I. Collins*, and *T. Reeve*, two of the Ranters taken in More-lane, at the Generall Seſſions of Goal-Delivery; holden in the Old-Baily the twentieth day, of this inſtant *Ianuary*, the Penalties that are inflicted upon them. The proceedings againſt one Parſon *Williams* for having four wives, and *Iohn Iackſon* a Scots Miniſter, condemned to be drawn, hanged, and quartered, for proclaiming *Charles Stuart*, King of England, with the ſtrange and wonderfull judgement of God ſhewed upon one *T. Kendall*, a Ranter in Drury-lane who fell down dead as he was affirming that there is no God, or hell to puniſh.   Publiſhed according to Order.

The Black Dogg hath bewitched us.

I. Collins.
T. Reeve.

Ian. 21

London, Printed by B. *Alſop*, 1652.   1650

Strange
NEWES
From the
OLD-BAYLY
or
The Proofs, Examinations, Declarations, Indictments
and Conviction of the Ranters, at the Sessions of
Gaole-delivery, held in the Old Bayly, the
18, 19, and 20 of this instant January;
with the Arraignment of *John Jackson*
a Scotch Minister, for proclaiming
Charls Stuart King of *England*

Several eminent tryals were this Sessions in the Old-Baily holden the 18 and 19 of this instant January, whereof I shall for the satisfaction and profit of the Reader speak in order, as followeth. First, One *John Jackson* a Scotch Minister, was indicted of high treason for proclaiming *Charles Stuart* King of England; at the first he refused to plead, because his Indictment was laid against *John Jackson* Cler. saying, that he was not a Clerk, but a Minister of the Gospel of Jesus Christ; but at length he pleaded, and was convicted: yet of such an undaunted spirit was this Parson, that in the very face of the Court, he prayed God to blesse King *Charles*, &c. His judgement was, to return from whence he came, and from thence to be carried on a Sledge to the place of execution, and there to be hanged untill he were half dead, and so to be cut down, his body ripped open, his bowels openly burnt, and his quarters to be disposed of as the State shall think fit. After he had received judgment, and was gone from the Bar, an acquaintance of his came to him, and asked how he did? to whom he replied, that he was never better, never so full of joy and inward peace and comfort as now: and notwithstanding his imprecations and obstinacie against the present Government, besides his wilfull forfeiture of life, and making himself a Traytor within the very expresse words of the Act, yet in the midst of judgement he hath found such mercy and favour, that he is reprieved, and his execution is respited.

One *Williams* (another Clergie man) was convicted for having 3 or 4 wives living at one time; he hath gone by several names, as Sir *John*, Sir *Thomas,* &c. He pleaded to the first Indictment, Guiltie, to that and all other within the compasse of Clergie: so he was burnt in the hand; and for that it was thought he had favour, he had a second touch, which was put more home.

Two of the Ranters which were taken in More-lane, the first of *Novemb,* last, *viz. Jo. Collins,* and *Tho. Reeve,* were indicted upon the late act against blasphemy, &c. and one *J. Gold,* and other persons of credit were examined as witnesses, and fully proved such wicked blasphemous words and actions, that the like was never heard before any Bench, neither in modesty can I relate in such broad speeches as were then delivered, upon oath for truth setting forth the Diabolicall practises of these wretched creatures, yet having promised to give you some satisfaction I shall give you some of the perticulars proved, *vizt.*

That this *Collins, Reeves*, and others were sitting at table, eating of a piece of Beef, one of them took it in his hand, tearing it asunder said to the other, *This is the flesh of Christ*, take and eat.

The other took a cup of Ale and threw it into the chimney corner, saying, *There is the bloud of Christ*. And having some discourse of God it was proved that one of these said, *That he could go into the house of Office, and make a God every morning*, by easing of his body, and blowing through two pieces of Tobacco pipes he said, *That was the breath of God.* There was also proved many other blasphemous words and uncivil behaviour, as the kissing of one anothers Breeches, more lively represented by this figure:

The indictment was found *Billa vera*, and according to the Act, they were fined and are sentenced to suffer for this first offence, six moneths imprisonment.

Shakespear and *Glover*, should also have received a tryall this Sessions, but in regard they appeared not till the last day, when tryall was over, they are referred for a tryall untill the next Sessions.

Some have confessed, that they have had often meetings, whereat both men and women presented themselves stark naked one to the other, in a most beastly manner. And after the satisfying their carnall and beastly lust, some have a sport that they call whipping of the Whore: other call for musick, and fall to revelling and dancing.

Into which kind of company we are informed some pretty young Ladies have been drawn, of whom (in favour to their sex), I shall rather chuse to be silent, then lay open the frailties of the weaker vesse.

I shall therefore onely mention one merry Christmas Frolick in relation to women, which is advertised to be acted at Banbury in the County of Oxford, where four or five women being very merry, and having but one man in their company, they agreed together to have a bout at Hot-cockles upon the bare breech, unto which full consent or approbation was given by all parties, and one of the women would draw cuts with the man, which should lie down first, and it fell to the womans share, and thereunto she presently submitted; the man being something eager of the sport, set it so home, that it made her whole body to rebound, for which they all consulted together to revenge the matter, and therefore they caused him to untrusse; and having of him down, either by their confederacy, or his own ill guesse who it was that hit him, he was so well paid for his Knavery that he was scarce able to turn himself in his bed two or three nights after.

Much more time and paper might be spent in setting forth the vanity of these people, which were labor and cost well bestowed, if that others would be debarred thereby from running into the same excesse of ryot; but considering how prone men are to commit wickednesse, and apt to let slip that which is good, and retain that which is evil, I have purposely omitted many things, which without wronging to the persons, or wresting the truth, might have been spoken; for it is safer for every one to look unto his own heart and ways then to neglect that (which is a duty) and pry into the actions of others; for although those that we have spoken of, may be compared to those the Psalmist speaks of, saying, *The wickednesse of the ungodly saith in his heart, that there is no fear of God before his eyes:* yet is there another sort of people. (and I fear they are not a few) which are in secret haters and despisers of God (as every wicked natural man is) yea, how many close and secret Blasphemers and Atheists are there in our days, that with the Prophets *Fool, say in their hearts, that there is no God,* though they may be so wise as verbally not to declare it?

There is one notable example of God's judgement upon an open prophane Ranter, which were it laid to heart would be suffcient to deter all that should ever hear thereof from uttering all grosse and wicked blasphemies. It is not above three daies, since Gods immediate hand was stretched out in severe punishing of *Kendall* in Drury-lane. This *Kendall* was discoursing with a woman which he called his Fellow-Creature, and was perswading her to have his pleasure with her, and said there was no God or Divell, affirming that all things came by nature, &c. whereupon it is said that she gave consent and appointed him a place where he should meet her.

When they had made this wicked compact and agreement together they parted with an intention to go two several waies, and meet again at the place assigned, but the man was no sooner gone from her, but he was suddenly strook dead in the place to the great amazement and astonishing of many beholders. It is further related that this man did often in severall companies where he came utter such like wicked and Atheisticall speeches and did frame some arguments to ground a discourse to maintain his Diabolicall opinions, which though for a time the patience and forbearance of the Lord did permit and suffer yet doth not one title of his word fall to the ground, for although *A sinner doth wickedly an hundred times, and his days be prolonged, yet remember for all this he must come to judgement.* Then will they confesse and gnashing their teeth say, *We fools thought the ways of God inesse madnesse, behold they are happy, and we are miserable and tormented.*

FINIS

8. The Ranters Monster *(30 March 1652) E.658 (6)*

RANTERS
MONSTER:
Being a true Relation of one MARY ADAMS
living at *Tillingham* in *Essex*, who named her self the Virgin
Mary, blasphemously affirming, That she was conceived with
child by the Holy Ghost; that from her should spring forth
the Savior of the world; and that all those that did not believe
in him were damn'd : With the manner how she was deliver'd
of the ugliest ill-shapen *Monster* that ever eyes beheld, and afterwards rotted away in prison : *To the great admiration of all*
those that shall read the ensuing subject; the like never before heard of.

London, Printed for *George Horton*, 1652. March 30

Strange and terrible News from Essex; being a true Relation of the most impious life, and blasphemous actions of one Mary Adams, who named her self the Virgin Mary, and said that she was conceived with child of the Holy Ghost: but being cast into prison, soon after she was delivered of the ugliest ill-shapen Monster that ever eyes beheld.

In the County of *Essex* at a place called *Tillingham*, there lived one *Mary Adams*, who said that she was the Virgin *Mary*, and that she was conceived with child by the Holy Ghost, and how all the Gospel that had bin taught heretofore, was false; and that which was within her she said was the true Messias; for she obstinately and very impiously affirmed, that Christ was not yet come in the flesh; but that she was to bring forth the Savior of the World, and that all those that did not believe in him were damn'd: For which blasphemous words, and wicked opinion of hers, Mr. *Hadley* the Minister caused her to be apprehended & cast into prison, until the time came that she was to be delivered; At which time, when the Midwife and other good women of the Parish came to her, they did their best endeavors to bring her to a safe deliverance, but could not prevail, so that there she lay in exceeding great misery and torment for the space of 8 dayes and nights; and upon the ninth day about 7 of the clock in the forenoon, she was delivered of the most ugliest ill-shapen *Monster* that ever eyes beheld; which being dead born, they buried it with speed, for it was so loathsome to behold, that the womens hearts trembled to look upon it; for it had neither hands nor feet, but claws like a Toad in the place where the hands should have been, and every part was odious to behold.

And as for *Mary Adams*, which had named her self to be the Virgin *Mary*, she rotted and consumed as she lay, being from the head to the foot as full of botches, blains, boils & stinking scabs, as ever one could stand by another. But her latter end was miserable, for the women that was about her, seeing there was no hopes of her life, desired her to pray, and to ask forgiveness for her sins, she answered, *That her heart was so hardened in wickedness, that she had no power to repent*; but desired one of the women to lend her a knife to pare her nails, which when she had made use of, she laid the knife aside till such time the women were gone, and afterwards ript up her bowels with the same knife.

This *Mary Adams* was descended of good parentage, and for many yeares deported her self both in a civil life and conversation being a great frequenter of the Church, and a most excellent pattern of true Holiness, till at last she fell off from these divine and glorious principles, to the most Heretical and undeniable way of *Anabaptisme*; and to the end that she might become a dear sister, and one of their society, desired to participate with them in their watry Element, and accordingly her former zeal to the divine Ordinance was extinguished and washed away by being rebaptized, or dipped: But before the expiration of many moneths she began to learn a new Exercise, and revolted from the *Brotherhoood*, to be one of the *Familists of Love*; but she had not long embraced that *Venerable Sect*, but she began to desire a further change, and immediately after turned *Ranter*, holding an Opinion, *That there was no God, no Heaven, no Hell; – but that the Creation came by providence*, with divers other Diabolical and blasphemous Tenets; amongst the rest, she said, *That as woman was made to be a helper for man, and that it was no sin to lie with any man, whether Batchelor, Widdower, or married; but a thing lawful, and adjured thereunto by Nature.*

This example may sufficiently serve *as a Caveat to all true Christians, that they presume not to offend their Heavenly Maker in such a high degree;* And the truth of this matter is affirmed by

Mr Hadley, **Minister.**

James Townsworth,	**Church-Wardens.**
Andrew Farmer,	

Richard Gittins, **Constable.**	
James Woodhouse,	
John Smith,	**Collectors.**
John Walton,	

William Jackson,	
Gilbert Pickering,	**Headboroughs.**
Thomas Watson.	

Another sad president I cannot but instance, which is an evident demonstration of the life and death of one *John Rogers* a Carpenter, who upon the 4. of *Jan.* being the Sabbath day, told his wife, that he had a piece of work in hand that he promised to make an end that very day, swearing the he would be so good as his word whatever followed after. His wife hearing him say so, endeavoured to disswade him from that presumptuous sin of Sabbath-breaking, and told him that God would bless his labour the better all the week after, and that he would find it better both for his soul and body, for that he remembred to keep holy the Sabbath day: To which her husband replyed, *That he that was born to be drown'd should never be hang'd.* Furthermore he said, *That if he were ordained to be saved, he should be saved, how wickedly soever he led his life; and if he was ordained to be damned, he should be damned, though he lived never so godly a life:* And so taking up his Tools at his back, went to his work, as he said he would do, having no other company but his Apprentice boy along with him; so when he came where his work was, he drew forth his Ax, and as he was hewing of a piece of Timber, the Ax glanced, and cut him on the leg whereby he fell down backwards, crying out that he had kill'd himself; which when his Apprentice perceived, caught him up, and held him by the arm, desiring him to go back again home with him, and he would do his best indeavor to guide him along on the way: No Villain, quoth he, I will never go home what ever betide me, neither shalt thou live to carry news what is become of me: so putting his hand in his pocket, pulled out a keen knife, swearing that he would kill the boy; At which words, the boy being afraid what would be done unto him, let go his hold, and ran away; and coming home told what his Master had done: Whereupon his wife called six of her neighbours to go along with her to see what was become of her husband, but when they came to the place where he was they found him lying on his back not quite dead, having with his knife stab'd himself in 8 several places; some of his guts lying two yards from him: his neighbours did their endeavors, but could not bring him home alive. The Lord in his mercy keep us all from vain opinions, hardness of heart, and from desperate deaths.

Here followeth another sad example which was done *Jan.* 7. in the County of *Yorke*, at *Rippon*, where lived one M. *Clerk*, who having a poor Tenant 4 miles off, that was behind hand of his Rent 7£ & od monies, took course of Law against the poor man, and threw him, his wife, and 3 children out of the hous on a bitter cold snowy day, they poor soules not knowing what to do, or whither to go for succor, and that poor lodging and houshold-stuff which they formerly had was kept from them: neither could the cries of the poor woman and her children any wais prevail with their greedy and covetous minded Landlord; but the more they sought to perswade him, the worse he was: At last there came some of the chiefest men of the Parish to perswade him that he would let them stay in his house a little time longer, til such time as they could procure some other place to dwell in. To which he answer'd, That he had rather make a Den for Devils of it, then that the poor folks should dwell there any longer: and there withall, he wisht that he might never depart out of the world in the right mind, if he would let them have one peny-worth of their goods to succour them in their need. But mark what came to pass; This M. *Clark* took horse and rid speedily away; but before he came home, his horse threw him in the street, and fell upon him, and with the fall bruised him so grievously, that the bloud issued forth of his mouth, insomuch that for two hours space he was not able to speak; But at the last when he came to his speech he raved and raged like a madman, crying out, that his sins were so great, and so many, that they could never be forgotten; and so in a sad and des-pairing manner he departed the World that very time, in the sight of many of his neighbors, not having so much grace as to say, *Lord have mercy upon me,* when he departed the World.

One thing I had almost omited, which is very remarkable, *viz.* That when the aforesaid *Mary Adams* was in prison, she used many Imprecations against

9. A Blow at the Root *(4 March 1650) E.594 (14)*

Title page and pp. 151–8.

A
Blow at the Root.
or, some
OBSERVATIONS
towards
A Discovery of the Subtilties and
Devices of Satan, practised against
the Church and Truth of
CHRIST,
as
In all Ages, so in these times especially.

Gen. 3.1. *Now the Serpent was more subtile than all the beasts of the field.*

2 Cor. 2.11. *Lest Satan should get an advantage of us for we are not ignorant of his devices.*

Febr. the 20. 1650.

I have perused this Discourse (intitled, *A Discovery of the subtilties of Satan, &c*) with much satisfaction and contentment, and approving it to be very learned, solid and judicious, I doe License it to be Printed and published as well worthy the reading of all who desire to be satisfied by such a Discovery.

Iohn Downam

London, Printed for *John Wright,* at the Kings Head in the Old Baily. 1650.

CHAP. XII.

The **Sixth** *Observation. How Satan labour's to introduce and establish certaine* **Principles,** *which are absolutely* **opposite** *to* **Gods** *declared counsells and purposes: and which also* **comprehend** *or make* **way** *for All manner of* **Evills** *in* **Opinion** *and* **Practice.**

Having been something *larger* upon some of the *former* Heads (which indeed are of largest *concernment*) than was *intended;* the *roome* so narrowes upon us now, that wee must of necessity be more *abrupt* than would be desired. But look *back* now, I beseech you upon the *Practises* before mentioned, and yee shall perceive, how *Satan* (with all subtilty and diligence) hath (by *them*) opened and cleared his *way* to his *work.* How he hath busied and employ'd himself in *making* and *fitting* his *Instruments [professed Saints:]* As also in *providing,* and furnishing them with *Materialls [New Lights:]* in contriving and emproving the fittest *Opportunities* and *Seasons,* to colour and further his *Busines [Times of Reformation,* and of *common calamities]* yee may see likewise what *paines* he takes *(removere prohibens)* to *remove* out of his way; or at least to obstruct and weaken, that which probably might *frustrate* his undertakings *[viz. The WORD of God].* As also to *undermine* shake and *shatter* in pieces the good old *building* of True *Religion,* in the feverall *parts* thereof; that it may have no fixed *Foundation* in the *Consciences* of men; but bee *swallow'd*-up (piece-meale) into that monstrous *Vacuum,* or bottomlesse *Gulfe* of *Skepticisme* and *uncertainty,* under pretence of *Scruples, Queries, Doubts, Questions, Disputes, &c.*

And now in the *next* place we should *Observe* how he falls to worke with his *owne* Building. What *Foundations* hee layes, what *superstruction* he reares, with what chosen-*pieces* he *heads* his *Corners,* what false *lights* hee beats out, with what *Artifice* he *workes,* and with what *cement* he *binds* together the manifold *heterogeneall* parts of his dark and Hellish *Fabrick.* But *this* wee must here (needs) fall *short of,* and but give a few *hints* and *glances* of what was *intended.*

But first of all let me *premise* this (to prevent *mistakes*) That *Satan confines himselfe to no particular fixed principles or practises, further than they conduce to his ends,* or *Serve his present turnes;* by them (as *Bridges*) to passe over to some *Designe* that lyes *beyond:* which, when hee has *done,* hee can *cut off* and break in pieces, that they be not made use of to his disadvantage. Thus he doth by some things already *mentioned,* and by some likewise that should now come to bee *propounded.* It is *Gods* Royalty to bee *semper idem;* it is the *Devills* cognisance to bee always *shifting* and *changing.* Shortly, and most *plainly,* ye may example it *thus.* An over-curious questioning of some things appertaining to *Religion* (against which yet I conceive, no cleare evidence can be given) disposeth to *Seperation: Seperation* is an ordinary step to *Anabaptisme; Anabaptisme* perfects it selfe in *Seeking,* being above *Ordinances,* and *questioning* every thing revealed in the *Scriptures,* and in high *Raptures* and *Revelations. This* determinates in *Levelling,* and (through that) runnes *compasse* (with some) to that strange and fearfull *straine* declared and taught in the late *Fiery flying Roll*; which state's the *perfection* of all Religion expresly *[in perfect Libertinisme]* So that Profaness ye may perceive, is the Devils *Alpha & Omega*.

For *there* Religion first findes us; and (if we suffer *him* to misguide our *Religion*) *thither* he will be sure againe to *bring* us. Now this is most certaine, That when a Soule is *misguided* to any of the above-mentioned, as it transports it selfe to the *next* stage *beyond*, and presseth on to that which is *before*, so it extreamly *despiseth* and slighteth that which is *behinde*; vilifying and *decrying* the steps and *degrees*, by which it *ascended* to that *cuspe* of imaginary perfection, wherein it conceits it selfe *culminating*. For *Satan* acts not-much-unlike your *Machiavelian* Statists; that *abandon* and *resume* the same *things* (upon feverall *pretences*) as they discerne them to *impede* or *assist* their *plots* and *designes*: carefully *demolishing* the *Fortifications* by which themselves have wonne the *Towne*, lest they should happen (by *them*) againe to *lose* it. And therefore *wonder* not if hee or his Instruments seeme to throw *downe* that sometimes which they had carefully *raised*, or to repaire that which they had demolished; (neither, for *this*, bee too forward to *charge* them with *changed* Intentions:) for it is ordinary with *Satan* to run *counter* and *double*; thereby to amuse such as would *trace* him, and repose himselfe and his Instruments, the *more* securely, in their deep Designes and *Stratagems*. This Hint premised, wee now proceed to *mention* (though we can *but* mention) some *few* of those *many* dangerous *Principles*, which (being absolutely *contrary* to Gods revealed *Counsells* and *Purposes*, or of a *radicall* and generall *influence* upon the *wayes* of men) might be called *Magnalia Satana*, the great stayes and *Pillars* of that frame of *Darknesse* which the Devill is busily raising in this erroneous *age*: or the *roots* that feed and nourish the many spreading and fruitfull *branches* of *Heresie* and *Prophanesse*. But (still I say) wonder not if some of them seeme to *interfere*, or bee inconsistent; For there is (you know) a mystery of Iniquity in these depths of Satan, *viz.*

1. *That the souls of man is mortall*, as is his *body*, whereof some (that so hold) acknowledge a *Resurrection*: others deny *that* also, and further say,

2. *That there is no other heaven nor hell but a mans owne Conscience here in this life.* Some againe,

3. That *all mankinde, yea and devills too, at last shall be saved.*

4. *That whatsoever is*, (be it Sensible or Intelligible) *is God; and whatsoever is done in the world, is done by God;* be it good or evill; punishment or *Sinne*.

5. That *it is a high degree of Christian emprovement for a man not to trouble himselfe at the sinnes of others, although they act as bad as the devill himselfe.* Whereas *Moses, David, Nehemiah, Jeremiah, Paul* and *Christ* himselfe expressed a quite contrary disposition; and much laid to heart the *sinnes* of the times, who yet were as well acquainted with the *Nature* and *extent* of the Divine *Decrees* as any *now* can be.

6. That *the Fall of man was not destructive, but perfective of the Image of God upon*

man. There's a large *Treatise* out in justification of this *Opinion:* and it goes for a glorious *sparke* of new *light.*

7. That *Revelations of the Spirit are to be preferred before the Scriptures, even in things that differ from the clear sense of the Scriptures:* and that such Revelations are *ordinary with the Saints in these times.* Truth it is, the pretence of Revelations hath *instrumented* and *assisted* great Designes for Civill-*changes,* first and last. Witnes *Numa Pompilius, Mahomet,* the holy maid of *Kent, &c.*

8. That *Divine providence may prescribe Duty, and bee a Warrant or Rule of action, in matters of highest concernment,* though they bee (seemingly) contrary to *Scripture*-rules and examples. (That is, for *themselves* that so hold when *providence* seems to bee *for* them: *not* for *others,* when *providence* takes against them.) That was the Divinity of the Sons of *Zerviah:* but not *Davids Rule,* I *Sam.*26.8. And indeed it is the best and greatest *plea* that the *Mahumetans* at this day pretend for *their* Religion. *God* (say they) *with an Almighty hand from heaven hath approved it,* with invincible prevailings against the *Christians, &c.* Whereas if that were a good *Rule,* the *Devils* are as obedient Creatures as the blessed *Angels* in heaven: And the *Jewes* in crycifying *Christ,* and *Judas* in betraying him, were as dutifull as the *Disciples* in *believing* on him: for they did *onely that,* and *all that* which the hand and counsell of *God* had *determined* before to bee done.

9. That *the Children of professed Christians are not to be baptized.* It troubles the Devill much that *Children* (from their Infancy) should be under an *engagement* to receive nurture and admonition in the *Lord:* to frequent the *Ordinances,* and to owne *Jesus Christ* by an external profession. If he could but contrive to prevent their comming into that engagement, hee might hope more easily to *keep* them out when they are grown up, than to *work* them out (so growne up) to a renouncing of *Christianity* which yet hee has brought *some* unto. But this referres to the *next.*

10. That *there ought not to be any Nationall Church under the Gospell.* The great *quarrel* against the *Baptizing of children,* is but in order to *this,* that *Nationall Churches* may bee *dissolved.* Then which, what more contrary to Gods declared Intentions? *I will give thee* (faith the *Father* to the *Messiah*) *the Nations for thine Inheritance. (Psalm 2.8)* And *all Nations shall flow unto it. Isa.3.2. And in that day, shall Israel be the third with Egypt and with Assyria – whom the Lord of Hosts shall blesse, saying, Blessed be Egypt, my people* (not, *my people of Egypt*) *and Assyria the worke of mine hands, and Israel mine Inheritance.* (Were not they to bee as Israel was?) And accordingly *Jesus Christ* commands and commissioneth his Disciples, *Matth. 28.19. Goe, and Disciple all Nations, Baptizing, and Teaching them, &c.* But the *Devill* doth at no hand *like* of this. But, whereas *Gods* great *worke* is to *Church the world,* (which in *Christ* he hath been reconciling to himselfe) the *Devils* counterworke is, *to Heathenize the Church.* Gods Commission is, to engage all we may, to the knowledge and profession of his *Truth:* but *Satans* plot is to *drive out* as many as he can *from* the Truth, and *Christ* himselfe (if he could) out of the world,

that so himselfe (and *Antichrist* his Vicegerent) may be *Lord* paramount, and suit his *Jurisdiction* to his *Title; The God of this world, 2 Cor. 4.4.*

11. *That to establish any one Religion,* (although it were true) *is a great Tyranny and Oppression: but to give liberty for all Religions is just, and equall.* Would yee know the true *Intention* of this *pretence?* It is surely this; *Pernicies multiplicata capitalier est, & nocentior qua e sola. Et, qua non profunt singula, multa juvent.* It is much more for the *Interest* of Satan that *all* manner of false Religions be *tolerated*, then that any *one* false Religion be *established;* That so by *all* meanes he may take some. For hee is not *practically* guilty of that Errour (himselfe) of resolving every thing into the Eternall *Decrees* of God (though he knowes well enough, that what is *decreed* must be *effected*) but most indefatigably applyes himselfe to the use of *Meanes.* And knowing the *Dispositions* of men to be very *divers*, and in many things *contrary*, would have somewhat wherewith to suit and humour *every ones* appetite and *lust.*

12. *That Christians should not fixe and settle upon any thing in Religion:* for (say they) *yee know not where God may be at his next remove.* Either the *Apostle Peter* (and others alike inspired) were much *mistaken*, or *this* is very *false* and *damnable.* See *2 Pet. 3.17. Yee therefore Brethren: – beware lest yee also being led away with the errour of the wicked, fall from your owne stedfastnesse. Gods* worke is to ground, *stablish*, strengthen and *settle* his People in the Truth, and to prejudice them against evill. But the *Devils* businesse is, to work us to an *indifferency* to *all* Religions, *till* we are outed of the *True*, and *then* this *Bridge* must be broken *downe*, and by pretence of some *extraordinary Rule* from *Revelation* or *Providence,* His Instruments will try to settle us upon some one *that* is false, or to tolerate *all* but the *Truth.*

13. Wee might yet descend deeper, and truely report how some of his Instruments expressely *deny the Godhead and Satisfaction of Christ.* Yea and some horridly *deny* and *scorne* all that is written in the holy *Scriptures.*

14. *That the Church is to be visibly victorious and superior to the world.* And when *Providence* hath possessed any of *Power* and *Advantages*, they ought to keep and make them good.

15. That *there is no True Church or Ordinances now in being upon earth:* Or, as others, *that there is no being of the true Church* unless in that which they call a particular-*Church-way; that is, by gathering Churches out of Churches.*

16. *Ubi res postulat fides & pacta posthabeantur:* that the most solemne *Obligations* may bee throwne *off*, when *Providence* urgeth with some conceived *Necessity;* and when men by so doing may present themselves some faire *advantage* or *security.* And that which hath been judged worthy of Death in *others*, may bee done by *themselves* for good ends.

17. *That there is no Originall of Power or Authority in the world but the Sword.*

These are but a *few* of many that are now adayes *whetted* upon the spirits of such as are disposed to receive them: The sad *Influence* of which, upon the *judgement* and *Practise* of men wee must not *here* enlarge to *demonstrate* in particulars. Being *enforced* not onely to *contract this* matter in *hand*, but to exhibit a meere *Skeleton* (and scarcely that) of the other halfe of the *Observations* that here should *follow*.

The VII. Observation.

That he endeavours to implant and settle these soule-destroying Principles in the Consciences *of men.* Whereby,

1. The soule is *prejudiced* against all *sense* of the *evill* that is in them: and entertaines with suspition and *distaste*, whatsoever tends to *oppose* them.

2. The Person is *ingaged* to act more *vigorously* and *zealously*, to maintaine and propagate such Principles: They are bound in *Conscience* to doe it. And men will Sacrifice their *lives* for their *Conscience*.

3. Hereby Satan *credits* his businesse (in the hands of his Instruments) with the plausible notion of Duty, and *Necessity*: of doing God good *service*, (in the things whereby they most dishonour him, and strongly promote the Devills *Interest*.) – It is their *Conscience*.

4. And questionlesse it *doubles* his *content*, to see how handsomly his Plot *succeeds*, to *ruine* Religion under *pretence* of Transcendent improvements in *Religion*: and to destroy *Conscience by Conscience*: to see poore soules doe his worke *devoutly*, and Sacrifice their endeavours to his *Service*, as the true God.

The VIII. Observation.

Lest these, or any other *Stratagems* of his, should at any time be *discovered* and *opposed*, by any reall, vigorous, and sincerely-intended *Reformation*; He hath of late brought forth a *New*-Device (scarce ever heard of before in the world:) viz. *to exempt, priviledge, and for-ever to secure his Agents and Brokers,* (The Seminaries and Teachers of such soule-murdering Doctrines) *from being molested, discouraged or disturbed in his worke, by any Government or Discipline, Ecclesiasticall or Civill.* And this Privilege to be *Universall* and *Perpetuall*; to be established at *once* for All, without *Example* or *Experience*. This was a Grand contrivance indeed, (to be seene more at large in the late *Agreement of the People*:) wherein yet hee seems to be over-reacht by *some*, who have made use of that *Instrument* to serve their *owne* Turnes. And yet hee wants not those that retaines the same *Principles*, and carry on the same *Interest*; *viz*. Utterly to *abolish* all *Magistracy*; or at least so to *binde* their hands (or rather to *cut* them quite off) that they may never bee able to serve that *God* (whose Vicegerents they *ought* to bee, and whose Power they *represent*) in the *Protection* or *Propagation* of *His Gospel*; or in defence of his universally-allowed *Rights*, from the Barbarous and Savage *Assaults* of Monstrous men.

10. Title page of The Joviall Crew *by S[amuel] S[heppard] (6 January 1651)*
E.621 (7).

THE
JOVIALL CREVV, 7

OR,

The Devill turn'd *RANTER*:

Being a Character of

The roaring Ranters *of thefe* Times.

Reprefented in a

COMEDIE,

CONTAINING

A true Difcovery of the curfed Con-
verfations, prodigious Pranks, monftrous
Meetings, private Performances, rude Revellings,
garrulous Greetings, impious and incorrigible
Deporements of a Sect (lately fprung up a-
mongft us) called *Ranters*.

Their Names forted to their feverall Natures,
and both lively prefented in Action.

Jan: 6

1650

London: Printed for *W. Ley.* 1651.

11. Title page of Bloudy Newse from the North *by Samuel Tilbury (20 January 1651) E.622 (1)*

Bloudy Newſe from the North,

A N D

The Ranting *Adamites* Declaration con-

cerning the King of *Scotland*, with their new League, Covenant, and Proteſta-
tion; their denying the great God of Heaven, and burning his ſacred vvord
and Bible; the name of a new God by them choſen, and his Speech and pro-
miſe unto them; their new Law, and grand Court; their Arraignment and
Tryal, and a Copy of the ſeveral Articles and Indictment; with the ſeveral
ſentences to be inflicted upon divers offenders, together with their names.
Alſo, a bloudy Plot diſcovered, concerning their Reſolution to murther all
thoſe that will not turn *Ranters*; put in execution at *York*, to the aſtoniſh-
ment and admiration of the Reader, that ſhall diligently peruſe this inſuing
Subject, never before heard of.

*J*an: 20 *Publiſhed according to Order.* 1650

LONDON, *Printed by* J. C. 1650.

12. Title page of The Declaration of John Robins *by G.H. (2 June 1651)* E.629 *(13).*

Note the adaptation of the woodcuts from M. Stubs, *The Ranters Declaration.*

THE

DECLARATION

OF

JOHN ROBINS, the falſe Prophet, otherwiſe called the *Shakers* God, and *Joſhua Beck*, and *John King*, the two falſe Diſciples, with the reſt of their Fellow-Creatures now priſoners in the New-priſon at *Clarkenwell* : Deliverd to divers of the Gentry and Citizens, who on *Thurſday*, *Friday*, and *Saturday* laſt reſorted thither to diſpute with them : With the Citizens Propoſals to the ſaid *John Robins*, concerning his Opinion and Judgement, and his Anſwer thereunto : Together with his Propheſie of what is to come to paſs this year, 1651, & the ſtrange things revealed to him : his Religion, Principles, and Creed : as alſo his blaſphemous Tenents, in attributing an inſpiration from the Holy Ghoſt : with the manner of their Diet, and his Woe pronounced concerning all thoſe that drink Ale. By G. H. an Ear-witneſs.

London, Printed by R. *Wood*, 1 6 5 1. June 2. 1651.

Index

205

DATE DUE

DEC 23			
DEC 0 8 1993			

DEMCO 38-297